I0804194

The publication of this book was made possible by the generosity of the HENRY REGNERY LEGACY FUND *at the Intercollegiate Studies Institute.*

The Lecturer's Art

Gems *of* American History

Essays by

Walter A. McDougall

Encounter Books
INTERCOLLEGIATE STUDIES INSTITUTE
New York • London

First American edition published in 2025 by Encounter Books, an activity of Encounter for Culture and Education, Inc., a nonprofit, tax-exempt corporation.
Encounter Books website address: www.encounterbooks.com

Manufactured in the United States and printed on acid-free paper. The paper used in this publication meets the minimum requirements of ANSI/NISO Z39.48–1992 (R 1997) (*Permanence of Paper*).

FIRST AMERICAN EDITION

LIBRARY OF CONGRESS CATALOGING-IN-PUBLICATION DATA IS AVAILABLE

Information for this title can be found at the Library of Congress website under the following ISBN 978-1-64177-433-8 and LCCN 2025930292.

To all my students in the past, the present,
and (God willing) the future.

CONTENTS

"If history were taught in the form of stories,
it would never be forgotten."

—Rudyard Kipling

PREFACE

I was born into a family of performers. My father was a patent attorney renowned for his eloquence and erudition. My mother was a frustrated actress. My oldest brother was an actor at New Trier High School and Amherst College who later pursued careers in radio and politics. My next oldest brother was the Illinois state champion diver on the high school swim team, won a Baker Scholarship at Harvard University, and became a legendary professor of business administration. My younger brother studied drama at Emerson College and pursued careers as a disc jockey and character actor at gigs including Disney World. Big talkers all.

Now, according to the "middle child syndrome," the second of three children usually gets the least attention from his or her parents and grows up introverted, intimidated, but highly motivated. Psychologists think the syndrome is worse when the children are all the same sex. Imagine, therefore, my plight as the third of four boys. I made no big splash in high school. I never even had the courage to try out for Little League baseball. I excelled only in schoolwork, at least until my senior year in college, which I spent drinking beer and playing poker with my fraternity brothers. It was 1968, after all, and we knew that after graduation we would be facing the military draft at the height of the Vietnam War.

Nor did I have a clue what I wanted to do for a living. I majored in history because I had always been fascinated by geography and stories about long ago and far away. But I never consciously chose an academic career and became an historian because, well, I never decided to do anything else. So I applied to graduate schools almost by default, knowing that I would be enlisting in the Army. I naively figured that by the time my hitch was over I would have a better idea of what I wanted to do. But no one who survived a year of combat in Vietnam thought about anything other than coming home in one piece. So after my discharge I just claimed my place in the graduate program at the University of Chicago and began to climb the academic ladder.

Nor did I really choose Chicago (which probably admitted me because that was the alma mater of both of my parents). But the training I received there could not have been better because the faculty members were brilliant and inspiring. I worked my tail off and breezed to a PhD in just four and a half years under the principal guidance of the great world historian William H. McNeill. But one thing was lacking. Since Chicago had few undergraduates (its college was very small) they were all taught by standing faculty with no teaching assistants. That meant that we graduate students got no experience doing what we all hoped to spend the rest of our careers doing, namely teaching. I was blessed to be offered an Assistant Professorship at the University of California, Berkeley, in 1975, but had no idea when I arrived there whether I would be any good at teaching, much less enjoy it.

By golly, I was...and I did. No sooner had I presided over my first class that fall that I knew this was my calling. Word quickly spread around campus that McDougall's lectures were awesome and in just two years my enrollments were exceeding three hundred students. Of course, it helped that my subject—European diplomatic history from the French Revolution to the present—was gripping and dramatic. It also helped that I had numerous role models among the excellent teachers whose classes I took at New Trier, Amherst, and Chicago. But there was no doubt that I possessed a knack (to cite the tired cliché) for "making history come alive."

Had my personality changed such that I ceased to be a shy introvert beset by the middle-child syndrome? Not at all. I was as nervous as a long-tailed cat in a room full of rocking chairs before every lecture—and I still am today, nearly fifty years later. But those nerves, probably born of a fear of humiliation, have always motivated me to prepare lectures with exceptional care. I write them out word for word so that everything in class is scripted save for an occasional aside. But I never appear to be reciting words off a page. Rather, I always retain eye contact with the audience, move around occasionally, gesticulate when to do so enhances what I am saying, and alter my volume and tone of voice when appropriate. Moreover, since the lectures are written out I can calibrate their length within a minute or two. That ensures that I never drone on too long and risk losing my the audience. My lectures, like chapters in a book, are self-contained units with beginnings, middles, and ends (sometimes dramatic ones), because I recall how annoyed I had been whenever a teacher glanced at the clock and said, "We'll pick up here next time."

Visual aids are imperative, especially for diplomatic history, given its reliance on maps. Since the lectures in this volume are not strictly about international relations they can be read as essays without visual aides. But my classroom lectures are always accompanied by elaborate, colorful, and informative PowerPoint presentations. Yes, slide shows need not be a MEGO ("my eyes glaze over") even though many boring speakers flash slides containing nothing but text, which they proceed to read verbatim. My PowerPoints always contain vivid pictures. Back in the dear, dead days of the twentieth century I would illustrate lectures with plates and maps using an overhead projector. I even delayed learning PowerPoint when it first appeared because I am frightened by all new technology. But once initiated I fell in love with its possibilities and have enjoyed composing slide shows. To be sure, it is time-consuming to compose as many as twenty-five slides per lecture, as I do. But the time is well spent. Every slide contains pictures of historical figures, events, and maps, plus a few words of explanation about why the items are important. I also post the PowerPoint presentations online so that students can take a few minutes to review them later and recall the main points made in the lectures. I also post detailed outlines of each lecture's content so that students have a ready-made syllabus of the whole course.

Finally, since I am drafting texts meant to be read out loud, my technique is to "listen" to every sentence I type, keeping an ear out for cadence and clarity and conforming as best I can to the rules of elegant style. Some years ago it occurred to me to write a brief guide to self-editing for my students, which I have appended to this preface. The agreeable result of listening to myself as I write is that the text works both as an oral presentation and a published essay. I hope the readers of this volume will reach the same conclusion.

★ ★ ★

Who among us really controls the trajectories of our own lives? I certainly haven't, beginning with that psychological impact of my place in the family's pecking order. I did not really choose Amherst College either, but just followed my brothers there as a matter of course. Service in the armed forces (rather than dodging the draft) was an expression of duty and patriotism, but certainly not choice. My brushes with death (I've had at least six) were—with the exception of two automobile accidents—out of my control. My good fortune in becoming a student of McNeill at Chicago, then getting hired by Berkeley to teach European diplomatic history, was utterly serendipitous. But that also landed me in an agonizing battle for tenure which lasted eight years because the leftist wing of the history faculty savaged my first book (*France's Rhineland Diplomacy 1914–1924: The Last Bid for a Balance of Power in Europe* [1978]) in hopes that I would be bounced. But that hostility was a blessing in disguise because it provoked me to rebel against everyone's alleged expectations. I decided to write a book about the history of the Space Age which won the Pulitzer Prize *(The Heavens and the Earth: A Political History of the Space Age* [1985]). That, in turn, got the attention of a search committee at the University of Pennsylvania charged with hiring a chaired professor to direct its International Relations Program.

Psychologists will also tell you that the three most stressful things one can do in the course of an ordinary life are to change jobs, change cities, and change marital status. I did all three at once in 1988. Leaving the Bay Area was not easy, but I have had few regrets because Penn, Philadelphia's Foreign Policy Research Institute, and the suburb where my wife and I reside have been congenial settings for thirty-four years now and counting. Albeit I did choose to write my next book as a sort of long farewell to the West Coast (*Let the Sea Make a Noise: A History of the North Pacific from Magellan to MacArthur* [1993]).

Another unexpected career twist came the year I arrived at Penn. Since the department's American diplomatic historian was going on an extended leave, the chair asked whether I could also teach U.S. history. It meant working up a new lecture course like a rookie Assistant Professor, but I leapt at the opportunity because I relish breaking new ground. It teaches you so much new stuff. I continued to teach European and East Asian history, but was so fond of my American course that I kept it in my rotation after the absent professor returned. It also inspired my next book (*Promised Land, Crusader State: The American Encounter with the World Since 1776* [1997]). Three years later Dr. Serendipity again took control of my life when editors at HarperCollins asked if I was interested in writing a grand synthesis of American domestic as well as international history. That project metastasized into three more weighty volumes over a fifteen-year period (*Freedom Just Around the Corner: A New American History 1585–1828* [2004]; *Throes of Democracy: The*

American Civil War Era 1829–1877 [2007]; and *The Tragedy of U.S. Foreign Policy: How American Civil Religion Betrayed the National Interest* [2016]). N.B.: The abominable example of "the pathetic fallacy" in that last title was the publisher's doing, not mine.

So it was that I gained such a reputation as an American historian that people today are surprised to learn I was originally trained in European history. Since the essays in this collection date from that latter phase of my career they all bear on important themes in American history. My hope is that readers find them entertaining as well as informative, and I invite them to share their reactions with me via email (wamcd@sas.upenn.edu). Thank you for your kind attention.

—Walter A. McDougall,
Bryn Mawr, Pennsylvania, December 2024

★ ★ ★

Now here are those stylistic instructions I distribute to students every semester.

Tips on Editing Your Own Work to Achieve a Crisp Writing Style

PASSIVE VOICE is a construction in which the object of a sentence (that which is being acted upon) is turned into the subject, such as "The 1954 Geneva Accords were not seen as a tolerable solution to the problems of Southeast Asia." Passive voice is almost always poor style because, well, it's just passive. It can also be an author's dodge because it does not require one to identify who was even doing the action, much less how or why. The essence of historical writing is to explain cause and effect. That is, someone (the subject noun) does something (the verb) to something or someone (the direct object) for a reason or reasons you, the historian, need to explain. A normal active voice sentence contains all elements of that causal chain. Such as: "The Eisenhower Administration refused to adhere to the Geneva Accords lest it legitimize an expansion of Communist power." Here you have a clear causal relationship and some added information besides. Always try to rewrite passive voice sentences, choosing actors (not abstractions) as your subject, plus a vivid verb.

VIVID NOUNS AND VERBS are always preferable to flat nouns and verbs, even when the latter are jazzed up by modifying adjectives and adverbs. If you are tempted to use words such as "very" or "somewhat" or "mostly" chances are you need to pick a more expressive noun or verb (think "torrid" rather than "very hot," or "pummeled" rather than "badly beat").

"APPROPRIATE" is never appropriate because it means nothing (which explains why politicians always promise to take "appropriate action at the appropriate time"). Without accompanying standards of propriety the adjective "appropriate" is a waste of four syllables.

Never write **"FEEL"** or **"FELT"** unless you really mean it. "To feel" means to harbor some emotion, but in our touchy-feely era of "self-esteem" and "getting in touch with our feelings" the word has become an icky substitute for "to think." Of course, sometimes historians should address emotional forces as in "The French felt betrayed when the U.S. failed to ratify the Versailles Treaty." But never write a sentence such as "The Kaiser's advisors felt victory was possible" when you really mean they "thought," "concluded," "believed," or "calculated." His generals turned out to be wrong, but they were making a rational, not an emotional, judgment.

THERE are many poor ways to begin a sentence, but perhaps the worst is with "There." Like passive voice, this blank substitute for a real subject noun is a vague construction that conveys little or no information, as in "There was a lot of doubt about Churchill's strategy to attack in the Mediterranean." Who doubted the strategy, when, and for what reason? Say instead: "In 1942 Generals Marshall and Eisenhower feared Churchill's Mediterranean strategy offered no chance of a decisive victory." Now we know the answers to who, when, and why.

IT is also rarely good style to start a sentence with "It."

AND the same goes for sentences beginning with "And."

If **AWK** appears in the margin of your graded essay it means your sentence is awkward, not that a seagull has flown into your prose. As in: "Sometimes AWK indicates run-on sentences, which one often finds in high school papers that have not been carefully proofread because that is something they are too lazy to do or else think they can just rely on spell-check, a good example of how computers, which in other ways are so useful, actually hurt American education." Here we have awkward syntax (sentence structure), run-on subordinate clauses, passive voice, and a missing antecedent (to whom does "they" refer: "high school papers"!?).

Speaking of **ANTECEDENTS**, be sure that your pronouns agree (singular or plural) with the nouns to which they refer. "Germany's policy was based on a miscalculation in 1939 because they figured Britain and France would never go to war over Danzig" is wrong because "they" has no antecedent. Write instead, "Hitler's strategy...because he figured...." or else "Nazi strategists miscalculated...because they...."

Learn to form the **POSSESSIVE**. It's = it is. Its = the possessive form of "it." Czechs = the simple plural. Czech's = the possessive form of one Czech person. Czechs' = the plural possessive for multiple Czechs.

Do not use **ABBREVIATIONS** (e.g., WW2) or **CONTRACTIONS** (e.g., "they'd" for "they would" or "didn't" for "did not"). Spell out words in a fine essay. The only major exception is the abbreviation "U.S." when employed as a nominative modifier as in "U.S. foreign policy..." That's O.K.

On the other hand, **ACRONYMS** (e.g., NATO or EU) are to be preferred so long as you spell out what they stand for upon first mention.

By the way, "e.g." is shorthand for the Latin phrase *exempli gratia* meaning "for the sake of an example." Do not confuse it with "i.e.," shorthand for *id est,* which means "that is."

If **SI** appears in the margin of your essay a **SPLIT INFINITIVE** is bleeding to death somewhere in your sentence. That means you have inserted an adverb between "to" and its verb stem, as in "to covertly support the Polish resistance." Write instead, "to support the Polish resistance covertly" or better yet, "to give covert support to the Polish resistance." Alas, even top U.S. newspapers and magazines have surrendered to the splitters of helpless infinitives, but that does not make it right.

"WORDY" speaks for itself. Think instead of a zippy noun, verb, or adjective that can substitute for a garrulous phrase. Instead of "The leaders of East Germany, who had always supported a more aggressive strategy toward the Allied presence in West Berlin, felt that the time was ripe to ask the Soviet Union to give the green light for decisive action" write "East German leaders had always itched for the chance to seal off West Berlin. Now they pleaded with Moscow to strike." Hear how the latter is much shorter and punchier? You can often create crisper sentences by substituting a vivid verb or noun for clunky adverbs, adjectives, or phrases.

COLLOQ is shorthand for a colloquialism, or slang, as in "De Gaulle was so ticked off at the British for he way he was treated during World War II that he black-balled them from the European Community." Sounds like a fraternity rush. Say instead, "De Gaulle, still bitter over his wartime snub from *les Anglo-Saxons*, relished the chance to veto Britain's application to the European Community."

Beware of **DANGLING PARTICIPLES** that fall off cliffs into the dreaded pit where B– students spend all eternity. "Flying back home from Munich, sighs of relief washed over Neville Chamberlain for saving the peace" literally means those "sighs" were the ones taking wing over the English Channel. Write instead, "After he flew home from Munich, Neville Chamberlain was greeted with sighs of relief." But since that is passive voice, better yet write: "The British public greeted Neville Chamberlain with sighs of relief when his airplane touched down at Heathrow Airport."

REDUNDANT means you use the same word or phrase repeatedly in a sentence or paragraph. Check for this when you proofread and substitute pronouns or synonyms. Thus, instead of writing "the United States" over and over again, refer at times to "America" or "the Truman Administration." Better yet, when possible, specify the precise actors to convey more information, as in "the State Department" or "U.S. military commanders."

Likewise, **REPETITIVE** means you are making the same point two or more times. That is tedious for the reader and wasteful of precious space if you have a page limit. A somewhat repetitive summary at the end of an essay is O.K., but no good reason exists to say something over again in the body of a text.

Avoid **SEMI-COLONS**, which make for choppy, often run-on sentences. When tempted to use one, try a period plus a new sentence or else a hyphen. To be sure, semi-colons are correct in a list that follows a colon, as in "The Versailles Treaty contained four main provisions to enhance French security against Germany: the Anglo-American alliance; German disarmament; the demilitarized zone; and a fifteen-year Allied occupation of the Rhine." Otherwise, semi-colons are nearly always bad news.

How many **COMMAS** are too many or too few? Listen to your prose as if you were reading aloud and make common-sense judgments about where punctuation is needed to assist the reader's understanding. But in all cases, if you open a phrase with a comma you must close it with a comma (or period if the end of the sentence). Consider: "The frequent turnover of governments, a perennial weakness of the Third Republic helped paralyze French foreign policy in the 1930s." You need a comma after "Republic" to close the phrase begun with "a perennial."

ELLIPSES are a mystery, and not only in mathematics. The word refers to dots. When skipping over text in mid-sentence of a quotation insert three dots: "From Stettin . . . to Trieste . . . an Iron Curtain has descended upon the continent." When skipping over text that would have concluded a sentence insert four dots: "From Stettin on the Baltic to Trieste on the Adriatic an Iron Curtain has descended. . . ." Why four? The fourth is the period ending the sentence!

ENDING QUOTATIONS can be a vexation, but the current (arbitrary) rule is that the close-quote marks reside outside the concluding punctuation in a sentence. See the Churchill quotations above. The correct order is (1) final word; (2) period, question mark, or exclamation; (3) close-quote. But if the punctuation is yours then it falls at the end, outside the close quotes. As in: Why did Churchill use the provocative phrase "Iron Curtain"?

What about **FOOTNOTE** form? Here I'm easy. Any accepted form is fine so long as you are consistent. Standard footnote form requires a full citation upon first mention of a source, then a short version thereafter: 1. Felix Gilbert and David Clay Large, *The End of the European Era* (New York: Norton, 2002), p. 66. And subsequently: 4. Gilbert, *European Era*, p. 103. Standard endnote form is the same except the notes are appear on a separate page. Standard social science form consists of a simple parenthesis at the end of the quoted sentence in your text, as in "Colonel House thought he must 'call the President's attention to the perils of such a treaty'" (Kissinger, p. 238). If you use social science method, however, you must add a bibliography with full citations at the end.

Do you **OVERQUOTE**? Many students do, either from lack of self-confidence, fear of plagiarism, or the erroneous belief they must document every fact they present. In truth, quotations should be rare because too many of them break up the flow of your prose and give your essay a cut-and-paste look. In my judgment direct quotations (rather than paraphrases) are advisable only in the following three instances: (1) the fact or idea you cite is so surprising and/or little known that the reader will want to know where you got it; (2) the words quoted are from a primary source critical to proving your argument; or (3) whether primary or secondary (i.e., some other historian) the quoted phrase is so felicitous that to paraphrase it would be a shame (i.e., "I couldn't have said it better myself"). In all other cases, write in your own words and preserve the flow of the story you're telling. Finally, you are free to assume a good deal of knowledge from your reader. We are studying the same subjects and reading the same books, so you can assume we are familiar with the Weimar Republic or the gold standard and do not need a quote or citation to persuade us that Clemenceau represented France at the Paris Peace Conference.

At all times the best principle for elegant writing style is get it clear in your mind what you want to say, then say it in the most efficient, effective words. That does not mean you should have the whole essay in your head before you begin. On the contrary! That will just give you writer's block. In fact, I advise you to pay little attention to style while writing your first draft. Just concentrate on stating your argument(s) and assembling your facts. But then do a serious second draft which applies the advice above on how to edit your own work. Ask of every sentence, "Is this exactly what I mean to convey, and is it the sharpest, clearest way to convey it?" Once your polished second draft is complete, one final proofread is all that remains.

BONUS TIPS from George Orwell's rules of writing which appeared in his essay on "Politics and the English Language" published in April 1946. The date matters. Orwell's essay expressed his disgust with the way totalitarian regimes and modernist movements generally had polluted the language so as to obscure clarity and truth. Since then verbal pollution has only increased thanks to the corruption of American rhetoric, decline in the quality of education, and spread of viruses such as political correctness and cancel culture. But these rules are generic and apply under all circumstances:

(i) Never use a metaphor, simile, or other figure of speech that you are used to seeing in print.

(ii) Never use a long word where a short one will do.

(iii) If it is possible to cut a word out, always cut it out.
(iv) Never use the passive when you can use the active voice.
(v) Never use a foreign phrase, scientific word, or jargon if you can think of an everyday English equivalent.
(vi) Break any of these rules sooner than write something that sounds utterly barbarous.

THE END

★ 1 ★

AMERICA'S MACHIAVELLIAN MOMENT

Origins of the Atlantic Republican Tradition[1]

What does it mean to speak of American exceptionalism? If it just means unique then the claim is unexceptional because no two countries are alike. If it means that Americans believe their country is special, then again that is nothing exceptional because all great nations have cherished flattering myths. If it means that Americans are exceptionally virtuous given their devotion to liberty, equality, justice, prosperity, social mobility, and peace, then ipso facto they have also been exceptionally vicious for having fallen so short of those ideals. If it means that Americans are exempted from the laws of entropy because—as the German statesman Otto von Bismarck reportedly quipped—"God looks after fools, drunks, and the United States of America," then such exceptionalism can only be proven *sub specie aeternitatis*. Indeed, the very illusion that one's nation is under divine dispensation may perversely inspire the pride that goeth before a fall or the many bad ends to which reckless adolescents are prone. Finally, if exceptionalism means that America's "indispensable" status renders the nation exempt from the rules of behavior *it makes and enforces on other nations,* then enemies, neutrals, and allies alike are sure to push back.

So "exceptionalism" is more trouble than it's worth: it either means nothing or altogether too much. But the principal reason to banish the term from historical discourse is that the moniker did not even exist until the mid-twentieth century. No Puritan colonist, Founding Father, Civil War statesman, nineteenth-century poet, pastor, or propagandist ever invoked the term. To be sure, Alexis de Tocqueville in the 1830s called America's geography exceptional insofar as it was separated from Europe, and the German sociologist Werner Sombart in the 1890s thought American society an exception to Europe's rules insofar as Socialism had little appeal for the American working class. But neither employed the noun "American exceptionalism."

Indeed, the first ones who did—Pope Leo XIII in the 1890s and the American Communist Jay Lovestone in the 1930s—used exceptionalism as a term of opprobrium because they feared the nation's liberalism, individualism, and prosperity rendered its people immune to their own universalist appeals. Not until the 1950s did Max Lerner, Daniel Boorstin, and many other historians turn American exceptionalism into a badge of honor and trace its roots all the way back to Puritan New England. Finally, Presidents John F. Kennedy and Ronald Reagan made American exceptionalism a benign household phrase in order to assure their national congregations that they were on the side of the angels during the Cold War. But after the end of the Cold War the malign implications of exceptionalism became quickly apparent when American elites assumed their own "exceptional" values and institutions would become universal whether or not other cultures wanted them.

So what if the *ur*-historical claims made for American exceptionalism amount to a civil religious myth? Do not the truths they symbolize about the nation's New World character remain valid? Not really, because common sense tells us New Worlds cannot baptize themselves. Only people from a self-conscious Old World can conjure a New World, which is exactly what happened in the centuries since 1492. As a British skeptic has observed, "not even the Puritans were impelled by a unique or exceptional American impulse. On the contrary, they were products of European education, European culture, European piety, and were engaged in a great European quarrel [the Protestant Reformation]." Some 140 years later the thirteen colonies' representatives did gather in Philadelphia to reject European rule, but the principles they invoked were "the beliefs of the English Revolution and the Whig tradition, in the English, Scottish, and French Enlightenments, and in the ancient principles of English Common Law—in short, in the core beliefs of a European civilization."

Historians have in fact dug deeply into the political theories of early modern Britain and unearthed the ideas that led, in the fulness of time, to the American Founding. One familiar source is the Bible, especially the Hebrew Republicanism mandated in the book of Deuteronomy and realized during the three centuries after the conquest of Canaan as recounted in the book of Judges. Former Chief Rabbi of the United Kingdom Sir Jonathan Sacks, has explained that the Covenant made by the Lord through Moses was a blessing but also a curse: a blessing if the children of Israel obeyed God's commandments, but a curse if they turned away to other gods in the Promised Land. "See, I have set before you today life and good, death and evil. . . . Therefore, choose life, that you and your offspring may live."

Thus did the Torah establish, for the first time in history, the spiritual principle of free will, but Rabbi Sacks points out that it also established three political principles. First, divine sovereignty does not remove human responsibility. Moses warns the people that unless they remain faithful, neither armies nor allies can save them. Second, the Israelites are collectively responsible: the archetype for what the American Founders called "We the People." As Michael Walzer put it in *God's Shadow: Politics in the Hebrew Bible*, the twelve tribes constituted an "almost democracy." Third, this political order was centered on God because He was the law-giver. Hence the Israelites were the first to imagine themselves "one nation under God."

Rabbi Sacks has also explained why many English scholars in the mid-seventeenth century suddenly became eager to learn Hebrew and read rabbinical *midrash* literature. They wanted to know whether the Bible ordained monarchy or condemned it, in which case Parliament's Puritan rebellion against King Charles I in the 1640s was God's will. In Deuteronomy chapter 17 Moses prophesies that the Israelites will eventually desire a king, and he warns them to appoint only kings chosen by the Lord who adhere strictly to the law. Evidently, therefore, the Lord does permit monarchy. But in 1 Samuel chapter 8 the prophet is angered when the Israelites demand a king "so as to be like all the nations." The Lord laments this because it is He whom the people have rejected. Yet He instructs Samuel to anoint for them a king. In so doing the Lord established the principle of popular sovereignty—government by consent of the governed. Predictably—as prophesied by both Moses and Samuel—the kings and their subjects in the unified monarchy, then in divided Judah and Israel, apostasize and suffer under a nearly unbroken succession of wicked kings until at last both kingdoms are conquered. Such was the price to be paid by free people who failed to do justice, love kindness, and walk humbly with their God.

Professor Eric Nelson, in his book *The Hebrew Republic: Jewish Sources and the Transformation of European Political Thought*, has studied in depth the supporters of Oliver Cromwell's republican experiment who pored over these Old Testament texts and their rabbinical commentary. The process was greatly enabled when Cromwell dramatically repealed the expulsion of Jews from England, which dated from the year 1290. For instance, the poet and statesman John Milton concluded that the Lord permitted monarchy but nevertheless condemned it as tantamount to idolatry. Algernon Sydney and James Harrington likewise damned monarchy for sacred as well as secular reasons and endorsed republicanism. Moreover, Professor Nelson shows that Sydney and Harrington derived corollaries from their Hebrew Republicanism, including the periodic redistribution of wealth (the Torah's "jubilee years") and—most surprisingly—religious toleration.

To be sure, Britain's Puritan Commonwealth did not long survive Cromwell's death. Parliament restored the Stuart king and Anglican church in 1660. But the ideas survived and partially triumphed in Britain's Glorious Revolution of 1688. A century later those same ideas inspired colonists such as John Witherspoon, the Scots-Presbyterian president of the College of New Jersey (as Princeton was originally known) who educated James Madison and a host of other American Founders.

All that is deep background to a very familiar event. In 1774 Tom Paine sailed from England to Philadelphia and within eighteen months published the pamphlet that persuaded Congress to declare independence. Paine himself was an Enlightenment skeptic who had no use for religion. Yet the central argument of *Common Sense* was precisely God's prophecies about the evils of monarchy. Paine had lifted the argument from John Milton.

Thus, Hebrew Republicanism, filtered through early modern England and transplanted to the colonies, was one familiar source of American institutions and values, and explains why clergymen throughout the colonies—not just in New England—preached revolution from their pulpits, made the Exodus their metaphor, told Americans they were a new chosen people, and sang with their congregations the revolutionary hymn: "To the king they shall sing hallelujah / And all the continent shall sing / Down with this earthly king: no king but God!"

But so, too, did another, much less familiar, source exist, one which republican philosophers of the seventeenth and eighteenth centuries consciously suppressed lest they repel their audiences. That second source was such a surprise to historians that they did not even stumble on it until the mid-twentieth century. That second source was born in southern, Catholic Europe and seemed the antithesis of Biblical morality. That second inspiration for the English Commonwealthmen was the notorious observer of Renaissance statecraft and founder of modern political science, Niccolò Machiavelli.

Everyone knows his essay *The Prince* because it is short, provocative, and quotable: what the French call a *succès de scandale*. In it Machiavelli seemed to advocate arbitrary rule, ruthless tactics, deceit, brute force, and the principle that the ends justify the means. He had no use for established religion except as a sedative for the lower classes and believed moral corruption necessary for political success. The kindest label given to him is realist. The worst is monster. In England he was so notorious that "Old Nick" even became a sobriquet for the devil. Later we shall challenge that stereotype. But first, let us tour a city some of you surely know well, but which I only came to know recently when I gazed into a distant mirror.

In 1978 Barbara Tuchman wrote a book called *A Distant Mirror: The Calamitous 14th Century,* in which she described the serial crises that wrecked the High Medieval Era. They included the bubonic plague, which killed a third to a half of all Europeans, the Hundred Years War between England and France, the terrible Muslim onslaught of the Ottoman Turkish Empire, the crisis of religious authority born of a papal schism, and more. By "distant mirror" she meant to imply that the 1970s reflected similar existential crises.

I thought Tuchman's analogy overwrought. The Vietnam War, OPEC oil embargo, stagflation, and Watergate were certainly bad, but hardly equivalent to those Medieval calamities. Nevertheless, over my long career I have come to appreciate distant mirrors, because the High Medieval Era also reflects so much that we value today and flatter ourselves to think of as modern. Consider this list of ideas and institutions whose roots lie in the Middle Ages: the rule of law, English Common Law, the separation of church and state, limited monarchy, parliamentary government (*Magna Carta* dates from 1215), universities first founded in the eleventh and twelfth centuries, natural rights (the first expression of what we call human rights), rural and commercial capitalism, all sorts of technological breakthroughs from the moldboard plow and mechanical clock to the waterwheel and the printing press, and the restless, curious, ambitious spirit that moved Europeans to build ocean-going ships and begin to map the world.

We only think of the Medieval era as stagnant, superstitious, and brutal because Renaissance humanists imagined their own era a rebirth of ancient Greece and Rome, hence they dismissed the Medieval millennium rather than admit the obvious fact that the Renaissance itself had grown out of it. The Puritan John Adams, who certainly had no love for the Catholic Church, grudgingly granted that fact when he wrote that somehow "people in the middle ages became more intelligent in general."

The distant mirror also reflects exquisite beauty, which is something I learned when I finally accompanied my wife on a journey to Italy. I say "accompanied" because she did all the logistics and planning and I just followed her lead like a joyful dog out for a walk. Everything about Italy—the history, art, architecture, scenery, and cuisine—was sublime. But for me the capstone was Venice.

Americans take pride in having lived under their Constitution for 230 years. The British have lived under their unwritten Constitution for 330 years. But *La Serenissima Repubblica di Venetia* lasted more than a thousand years, from the 700s until 1797, when that brigand Napoleon abolished it. Imagine peering into churches built four or five hundred years before Christopher Columbus discovered America!

The islands in the lagoons at the northern edge of the Adriatic Sea were first settled by refugees from the Lombards, one of the barbarian tribes that overran ancient Rome. Then Venice was reinforced by the Lombards themselves as they fled from the Frankish armies of Charlemagne, who invaded Italy around the year 800.

For a few centuries the colony's politics were turbulent, but the creative Venetians took advantage of their unique geography to consolidate a city-state devoted to sea power, aggressive commerce, and precocious republican institutions. Their leader was an elected duke, or Doge, who served for life under a sacred pledge not to abuse his powers. As the centuries passed his executive powers came to be checked and balanced by a Senate, a Great Council, an executive Council in charge of war and diplomacy, and special councils for other functions, including a secret bureau for internal security and another for naval construction and recruitment. By the fourteenth century the Venetians had fashioned a thalassocracy—a maritime empire—throughout the Adriatic and eastern Mediterranean, and pioneered trade routes to northern Europe, the Byzantine Empire, the Ottoman Empire, Persia, and thanks to Marco Polo, China.

This surprisingly modern commercial republic in the midst of Medieval Europe grew immensely wealthy thanks to its shrewd Doges, Councils, and merchants, and thanks to the intelligence gathered by permanent embassies stationed abroad. Venetians outfitted the Crusades and claimed the lion's share of the plunder. Venetians monopolized the spice trade. Venetians patronized exquisite art, music, and public works. But perhaps their most impressive achievement was the city-state's highly developed *civil* religion. Venice was nominally Roman Catholic, but also receptive to anyone who contributed to its prosperity, be they Muslims, Jews, Greek Orthodox, and later Protestant Germans, Britons, and Dutch.

What Venetians really worshiped was the city itself, symbolized by its patron saint, Mark the Evangelist, whose very bones a Venetian expedition, in the year 828, purloined from a crypt in Alexandria, Egypt. According to legend, the raiders smuggled the relics past Muslim officials by stuffing them inside a shipment of pork. The iconographic symbol for St. Mark is a wingèd lion, which one encounters all over Venice to this day. The city fathers honored the Catholic Church calendar but also celebrated civic triumphs with feasts, carnivals, and liturgies. The Doge's palace is a treasury of frescoes and sculptures displaying the glorious history of Venice and celebrating its republican virtue.

The *Sala del Maggior Consiglio* is the largest room in Europe. There the Great Council's 1,500 members convened in a spirit of equality under a frieze ringing the ceiling with busts of the first seventy-six doges. The hall's grand fresco by Tintoretto was supposed to depict the coronation of the Virgin Mary as Queen of Heaven, but Tintoretto's son, who completed this largest painting in Europe, changed the theme to "The Virgin Mary Interceding with Christ on Behalf of Venice." Many more frescoes pay obeisance to Neptune and Mars, the Classical gods of the sea and of war, as if the Venetians were hedging their bets. Most tellingly, the Doge's palace and St. Mark's Basilica are literally joined at the hip in proud expression of the civil religion.

In war and diplomacy the Venetians shunned entangling alliances except in emergencies when they would organize coalitions. The most famous was the Holy League, whose combined fleets routed the Ottoman Turks in the 1571 Battle of Lepanto. Tintoretto, conveniently forgetting the other members of that coalition, commemorated the battle in a grand allegory entitled "The Triumph of Venice."

Alas, by the sixteenth century Venice was beginning to suffer the effects of dire historical trends which hurled it into a long, languid decline: the Ottoman conquest of Byzantium in 1453, the Spanish and Portuguese discoveries of sea routes to America and India in the 1490s, the perennial wars following the invasion of Italy by France and the Holy Roman Empire after 1494, and the rise of national monarchies in Spain, France, and England. It speaks to the credit of Venetian institutions, civil religion, and artistic genius that the city's brilliant sunset lingered all the way down to the French Revolution.

What has that distant mirror to do with England, much less the United States? A great deal, it turns out, and not only because those countries came to resemble the Venetian commercial republic in many ways, but specifically because of what J. G. A. Pocock described in his 1975 classic *The Machiavellian Moment: Florentine Political Thought and the Atlantic Republican Tradition*. In it he argued that the modern political theory of eighteenth-century America mirrored that of seventeenth-century England, which in turn mirrored that of sixteenth-century Italy. Pocock drew on the writings of Renaissance figures such as Francesco Guicciardini, but especially Machiavalli's lengthy treatises such as the *Discourses on Livy* and *Florentine Histories*, written between 1510 and 1530. Pocock meant to educate English readers on the *real* Machiavelli, the brilliant and brutally honest student of politics whose purpose was not to advocate cruelty and deceit but to describe, empirically, how most real princes behave in the real world. Hence, it behooved even high-minded princes to act likewise if only to defend their subjects' liberty and well-being. To be sure, Machiavelli was hostile to the Christianity of his day, but that is not surprising given the Papacy had plummeted to its decadent nadir during the Renaissance. But his purpose in separating moral judgments from the facts of political life was simply scientific.

What is more, Machiavelli did not mean the word "prince" to imply a dynastic ruler, but anyone in charge of a state, be he a nobleman like the Duke of Milan, a plutocrat like Lorenzo di Medici, or a military *condottieri* like Francesco Sforza. Indeed, he preferred that princes, whatever their background, be men of *virtú,* that Renaissance ideal which meant not Christian virtue but ancient Roman ideals such as manliness, energy, guile, and courage. And he insisted that princes—as opposed to tyrants—use their power on behalf of "the common good." In the *Discourses on Livy*, that ancient chronicler of the rise and fall of the Roman Republic, Machiavelli made clear his own preference for republican government. But that very preference made it imperative for him to learn from the histories of Classical Greece and Rome why republics so often succumbed to tyranny, anarchy, or conquest, or aborted in the manner of Renaissance Italy's ephemeral republics. His voyage of discovery—Machiavelli likened himself to Columbus—taught him surprising things, including the positive value of factionalism because competition among rival parties fostered a division of powers and checks and balances. He thus considered it healthy for a state to include plebeian or populist factions opposed to patrician or princely factions, and he welcomed the occasional tumults that resulted because they inspired the reforms periodically needed to rejuvenate a republic. He advocated an independent judiciary. Finally, he promoted commercial and military expansion because he understood the well-springs of republics to be popular greed and fear.

Machiavelli and Guicciardini were natives of Florence, but for both the model republic was Venice, and by "Machiavellian moment" Pocock meant a historical conjuncture when the founders of a republic confront the question of how to build durable institutions like those of Venice. But Machiavelli's reputation was besmirched during a tormented life in which he suffered exile and torture, and it only grew worse after his death. The Catholic Church banned his books. Protestants reviled him because he denied natural rights and advocated republicanism on strictly utilitarian grounds. That is, he believed that people preferred liberty, not because they valued its intrinsic dignity or had any natural right to it, but simply because it worked: "cities have not grown either in dominion or riches when not in a condition of liberty."

But for that same reason Machiavelli's science of politics lived on among practical men intent on propagating and preserving conditions of liberty. So it was, a century later and half a continent away, when a Parliament declared its king a tyrant, waged civil war against him, cut off his head, then founded a republic in 1649, that England faced its own Machiavellian moment.

The leader of the Parliamentary army, Oliver Cromwell, claimed his purpose was to establish a godly Commonwealth, but he in fact exploited power in the manner of a Machiavellian prince to make himself Lord Protector, in effect a military dictator whose regime oppressed the English and crushed the Irish and Scots. Yet the Commonwealth did create space for republican thought to flourish, and into that space rushed such creative thinkers as Marchamont Nedham and James Harrington, whose greatest works, *The Excellencie of a Free State* and the *Commonwealth of Oceana*, respectively, were both published in 1656. They restated, refined, and adapted Classical Republican ideas about liberty emerging from the tensions between patricians and populists, the importance of mixed government and checks and balances, and the value of tumults, commerce, and war. Harrington even cited Machiavelli as his principal source, and the utopia he described in his famous *Oceana* was not really utopian. It was simply the Venetian republic with English characteristics, in which a natural aristocracy expertly trained in commerce, science, and law governs the republic in the best interests of all. Nowhere else was there "so undisturbed and constant a tranquillity and peace," wrote Harrington, because civil perfection "hath no pattern in the universal world, except that of Venice."

Of course, Harrington's grand design was never attempted because the English people and Parliament grew weary of Cromwell's authoritarian zeal and restored the Stuart monarchy after his death. But the Classical Republicanism largely inspired by Machiavelli did not die. On the contrary, it stormed back forcefully during the

Restoration in the works of philosophers such as Algernon Sydney, whose *Discourses Concerning Government* of 1680 was an assault on monarchy (indeed, so brazen an assault that it cost Sydney his life). His contemporary John Locke was more prudent. He escaped charges of treason by fudging his opposition to monarchy and then coming to terms with a limited, constitutional monarchy in his *Two Treatises on Government* of 1689. Locke was also discreet in that he never revealed how profound Machiavelli's influence had been on his thought. He was in fact an avid collector of the Florentine's writings, studied them with care, shared his antipathy toward religious moralizing, and diverged from Machiavelli only insofar as he favored peaceful commerce rather than martial expansion.

But Machiavelli got that right as well: popular regimes are just as belligerent as autocratic regimes. For the so-called Glorious Revolution defended by Locke was in fact an inglorious coup d'état by a war party in Parliament and the Army that called itself Whig. The Whigs then drove James II into exile for the crimes of baptizing his son a Catholic, emulating Louis XIV's absolute monarchy, and pursuing peaceful relations with France. Whereupon the Whigs invited James's Protestant daughter Mary and her husband, the Dutch *stadtholder* William of Orange, to reign over England and join them in launching the first in a long series of conflicts which the colonists in America would come to call the French and Indian wars.

The Whigs also pursued an ambitious domestic agenda of a decidedly Republican cast. Between 1689 and 1707 they established Parliamentary supremacy over the crown, the Bill of Rights, the Act of Succession banning Catholics, the Act of Union with Scotland, and the Bank of England to fund a floating national debt to finance Britain's imperial wars.

Over the course of the eighteenth century those institutions made Britain the world's greatest power. Moreover, it was during that century that the intellectual movement called the Enlightenment spread throughout Europe and across the ocean to the quickly maturing American colonies. The hyper-rational, social-scientific character of the Enlightenment sharply circumscribed the influence of sectarian religion on statecraft. So it is not surprising that Machiavelli became more influential (if not more respectable) than he had been during the era of the Wars of Religion. The Frenchman Charles-Louis de Montesquieu, the Scotsman David Hume, and the American Benjamin Franklin were just a few of the eighteenth-century philosophers who postulated that Christian virtue was a fragile foundation on which to build a republic. Rather, republican durability required precisely those sturdy institutions the Whigs had established, indeed institutions that resembled Venetian ones so closely that Montesquieu even called Britain "a republic in monarchical disguise."

In 1705 the Dutchman Bernard Mandeville observed those institutions and wrote a satire *The Fable of the Bees*, describing the Machiavellian modes by which Whigs pursued parliamentary, commercial, and imperial power: "Thus every Part was full of Vice, / Yet the whole Mass a Paradice... And Vertue, who from Politicks / Had learn'd a Thousand cunning Tricks, / Was, by their happy Influence, / Made Friends with Vice: And ever since / The worst of all the Multitude / Did something for the common Good."

Henry St. John Bolingbroke, in his 1738 classic *The Patriot King*, even reconciled monarchy with republicanism when he admonished kings to imagine themselves the nation's chief executive on behalf of the public interest. Delegates at the Constitutional Convention had that book much on their minds while designing of the office of President of the United States.

Which brings us at last to America. So far it would appear that I fully endorse Pocock's thesis about the direct reflections of sixteenth-century Florentine thought on seventeenth-century English ideas and eighteenth-century American ones. In fact, I do not, because various intellectual historians have challenged Pocock since 1974. One of the more prominent, Hillsdale College Professor Paul Rahe, summed up their findings as follows: while all agree with Pocock that Machiavelli had considerable influence on later British and American thought, they believe the cause-and-effect connections he drew from one Machiavellian moment to the next are too direct. They caution that historical actors should not be read as semi-conscious speakers of someone else's political language but as fully conscious agents for whom Machiavellian insights, while important, must be weighed alongside other sources as well as their own experiences. In any event, Machiavelli's legacy was bound to become diffuse during the 250 years separating Renaissance Florence from colonial Philadelphia.

Finally, we must remember that men such as Franklin, George Washington, Thomas Jefferson, Alexander Hamilton, James Madison, and John Adams were not abstract theorists like Harrington, Sydney, or Locke. Rather, they were statesmen-practitioners engaged in designing real institutions they hoped would foster justice as well as liberty and prosperity. That moral imperative precluded a wholesale adoption of the Florentine's system. Indeed, Washington, however realistic his statecraft in war and peace, displayed a character the very opposite from that of a serpentine Machiavellian prince. Nevertheless, the years between the summoning of the First Continental Congress in 1774 and the ratification of the Constitution in 1789 were assuredly another Machiavellian moment in that earnest men deliberated on how to craft a republic that might endure like the Venetian one.

For instance, the Founders all saw the wisdom of such Machiavellian notions as separation of powers, checks and balances, an independent judiciary, sacrosanct private property, robust commerce, and occasional political tumult. Recall that Jefferson wrote: "I hold it that a little rebellion now and then is a good thing, and as necessary in the political world as storms in the physical." Jefferson and Madison never admitted to having Machiavellian ideas, but they were influenced by people who did, such as Sydney, Locke, Montesquieu, and Hume, and their libraries contained Machiavelli's works. For Madison, Machiavelli had been assigned reading at Witherspoon's college, and one of his most trenchant contributions to the Constitution—the celebration of political factionalism—was a Machiavellian insight. To be sure, Madison's abhorrence of war was certainly not Machiavellian, but his arch-rival Hamilton thoroughly agreed with the Florentine's observations that republics are warlike and that successful ones need an energetic executive ready and willing to prepare for war.

No American devoted more thought to the Florentine's writings than John Adams. He not only studied his works but quoted extensively from the *Discourses on Livy* and *Florentine Histories* in his own *Defense of the Constitutions of the United States of America* published in 1788. Moreover, Adams drew heavily on English Commonwealthmen such as Nedham and Harrington, whom he also discussed at some length in his *Defense*. Needless to add, the New England Puritan also critiqued Machiavelli on various constitutional points and broke with him entirely on moral questions. Adams, like Washington, believed religious faith to be an indispensable buttress for a healthy republic, and he obviously thought it possible to fashion a republic through collective reflection rather than princely force and deceit.

Perhaps therein lies the most trenchant critique of Pocock's thesis because the American Founders, while eminently practical men, were not strictly utilitarian... which brings us full circle back to the Bible. The historian Russell Kirk, in his classic treatise *The Roots of American Order*, has explained that whereas the U.S. Constitution owed little to the example of the Israelites as recounted in Deuteronomy and Judges, the Founders' moral order could not have existed without it. Kirk noted that in John Adams's corpus of works, which drew so heavily on Machiavelli's studies of Greece and Rome, one finds no account of Israel and Judah. Yet Adams understood their true import. In 1809 he wrote, "I insist that the Hebrews have done more to civilize men than any other nation. [Even if I were an atheist who believes] that all is ordered by chance, I should believe that chance had ordered the Jews to preserve and propagate to all mankind the doctrine of a supreme, intelligent, wise, almighty sovereign of the universe, which is the essential principle of all morality, and consequently all civilization."

So what do we find when we dig for the roots of the Atlantic republican tradition? We find that American institutions derived from a Classical Republicanism leavened by Hebrew Republicanism; a Machiavellian body quickened by a Biblical spirit; a civil government inspired by a civil religion. I therefore agree with Professor Rahe that while no American Founder adopted Machiavelli's ideas without at least some reservations, the Founders and those who came after them nevertheless owed Machiavelli a very great debt. Rahe concludes: "To sort out the character of the American Revolution... one would do well to begin with the astonishing wave of political speculation that took place in the English revolution, which itself was a product of that great revolution initiated in 16th century Florence... by the sage after whom the devil himself came to be called Old Nick."

★ 2 ★

BENJAMIN FRANKLIN AND THE CRISIS OF THE BRITISH EMPIRE[1]

On a cool, dank afternoon in December 1773 two men met in London's Kensington Gardens for the purpose of killing each other.

John Temple, who had served as a customs official in New England, had little experience with weapons. William Whately, a banker, had none at all. But they fell upon each other without even waiting for their seconds to arrive. After both pistol shots went awry they thrashed at each other with swords for forty-five minutes in what one historian called "a clumsy, almost comical affair." When the banker suffered a serious wound onlookers finally separated the duelists. In fact, the two men barely knew each other, although both had ties to prominent people in Massachusetts and both had obtained access to a sheaf of confidential letters sent to Whately's now-deceased brother by Thomas Hutchinson, the colony's lieutenant-governor. Eight years before, during the agitation over the Stamp Act passed by Parliament, a Boston mob had sacked and burned the governor's elegant townhouse. So Hutchinson, himself a native of Massachusetts, had written those letters urging that British officials "abridge what are called English liberties" lest the angry colonists issue "a veritable declaration of independence." Somehow those inflammatory documents turned up in Boston in June 1773, and their publication provoked more riots plus a petition from the colony's assembly demanding Hutchinson's dismissal. Who had leaked the letters? For months suspicion in London had fallen on Whately or Temple, which caused each to accuse the other of lying and prompted their near-fatal duel.

That smoked out the real perpetrator. On December 25, 1773, a shocking letter appeared in the *London Advertiser* signed by a third party who confessed to leaking the correspondence. He was none other than the Deputy Postmaster for North America, Benjamin Franklin. A London resident since 1757, he served as the colonial agent for Massachusetts as well as Pennsylvania, and his motive had been to show the colony's leaders that one of their own—not the king or Parliament—had been responsible for the fact that their town was now occupied by Redcoats. Franklin had meant to promote reconciliation. Instead, he was obliged to write the speaker of the Massachusetts assembly Thomas Cushing: "I am told by some that it was imprudent to avow obtaining and sending those letters, for that the administration will resent it, but if it happens I must take the consequences."[2]

The consequences were not slow to arrive. On the evening of December 16, 1773, after a contest of wills between Bostonians and their royal officials over the payment of duties on tea, a mob boarded three East India Company ships and dumped 342 chests of tea into the harbor. On January 7, 1774, Whately filed suit against Franklin for purloining the Hutchinson letters. Two days later Franklin presented to the Privy Council the colonists' petition for Hutchinson's recall. On January 27 news of the Boston Tea Party struck London like lightning. Two days later Franklin was summoned to the Privy Council, where he was subjected to a vicious and carefully planned humiliation in the so-called Cockpit.

More than thirty peers, including the Chief Justice and Archbishop of Canterbury, were in rapt attendance. The spectator benches overflowed with dignitaries, very few of whom had any sympathy for the scheming American. Two who did were the Anglo-Irish statesman Edmund Burke, who served as colonial agent for New York, and Joseph Priestley, the famed chemist and friend of Franklin.

The historian Daniel Mark Epstein describes the scene: "At the head of the table, his figure inclined like a question mark or a scythe, rises the dark figure of the solicitor general, Alexander Wedderburn, a lawyer famed for eloquence and malice. A short, delicate, hawk-nosed man, Wedderburn pointed his finger at Franklin and pounded the table. He had come on behalf of Governor Hutchinson, Lord North, the King, the Empire, and the very principle of decency—to call Benjamin Franklin to account." Franklin, who later likened it to a bull-baiting, stood rigid and still for over an hour while the solicitor leveled vicious indictments. He accused him of inciting insurrection and of inspiring pamphlets which told Bostonians "of a hundred rights of they had not heard before, and a hundred grievances they had not felt." He accused him of leaking the Hutchinson letters for the purpose of undermining the governor's stoic efforts to calm his constituents. Finally, he verged on accusing Franklin of treason by suggesting he had become possessed by the idea of a Great American Republic. The Privy Council, needless to say, dismissed the Massachusetts petition out of hand. Franklin walked home alone, seething inside, and carefully packed away the elegant velvet suit he had donned for the occasion, swearing never to wear it again until he was somehow avenged. The following day he also learned he had been stripped of the postmaster duties he had performed with distinction for two decades.

Most historians (myself included) facilely concluded that Franklin's humiliation in the Cockpit was sufficient to explain his conversion to the American cause. But Wedderburn's arrogance did *not* change Franklin's loyalties. The story is much more complicated than that.

In our previous lecture we traced the American Founders' ideas all the way back to the Classical and Hebrew republicanism bequeathed by the Renaissance city-states of sixteenth-century Italy and the Cromwellian Commonwealth of seventeenth-century England. This time we shall stick much closer to home, for our subject is Benjamin Franklin and the crisis of the British Empire.

The first thing to realize about 1776 is that the declaration of independence was by no means inevitable. As the historian J. C. D. Clark writes at the start of his essay "What If There Had Been No American Revolution?": "History labours under a major handicap in societies suffused with a sense of their own righteousness or inevitability. Whether driven by secular ideologies, shared religious beliefs or consensual optimism, such societies devise intellectual strategies to blot out their earlier sense of the paths that were not taken... [despite] their attractiveness to those who, knowingly or unknowingly... made the fatal choices."

Americans, steeped in their powerful civil religion which takes for granted their righteous nation's inevitability, have trouble imagining paths not taken. Exhibit A is Franklin himself, who, far from being an American patriot, was a zealous advocate for British imperial unity to the very end. Yet, by the 1820s, Americans were already honoring Franklin as one of their greatest Founding Fathers and indeed the archetype of their national character.

Over the two centuries since his reputation has only grown. The historian Robert Spiller considered Franklin's life the "distinctive American story" because he was both pragmatic and idealistic, scientist and salesman, speculator and philanthropist. Gladys Meyer called him the embodiment of American liberalism because of his support for "free trade, self-government, liberty, equality, education, social mobility, freedom of speech, press, thought, and religion." William Dean Howells considered him the "most modern, most American" man of his time. And so on down to H.

W. Brands, whose biography published in 2000 named Franklin "the first—in the sense of foremost—American"; Walter Isaacson, whose 2003 biography called Franklin the "first American"; and Stacy Schiff, whose 2005 biography claimed he was an American even before it was possible to be one. In my own 2004 book I cited Franklin's penchant for hustling in both the positive and pejorative senses as a quintessential American trait. David Brooks, the prominent *New York Times* columnist, recently dubbed Ben "Our Founding Yuppie," and Elon Musk tersely remarked, "Franklin was pretty awesome."

Enough! You need hardly be told about Franklin's character and lifetime achievements as a printer, entrepreneur, and civic leader who helped to found his adopted city's first fire department, police patrol, masonic lodge, library, college, militia, and post office. Nor of his homespun humor and biting satire, nor his fame as a self-taught scientist and philosopher, nor of his taming of electricity and ingenious inventions.

Indeed, it seems only natural that Americans came quickly to identify themselves with Franklin's apparent virtues.

What then does one make of the judgment by the Pulitzer Prize–winning historian Gordon Wood, who insisted "the historic Franklin of the eighteenth century was never destined to be [an American] symbol. He was not even destined to be an American!"

That is our story, a story that starts not with Franklin's birth in Boston in 1706, flight to Philadelphia in 1723, founding of the *Pennsylvania Gazette* in 1729, publication of *Poor Richard's Almanac* beginning in 1733, or any of his civic or scientific achievements. That story begins in 1754, when Colonel George Washington of the Virginia militia led an expedition into the forests of western Pennsylvania in hopes of prying the French out of their recently founded Fort Duquesne at the confluence of the Allegheny and Monongahela rivers. Instead, Washington blundered into a battle that escalated into the climactic French and Indian War. Franklin, who was then forty-eight years old and comfortably retired from business, jumped into politics. On the local scale he was active in Pennsylvania's faction opposing the proprietor Thomas Penn. On a grander scale he served as postmaster for all the northern colonies. On the grandest scale, Franklin now championed Britain's geopolitical struggle for North America.

Pennsylvania had long been vexed by problems of self-defense inasmuch as its Quakers were pacifist and its assembly was strapped for funds given that the Penn family's vast estates were tax-exempt. Franklin took matters into his own hands by raising a militia paid for by lotteries and by representing his colony at the Albany Congress on the Hudson River. Sponsored by the British Board of Trade, the purpose of the congress was to entice the Six Nations Iroquois into a war alliance, but delegates also took the occasion to advance plans for a colonial alliance. One of them, coincidentally, was proposed by the young Thomas Hutchinson.

Franklin later recorded in his autobiography that many objections and difficulties were voiced but at length his own plan was adopted. It would have left imperial defense in the hands of the Crown but also envisioned an American President-General appointed by the King and a Grand Council of colonial delegates empowered to tax themselves.

His plan was dead on arrival because, Franklin wrote, the assemblies "were narrowly provincial in outlook, mutually jealous, and suspicious of any central taxing authority." Hence, "the assemblies did not adopt it, as they all thought there was too much *prerogative* in it, [while] in England it was judg'd to have too much of the *democratic*." He later rued those rejections because under his plan the colonies might have been able to defend themselves without British Redcoats, which in turn became one of the pretexts for taxing the colonists.

The war began badly for the Redcoats and colonial militias, whom the British were now beginning to call—with a tinge of contempt—"Americans." General Braddock's invasion of western Pennsylvania, for which Franklin helped to procure horses, wagons, and supplies, ended in disaster. But Anglo-colonial relations improved markedly over the course of the war under the wise leadership of Prime Minister William Pitt, who, among other things, reimbursed colonial assemblies for their military expenses. In 1759 and 1760 British regulars captured Québec and Montreal, and in the 1763 Peace of Paris the French were obliged to cede New France (Canada) to the British. Franklin exulted. The colonists, he wrote, were fortunate to live "under the best of kings... [and] happy in the vigor and wisdom of the administration...."

Charles Pratt and William Burke, two prominent English lawyers, were among the few who did not exult. They feared that removal of the French threat to the north and west of the thirteen colonies would perversely tempt their inhabitants to pursue independence. Franklin dismissed such fears, assuring the British such notions would never enter the colonists' heads.

By that time Franklin had become a more or less permanent expatriate, comfortably residing at Mrs. Stevenson's boarding house near Charing Cross in London. In 1757 Pennsylvanians had made him their colonial agent, charged with lobbying the Privy Council to rescind the Penn proprietorship and appoint a royal governor. In that he would fail, but in all other ways Ben flourished in the cosmopolitan capital. His twenty-eight-year-old son flourished even more. William Franklin, the illegitimate offspring of an unknown affair, had accompanied Ben to London in order to study law. William rose so quickly in aristocratic circles that in 1761 he was invited to attend the coronation of George III. The following year he married the daughter of a Barbados sugar planter, and the year after that Prime Minister Lord Bute arranged for his appointment as governor of New Jersey. Not surprisingly William became a devoted royalist, so much so that he later became the most prominent "Tory" during the American revolution.[3] But that lay thirteen years in the future. For the time being Ben was proud and even a bit envious of his over-achieving son.

In any event, Ben was also warmly received in British society. St. Andrews and Oxford universities bestowed honorary degrees on the scientist, the Royal Society welcomed him, and such luminaries as David Hume, Adam Smith, and Joseph Priestley befriended him. Ben, always alert to the main chance, also promoted a company hoping to get a royal charter for a new colony on the Ohio River. In all things Franklin's identity, interests, and ambitions were so intimately bound up with Britain that he projected his own loyalties onto his countrymen, saying they would never unite against a nation "with which they have so many connections and ties of blood, interest, and affection."

Reality suggested otherwise. For the climax of the Anglo-French struggle for North America served as prelude to an intramural conflict over the empire's future because it obliged all parties to ask a question few had posed, and none had answered, before. What was the British Empire, anyway?

Twelve of the thirteen colonies—all but Georgia—had been founded during the seventeenth century under charters granted by Stuart kings. The last of them, James II, took a personal interest in America because, as Duke of York, he had dispatched the expedition that conquered New Amsterdam. When he then assumed the throne in 1685 James planned to merge all the colonies into dominions modeled on the Spanish vice-royalties. Happily for the colonists the English Whig Party ousted King James in the Glorious Revolution of 1688, established Parliamentary supremacy and the Bill of Rights, and pretty much left the colonies to their own devices for fully seventy-five years. Such Salutary Neglect suited the colonists, whose assemblies became largely self-governing, and suited members of the Whig establishment, who exploited—at no expense to themselves—coastal plantations that served as sources of commodities and burgeoning markets for British manufactures.

So by 1763 Americans just took for granted that they were autonomous subjects of a king whose authority was checked by a Parliament whose own authority did not extend beyond the British isles. Few realized that over those same seventy-five years the British had lived through events that impressed on crown and Parliament alike the chilling potential for civil unrest. Scotland's Jacobite revolts on behalf of the Stuart pretenders in 1715, 1719, and 1745 had posed existential political threats, while social disorders became so endemic that in 1769 Franklin observed: "I have seen, within a year, riots in the country, about corn; riots about elections; riots about workhouses; riots of colliers; riots of weavers; riots of coal-bearers; riots of sawyers; riots of Wilkesites; riots of government chairmen; riots of smugglers in which customs officers and excisemen have been murdered and the King's vessels and troops fired at." So Parliament had become vigilant about threats to law and order, not least on the fringes of empire.

British notions of sovereignty had also hardened considerably in ways that escaped the colonists. The first volume of William Blackstone's commentaries on English Common Law, published in 1766, argued that sovereignty rests with the Crown-in-Parliament and "sovereignty admits of no degrees, but is always supreme [so] to level it is in effect to destroy it." Blackstone called John Locke's popular right to resist putative tyranny "a doctrine productive of anarchy," in all but the most extreme circumstances. (Incidentally, that same principle would be later invoked by Andrew Jackson and Abraham Lincoln when they equated nullification and secession with anarchy.)

Moreover, it is often forgotten that the British Empire after 1763 consisted almost entirely of the North American colonies and the

Caribbean sugar islands dependent on them for food and commerce. So we need not wonder why Crown and Parliament believed they must stand firm on sovereignty lest their whole empire dissolve.

Next, very few British or colonists anticipated the burdens that came with their victory over the French. For instance, all the Native Americans now became the King's subjects and must be protected and/or policed on a violent western frontier. An omen of what might ensue was Pontiac's Rebellion, a violent defense of ancestral tribal lands. The native insurgency was suppressed, but the generals estimated some 10,000 Redcoats might be needed to garrison forts at a cost of £300,000 per year. It was in hope of appeasing the Indians that George III declared the Proclamation Line of 1763, forbidding new pioneer settlements west of the Appalachians, including the Ohio Valley, over which the Anglo-French war had broken out in the first place.

Then there were all the Québecois, whom New Englanders had hated and feared for 140 years. They, too, were now the King's subjects and must be appeased. So Parliament began to talk openly about establishing the Catholic Church and even expanding Québec south to the Ohio River, thus nullifying the western claims of some of the colonies.

Finally, the British Treasury had nearly doubled the national debt over the course of the war from £75 million to £133 million until interest payments now consumed more than half the annual budget. Parliament expected Americans, who were among the chief beneficiaries of the victorious war, to share that fiscal burden, not to mention quit dodging the Navigation Acts through their habitual smuggling.

Yet those seemingly prudent efforts to meet Britain's new responsibilities outraged a critical mass of colonists because it seemed to them the British were violating all four historic spirits of English expansion. First was the hustling spirit of rural and commercial capitalism. Second was the crusading spirit of the Protestant Reformation. Third was the imperial spirit of rivalry with the Catholic colonial powers. Fourth was the civilizing spirit, which caused John Locke himself to argue that the English had a sort of "right of eminent domain" over the lands of indigent people such as the Irish and Native Americans. The colonists had been weaned on those spirits and so felt betrayed when the British had evidently become heretics in their own church!

Those were the external sources of imperial crisis. Let us turn now to the internal debilities of the otherwise admirable British government, especially the petty factionalism that inevitably corrupts uncontested one-party rule.

After three generations in power the Whig establishment was bereft of ideas. Its factions had become mere matters of personality, patronage, and pelf in the form of lobbies such as the Sugar Interest, the Tea Interest, the Merchant Interest, and the Landed Interest, or Squirearchy. William Pitt had vision, but his health began to fail in 1762. Young Edmund Burke also had vision, but as yet little influence. Otherwise, Parliament was rent by feckless coalitions, while the prime ministry fell in a dizzy succession from Bute to Grenville, Rockingham, Pitt, Grafton, and finally Lord North. Their policies toward the colonies were inconsistent, if not incoherent.

Yet another handicap faced by British authorities was the lack of a colonial ministry, a consequence of their never having faced an imperial crisis. The British army and Royal Navy were under separate commands, and the military as a whole was independent of the Board of Trade, which in turn shared authority over economic policy with the Customs Board and the Treasury. The only body which occasionally deliberated strategy for the empire was the Privy Council's sub-committee on Plantations. Thomas Pownall, who had served as governor of Massachusetts and whose brother was on the Board of Trade, abominated such confusion. In 1764 he published

The Administration of the Colonies, a critique of British governance and a cry for imperial unity along the lines of the Albany Congress. Four years later Parliament did get around to creating a Secretary of State for the Colonies. But since the other agencies clung jealously to their influence, the colonial ministers had little authority.

The timing of this imperial crisis was also unfortunate because it occurred during the final decades of mercantilist economic ascendancy. Adam Smith's *The Wealth of Nations*, which introduced the theories of free market economics, appeared coincidentally in 1776. But a generation would pass before his ideas caught on, and in the meantime British mercantile interests were determined to enforce their monopolies and suppress the de facto free trade that Americans practiced through their smuggling.

Edmund Burke later told Parliament, "The Americans have made a discovery, or think they have made one, that we mean to oppress them; we have made a discovery, or think we have made one, that they intend to rise in rebellion." In fact, all the elements of the imperial crisis I have just described suggest that there were no conspiracies on either side—just ignorance and incompetence.

Franklin had little grasp of the formidable barriers to wise colonial policies, and since some British leaders such as Pitt, Burke, and the radicals Isaac Barré and Charles Wilkes sometimes spoke in favor of conciliation Franklin wrongly believed America had friends in high places. The truth was—however much the British quarreled over details—they all took for granted Parliament's sovereign right to tax and regulate.

Something Franklin did understand well—having written about it as early as 1751—was demographics. He predicted the populations of the American colonies would double every twenty-five years, such that within a century "the greatest Number of Englishmen will be on this Side of the Water.... What an Accession of Power to the British Empire! What Increase of Trade and Navigation!" His numbers should have set off alarm bells, but instead they persuaded him that the prophecy of Bishop George Berkeley was coming true. In 1728 Berkeley had written of Britain's imperial destiny—"Westward the course of empire takes its way"—in his poem "Verses on the Prospect of Planting Arts and Learning in America."

In 1763 Franklin returned briefly to Philadelphia but was back in London the following year to lobby against Thomas Penn and promote an ambitious land speculation in the Ohio Valley. He arrived just as Parliament began to adjust to Britain's new imperial responsibilities, including provision of a civil administration and military defense of the frontier. Now under Salutary Neglect the colonists had been able to tame the few royal officials in their midst, and they never saw Redcoats in peacetime. But the Grenville ministry, aiming to standardize administration and raise revenue to cover the new imperial expenses, sponsored the 1764 Currency Act and 1765 Stamp Act. The former prohibited circulation of foreign coins and colonial scrip in favor of British currency, and the latter obliged Americans to conduct all their transactions from legal documents, contracts, licenses, bills of sale, land grants, wills, even playing cards on stamped paper which colonists would be obliged to purchase with their scarce British currency. For good measure, the Quartering Act also obliged Americans to garrison any soldiers deployed in their midst.

Franklin had not protested these measures. On the contrary, he positively recommended the Stamp Act, perhaps imagining that he himself—a postmaster and prominent printer—might profit as a dispenser of patronage.

It soon became apparent how badly he had miscalculated. American colonists finally did unite, but in disharmony, not harmony, with the British. A Stamp Tax Congress convened to petition Parliament for repeal. Sons of Liberty tarred and feathered British officials. That Boston mob burned Governor Hutchinson's mansion. Congress also declared a boycott of British goods, which cost merchants £2 million per year and made them perforce the only real "friends of America" insofar as they lobbied Parliament for repeal of the Stamp Act.

So Franklin, supposedly the colonies' principal spokesman, made a U-turn in his February 1766 testimony before Parliament. The Rockingham Whigs, who had toppled the Grenville Whigs, were looking for a way out of the fracas, and Franklin obligingly patronized them by speaking persuasively for over two hours.

He assured the house that the colonists' temper toward Britain had never been better than in 1763. But since then their temper had turned due to Parliament's currency restrictions, restraints on trade, and direct tax on stamps. Indeed, he explained, the consequences of any attempt to tax the colonists directly would lead to a total loss of respect and an embargo on British exports. Indeed, the most delicious passage in the seventeen pages of testimony was this final exchange. Question: "Would it be more for the interest of Great-Britain, to employ the hands of Virginia in tobacco, or in manufactures?" Franklin: "In tobacco, to be sure." Question: "What used to be the pride of the Americans?" Franklin: "To indulge in the fashions and manufactures of Great-Britain." Question: "What now is their pride?" Franklin: "To wear their old clothes over again, till they themselves can make new ones."

Following that appearance he agonized in a letter to a Scottish friend: "I have lived so great a Part of my Life in Britain, and have formed so many friendships in it, that I love it and wish its Prosperity, and therefore wish to see the Union on which alone I think it can be secur'd and establish'd. As to America, the Advantages of such a Union are not so apparent." Indeed, "Every Act of Oppression will sour their Tempers, greatly lessen if not annihilate the Profits of your Commerce with them, and hasten their final Revolt: For the Seeds of Liberty are universally sown there, and nothing can eradicate them. And yet, there remains among the People so much

Respect, Veneration and Affection for Britain, that, if cultivated prudently…they might be easily govern'd still for Ages, without Force or considerable Expense. But I do not see here a sufficient Quantity of the Wisdom that is needed to produce such a Conduct."

The Rockingham Whigs repealed the Stamp Act, but were careful to pair that with passage of the 1766 Declaratory Act, which reserved to Parliament "full power and authority to make laws and statutes of sufficient force and validity to bind the colonies and people of America…in all cases whatsoever." Two months later William Pitt, now the Earl of Chatham, became prime minister. It was he who created the Colonial Office and appointed Lord Hillsborough its chief. Franklin reported enthusiastically to Joseph Galloway, speaker of the Pennsylvania assembly: "We have the satisfaction to find that none of those whom we looked on as adversaries of America in the late struggles, are come to power…." Alas, that was another misunderstanding. For even though Chatham had favored repeal of the Stamp Act, he still meant to enforce the Quartering Act, which New York was defying, and to raise revenue in the colonies by imposing duties on their imported goods. Franklin had misled him into believing Americans would *not* protest indirect taxation.

That false assumption emboldened the Chancellor of the Exchequer Charles Townshend. For no British officials were more determined than Charles and his brother George to impose uniform imperial rule according to a contemporary theory of government called Enlightened Absolutism. George had chosen a military career. In 1745–46 he helped the Duke of Cumberland's army defeat the Jacobites, after which he imposed his ruthless regime on the Highland Scots. He later performed similar duties in Québec and in Ireland. Charles had chosen a political career, and upon being named Chancellor in 1767 he authored the plan for what came to be known as the Townshend Duties to be enforced by British customs houses. Moreover, the revenues gleaned from these tariffs would cover the costs of imperial administration and thus eliminate the "power of the purse" hitherto wielded by colonial assemblies. In the words of the historian Will Hay, "Where the Stamp Act had been a specific revenue measure, the Townshend duties were part of a systematic effort to bring the colonies to heel."

Franklin hoped for the best, especially when Charles Townshend died of a mysterious fever in September 1767, and spent most of the following year promoting his Ohio land schemes. But at length it turned out the Chatham ministry let him down on all counts. In August 1768 Lord Hillsborough finally replied to Pennsylvania's petition about revoking Penn's charter, and his answer was no. He also vetoed the Ohio project as a clear violation of the king's Proclamation Line. Franklin was crushed, but nevertheless informed Galloway that he thought it wise to "stay a little longer here, till I see what turn American Affairs are like to take." It is hard to avoid the conclusion that Franklin was in denial about sentiments in London and the colonies alike even as his own influence was evaporating rapidly.

So, too, was that of the colonial assemblies, whose relentless petitions against acts of Parliament were frankly becoming a bore. Most were addressed to the Privy Council in hopes that the King would take up the colonies' cause. That infuriated most Whigs, who styled themselves keepers of the flame regarding the Parliamentary supremacy won through the Glorious Revolution of 1688.

Meanwhile Parliament pressed on with the Townshend agenda by passing the Commissioners of Customs Act of 1767, which created a Customs Board with headquarters in Boston. Since the Board was charged with rigorous enforcement of the Navigation Acts and Townshend Duties it inevitably bred public disorder. That in turn caused General Thomas Gage, the British commander in North America, to request two regiments to be stationed in Boston. They arrived in October 1768. The city fell under an ominous cloud.

Yet another cabinet change occurred that same month because Chatham, once again ailing, stepped down in favor of the Duke of

Grafton. He inherited the wind blown up by the Townshend Duties because it turned out the colonists resisted indirect taxation as vehemently as direct taxation. By spring 1769 hundreds of merchants in Philadelphia, New York, and Boston declared a boycott on British goods, and the Virginia assembly renewed its Non-Importation Resolution. So the Grafton cabinet, under pressure from the Merchant and Sugar Interests, reluctantly asked Parliament to repeal the duties with the sole exception of tea.

At this nervous juncture comic confusion ensued thanks to one of the more outlandish scoundrels in British history. John Wilkes, the son of a gin distiller, had become notorious as a rabble-rousing populist. In 1763 he had published an article in the *North Briton Review*, Number 45, which savagely critiqued the King's speech at the opening of Parliament. Wilkes was also notorious for being an avid patron of the lewd, blasphemous Hellfire Club, which Sir Francis Dashwood hosted at his rural retreat, Medmenham Abbey. (Incidentally, the only American known to have frequented the Hellfire Club was Benjamin Franklin because Dashwood, Britain's Postmaster-General, was his direct superior.)

In 1764 Wilkes made the mistake of playing a practical joke on another Hellfire Club member, John Montagu, the Fourth Earl of Sandwich, who wasn't amused. He avenged himself by persuading Parliament to declare Wilkes an outlaw. Wilkes fled to France for a time, but returned to win his own seat in Parliament, whereupon he was jailed only to win another elections and obtain his release. Wilkes became a national obsession when he gave vocal support to the colonies, whose oppression he likened to his own. Indeed, so popular had he become in America that a town was named for him and his fellow radical: Wilkes-Barre, Pennsylvania.

That scandal helped to topple the Grafton ministry in January 1770, whereupon King George, having run through six prime ministers in eight years, decided to gamble on a new name. Frederick, Lord North displayed such deft political skills that his ministry would lasted a dozen years. But his longevity rested in great part on his determination to carry out the will of Parliament and the Crown with regard to the naughty colonists.

Now, the sole duty that Parliament had chosen to retain after the repeal of the Townshend was that tax on tea. But few people know that the act sharply *reduced* the retail price of tea. That was because its real purpose was not to raise revenue but to sustain the East India Company's monopoly by undercutting the price charged by foreign smugglers in America. If anything, that made colonists more dyspeptic! As the Massachusetts lawyer Daniel Leonard exclaimed: "Will not posterity be amazed when they are told that the present distraction took its rise from parliament's taking a shilling off the duty on a pound of tea, and replacing it with three pence?" For Bostonians reasoned that if Parliament claimed the right to impose a monopoly on tea, what monopoly might it not impose? So what Americans were really rebelling against was mercantilism, and what they were really defending was a smuggler's racket. It had nothing to do with taxation without representation, which no one took seriously on either side of the ocean.

As tensions rose the Redcoats became a menacing presence until the inevitable bloodshed, the Boston Massacre, occurred in March 1770. Irate New Englanders retaliated, most infamously by looting and burning a British revenue cutter that ran aground in Rhode Island. The clash between parents and children was finally beginning to clarify. If British customs officials guarded by soldiers succeeded in getting their way, colonial merchants would lose lucrative trade while Americans as a whole would become "slaves" to the British plutocrats who monopolized commerce and Parliament. That is why the governor of New York informed the Colonial Office that "even if the tea comes free of duty I understand it is to be considered as a monopoly . . . of dangerous tendency . . . to American liberties." That is why John Hancock, the richest merchant in Boston, made common cause with Sam Adams, the penurious rabble-rouser.

Franklin, desperate to reverse this dangerous drift, resorted to satire. (All told, he would publish ninety comedic items during his years in England using forty-two pseudonyms.) But the two major ones written in 1773 were barely veiled warnings and not very funny. In "An Edict by the King of Prussia" he asked readers to imagine how Britons would react if Frederick the Great made demands on them similar to those they made on the colonies. And in "Rules by Which a Great Empire Might Be Reduced to a Small One" he sarcastically instructed the British government that if its purpose was to shed its colonies then it was proceeding in just the right fashion.

Nobody paid attention. Franklin's cachet was dissolving. Wilkes's mobs might display sympathy for the American cause, but the King and Parliament held it in contempt, while British merchants, having twice lobbied for repeals, were in bad odor. Even the colonial agencies ceased to be factors because the tiresome Franklin now represented New Jersey, Massachusetts, and Georgia as well as Pennsylvania, whereas Delaware, Maryland, Virginia, and North Carolina did not have any representation at all. Such were the circumstances that likely persuaded Franklin he must somehow buy time, which meant he must cool colonial tempers, which meant he must risk sending those Hutchinson letters to Boston.

That was Franklin's ultimate miscalculation. The letters only rekindled the rage in Boston's taverns, and when the first East India Company ships dropped anchor in December 1773, hotheads staged the Boston Tea Party in a premeditated, theatrical act of defiance... indeed, of sedition, apparently inspired by Franklin's machinations.

In April 1774 Lord North sponsored bills to close Boston's port, revoke the colony's charter, suspend Massachusetts law, and oblige colonists to house Redcoats in their homes. "The Americans," he told Parliament, "have tarred and feathered your subjects, plundered your merchants, burnt your ships, denied all obedience to your laws and authority; yet so clement and forbearing has our conduct been that it is incumbent on us now to take a different course. Whatever may be the consequences, we must risk something; if we do not, all is over." Those Coercive Acts, or Intolerable Acts as they were called in America, forged a resolve among a critical mass of colonists such that their assemblies called for a Continental Congress. William Franklin, the royalist governor of New Jersey, urged the crown to preempt that by convening its own congress to include the governors, representatives of the assemblies, and "British gentlemen of abilities, moderation and candour commissioned by His Majesty." But the King ignored his suggestion while Parliament further inflamed New England by passing the Québec Act that June.

Did Benjamin Franklin turn American patriot after his humiliation in the Cockpit? He did not. Instead, he wrote to Speaker Cushing that a union of the friends of liberty in both houses of Parliament might soon repeal the Coercive Acts. It did not. He imagined the opposition might be victorious in the 1774 Parliamentary elections. It was not. He imagined another embargo of British trade might oblige a repeal. It would not. When Congress sent Franklin its Address to the Crown in December, he imagined it could change the King's mind. It could not. King George, deeming the Continental Congress illegitimate, refused even to read it.

No one miscalculated more thoroughly or more often than Franklin, in part because no one tried harder to heal the rift in the empire. In fact, some Britons—and Americans—suspected Franklin of playing a double game all along. He was too American for the British and too British for the Americans.

Yet Franklin was encouraged anew by confidential visits from several conciliatory MPs and by the surprise appearance in London of Josiah Quincy, Jr. As a member of Sam Adams's inner circle, his evident mission was to discern whether Franklin could be trusted and to explore possibilities for back-channel negotiations. The thirty-one-year-old Quincy fell entirely under the spell of Ben's "sagacity, judgment, morality, and benevolence. I was charmed." He returned home in expectation of providing a "singular service" and preventing "much calamity and producing much good to Boston... [and] all America." Whether that expectation was justified can never be known because Quincy caught tuberculosis on the return voyage and died just hours before his ship docked at Gloucester.

Meanwhile, the climax of Franklin's discussions with those MP's occurred on January 29, 1775, when the Earl of Chatham's elegant carriage pulled up in broad daylight at Franklin's house. He and Ben consulted for hours, after which Chatham drafted a series of bills he introduced to the House of Lords on February 1. They stipulated Parliament's supremacy and right to station troops in America, but repealed the Intolerable Acts and recognized the Continental Congress, in exchange for which the colonies would pledge to raise revenue for the crown.

Had Pitt presented those terms to Parliament back in 1765 the plan might have gained traction. Even now, the initial reception was positive, and Dartmouth, the Colonial Secretary, appeared to approve. But at that point the vindictive Earl of Sandwich stood up to denounce a plan that "could not have been composed by an English peer" and must have been authored—he stood staring at Franklin in the gallery above—by an American! The bills were defeated, 32 in favor and 68 opposed. A week later Parliament and the Crown declared Massachusetts to be in a state of rebellion.

The only resources left for peacemakers were the Rockingham Whigs, who hitherto had not taken a stand but now knew the hour had struck. So Edmund Burke, their most eloquent orator, delivered a spell-binding three-hour speech to a packed House of Commons on March 22. Citing the size and growth of the colonies' population, agriculture, shipping, forestry, manufactures, and commerce, he concluded the conflict could never be settled by force simply because Britain could never suppress them for long.

But even more salient than statistics, he essentially explained, was the American character:

> *Those people are Englishmen, sir, born with a free spirit. What is more, they are Englishmen in whom religion is neither worn out nor impaired.... Those people are Protestants, sir, and of that kind, which is most adverse to submission.... The Northern colonies profess various denominations, but commune in the same spirit of liberty. As for the Southerners, their spirit of liberty is still more high and haughty. That is because they are slave-holders, sir, and where this is the case in any part of the world, those who are free are by far the most proud and jealous.... What is more, no people on earth has made so general a study of law than the Americans, a study which renders men acute, inquisitive, dexterous, prompt in attack, ready in defence, and full of resources.... But even if the colonists were less numerous, less loving of liberty, less steeped in religion, less proud, they would still be irrepressible for the simple reason that Americans are full of chicane and take whatever they want. In any event, an Englishman is the least fit person on earth to argue another Englishman into slavery.*

Burke's motions to repeal the Intolerable Acts were defeated by a vote of 78 in favor and 270 opposed. Less than a month later the shooting began at Lexington and Concord.

★ ★ ★

Thus did the peripatetic, befuddled British elites, having backed down several times, finally decide to call the colonists' bluff. As the British historian Peter Thomas aptly concludes: "The [American] War of Independence was not a heroic enterprise, but the result of political miscalculation."

Franklin's fourteen-year mission for imperial unity had come to a ruinous end. The British crown issued a warrant for his arrest which was making its way through the courts when he boarded the Philadelphia packet at Portsmouth. But not before spending a last melancholy day with Joseph Priestley, who wrote in his diary: "While we read in the newspapers about the likelihood of an American war, Benjamin grew more and more emotional until he could no longer read through the tears in his eyes."

Franklin arrived in Philadelphia on May 5 and was instantly elected a delegate to the Second Continental Congress. But he still clung to a forlorn hope that George III might step forth as a *deus ex machina*, appease the colonists, and save imperial unity. Hence his final act as a British subject was to help the Quaker John Dickinson draft the Olive Branch Petition of July 1775. When the King again would not deign to read it, there kindled in Franklin's heart a seething hatred for George III he would carry to the grave.[4] Like Washington before him, Franklin became a reluctant republican because the British themselves had thwarted his grand imperial vision, and like Washington he went on to do more than any other Founder to secure the independence of the United States.

As the new nation's first diplomat Franklin sailed back to Europe to conclude the military alliance with France, which would turn the tide in the war. On the day that treaty was signed at Versailles in February 1778, Ben at last donned the velvet suit he had sworn not to wear until he was avenged for his ordeal in the Cockpit.

That same month Lord North belatedly offered to send a peace commission to America and seek a truce based on Parliament's waiver of rights to tax or legislate for the colonies, the withdrawal of all British soldiers, and no modification of charters without the colonists' assent. Imagine he had made that offer four years before. What might the consequences have been?

First, no War of Independence, of course. Second, no radical French Revolution because it was his participation in the American war that bankrupted Louis XVI and forced him to call the Estates General in 1789. Third, no War of 1812 because the British Empire would have remained intact. Fourth, possibly no American Civil War because the British Parliament abolished slavery—with compensation for slave-owners—in 1833, and an American Parliament would presumably have had the same authority. One might even imagine no Great War in 1914 because Imperial Germany might never have dared challenge a British Empire which included as dominions a by then industrialized North American continent. And if no Great War, perhaps no Communism, Fascism, World War II, or Cold War.

Doubtless other calamities would have befallen the nations over those two hundred years. History happens. But those that did occur might never have done so if Benjamin Franklin's dreams had come true. Yet in retrospect even he came to conclude—if only by way of self-exculpation—that the British imperial crisis had been providential. As he confessed to the delegates of the 1787 Constitutional Convention in Philadelphia: "The longer I live, the more convincing proofs I see of this truth—that God governs in the affairs of men. And if a sparrow cannot fall to the ground without his notice, is it probable that an empire can rise without his assistance?"

★ 3 ★

WILLIAM PENN, BENJAMIN FRANKLIN, AND THE AMERICAN FOUNDING

The Philadelphia Factor[1]

Several years ago the *Philadelphia Inquirer* reported proudly on the city's twentieth annual Welcome America! celebration. Its bold headline quoted Mayor Michael Nutter to the effect that "Philadelphia owns the Fourth of July." What evidence exists to substantiate that boast? Was the Philadelphia factor truly decisive to the American founding?

In his 1997 *History of the American People*, Paul Johnson summarized some of the evidence as follows:

> Amid this prosperous rural setting, it was natural for Philadelphia to become, in a very short time, the cultural capital of America. It can be argued, indeed, that Quaker Pennsylvania was the key state in American history. It was the last great flowering of Puritan political innovation, around its great city of brotherly love.... Its harbor at Philadelphia served as a national crossroads leading north, west, and south.... It became in time many things, which coexisted in harmony: the world centre of Quaker influence but a Presbyterian stronghold too, the national headquarters of American Baptists but a place where

> Catholics also…flourished, a center of Anglicanism but also a key location both for Lutherans and…many more German groups, such as Moravians and Mennonites. In due course it also housed the African Methodist Episcopal Church…. With all this, it was not surprising that Philadelphia was an early home of the printing press, adumbrating its role as the seat of the American Philosophical Society and birthplace of the Declaration of Independence.

Pennsylvania became known as the Keystone State even though it is not really a state but one of the four commonwealths, along with Massachusetts, Virginia, and Kentucky. As early as 1803 the Jeffersonian journal *Aurora*, published by Benjamin Franklin Bache, dubbed Pennsylvania "the keystone in the democratic arch." And ever since then most historians have agreed that Pennsylvania occupied a key position among the colonies by virtue of its demography, geography, and economic, cultural, and political importance. They have argued or simply assumed that Philadelphia was no accident but the *sine qua non* of the American Revolution.

But historians must always beware of prolepsis: the fallacy of interpreting the past in terms of an implicitly inevitable future; in short, to read history backwards. William Penn and Benjamin Franklin are cases in point because many eminent historians have heralded them as "proto-Americans" given their tolerance, egalitarianism, industry, enlightenment, and capacity for self-reinvention, "For better or worse, rightly or wrongly," wrote Charles Sanford, "Benjamin Franklin has been identified with the American national character. Though greater hero worship has been accorded to Washington and Lincoln, historians have almost unanimously judged Franklin to be more representative. He is the inventor of the American character and American way of life."

Thomas Carlyle called Franklin the "father of all Yankees," and Paul Elmer More said he was "America's Renaissance Man." Frederick

Jackson Turner dubbed him "the first great American" and H. W. Brands "the first American"—period. To Walter Isaacson he was "the multiple American"; to Jonathan Lyons "the Enlightened American"; to Gerardo Del Guercio "the inventor of the American Dream."

All that amounts to prolepsis because it assumes the United States was already "out there" on the horizon in 1723 when Franklin left his native Boston for Philadelphia or even in 1682 when William Penn received his colonial charter. But in truth Penn was an English imperial patriot who had no notion of planting the seeds of a new nation. And Franklin—as noted in a previous lecture—was also an imperial patriot until, at age sixty-eight, he reluctantly embraced the American cause. Indeed, very few of the Founding Fathers had any notion that they were about to establish a new nation. George Washington even wrote in a letter on October 9, 1774, just six months before Lexington and Concord: "I think I can announce it as a fact, that it is not the wish or interest of [the Massachusetts] government, or any other upon this continent, separately or collectively, to set up for independency... on the contrary, it is the ardent wish of the warmest advocates for liberty, that peace and tranquility, upon constitutional grounds, may be restored, and horrors of civil discord prevented." Can it be that American independence was not an inevitability but an improvisation?

To be sure, the political consciousness of the colonists coalesced quickly during the decade following 1765, when the Stamp Act initiated the imperial crisis. But independence seemed the least likely outcome, so much so that contemporary observers regarded the unfolding events with shock, dismay, and disbelief. As recently as 1763, when the Seven Years War, or last French and Indian War, ended in Anglo-American victory, colonists had toasted the health of King George III with gusto. Just a dozen years later the same colonists damned his eyes and reached for their muskets. And for what? The ostensible causes seemed wholly inadequate to explain the scale of the unfolding tragedy.

Joseph Galloway, Speaker of the Pennsylvania Assembly from 1766 to 1775, asked, "How then can it happen that a people so lately loyal, should so suddenly become universally disloyal, and firmly attached to republican Government, without any grievances or oppressions but those in anticipation?" Galloway hoped the discord had been exaggerated out of proportion and that reconciliation might still be effected. So historians—far from taking the future for granted—ought to have asked what might have happened had the British been more forthcoming or the colonists less hot-headed. Surely secession and civil war—which is what the American Revolution amounted to—needed more of a cause than a three-penny tax on tea.

Schoolbooks have always taught children that it was the principle of the thing: taxation without representation and the dangerous precedent of Parliamentary supremacy. That external excuse then became the ostensible justification because of the Americans' decision to declare independence. Jefferson had to argue, out of a "decent respect to the opinions of mankind," that the cause of the rupture was British oppression, hence his long (and boring) litany of grievances. But implicit in that pretension was the counter-factual that the revolution would *not* have occurred if wiser policies had prevailed in London. Instead, the six lords who served George III as prime ministers during that decade only exacerbated the crisis: Grenville was too narrow-minded, Townshend too clever by half, Hillsborough too arrogant, Pitt too infirm, Dartmouth too weak, North too stubborn, and King George too solicitous of all the above. But to suggest that American independence was a by-product of botched British policy did not suit the needs of the emerging American civil religion, which required that the national founding be not accidental but providential. So almost from the beginning historians depicted the birth of the United States as divinely inspired, taught American values to the next generation, and implicitly recommended them to the whole human race.

A second set of counter-factuals suggests what might have happened had the colonists been less hot-headed, less jealous of their autonomy from crown and Parliament. After all, the conquest of Canada had imposed new burdens, responsibilities, and costs on the British, which they naturally expected their North American colonists to share. Hence the King's Proclamation Line of 1763 prohibited new frontier settlements beyond the Appalachians out of deference to the Native Americans. The Québec Act of 1774 established rather than abolished the Catholic Church in Canada out of deference to the Québecois. The Sugar Act, Currency Act, Quartering Act, Stamp Act, and Townshend Duties were parliamentary attempts to pay down the national debt by raising revenue in the colonies. Of course, the angry colonists resisted, which provoked the Coercive Acts, and which Americans deemed "Intolerable." Yet all those measures, while necessary conditions, were still not sufficient to explain civil war and secession.

The sufficient cause could only be a new self-awareness, what John Adams called the revolution in men's minds that had to precede the political act of separation. That indeed occurred once those various provocations caused the colonists to inquire, for the first time, into the nature of the British Empire. The thirteen colonies had all been created by private companies with royal charters wholly independent of Parliament. Hence delegates to the First Continental Congress—even Quaker accommodationists such as Joseph Galloway and John Dickinson—were convinced that Parliament had no right to legislate for the colonies whether or not it was a matter of "taxation without representation."

In fact, Galloway proposed in September 1774 a constitutional plan for the empire providing for an *American* parliament to be chosen by the colonial assemblies and an *American* president-general to be appointed by the Crown. But even the moderate First Continental Congress voted down "taxation with representation" by six colonies to five. In January 1775 Lord North proposed that Parliament not legislate for the colonies but simply request the colonial assemblies to decide for themselves how to contribute to administration and defense. Congress rejected that, too. Finally, Josiah Tucker, Dean of Gloucester, suggested Parliament call the colonists' bluff and force independence upon them in the expectation they would come groveling back with an appeal to the crown. That proposal was never made, but it was certainly true that Americans' anger was never directed at King George until Tom Paine wrote *Common Sense* in 1776. So historians might well imagine that a self-governing American dominion under British sovereignty might have emerged from the crisis of the 1770s and might even survive to our day... if not for some *internal* reasons why American Patriots would settle for nothing less than independence.

A third set of counter-factual "what ifs" may be drawn from military history because the Americans' Glorious Cause could easily have aborted. What if the British had routed the Minutemen on Bunker Hill? What if Washington's army had been trapped on Long Island instead of slipping to the mainland under cover of fog? What if the British captain who had Washington in his sights during the Battle of Brandywine pulled the trigger? What if Washington had decided against marching his army five hundred miles from New York in the slim hope of trapping Cornwallis at Yorktown?

Given all those contingencies it would appear the birth of a United States of America was a fluke. Yet the same historical narrative suggests that what made the glorious fluke possible was the location, culture, and people of Philadelphia. If Washington was the indispensable man, then Philadelphia was the indispensable city that made possible the Declaration of Independence, victory in the Revolutionary War, and the triumph of the Constitution. At least that is what I mean to argue, beginning with some background on the unique colony founded on the Delaware River by Quakers.

A historian recently prefaced his new biography with a lament: "When I ask my students in the U.S. history survey who was William Penn, responses range from blank faces to the inevitable 'he's the guy on the Quaker Oats box.' Sadly, in 24 years of college teaching I have watched Penn and the Quakers slip ever deeper into the recesses of historical memory."

That is a shame, because Penn still casts a long shadow from his perch atop Philadelphia's City Hall, whence he gazes down on Penn's Landing to welcome all newcomers. He was the son of the famous Admiral William Penn, who captured Jamaica for Oliver Cromwell's Commonwealth but whose clandestine ties to the exiled Stuart dynasty paid off when Parliament restored Charles II to the throne in 1660. The King and his brother James, the Duke of York, promised the admiral upon his death in 1670 that they would look out for his son. But the son had improbably turned Quaker and thus pacifist, hostile to all authority and egalitarian to the point of treason. Why did the King in 1681 grant Penn an exclusive charter to lands as extensive as England itself? Was it simply to pay off a large gambling debt that Charles owed the admiral's estate? Or was it a ploy to lure Quakers out of the country? Or did Penn, who was already experienced in the colonization of New Jersey, know how to slip his petition past the Lords of Trade without notice? The likely answers are no, no, and no, because whatever personal motives might have been involved, the creation of Pennsylvania was premeditated statecraft on the part of the Stuarts. First, a strong colony on the Delaware would swallow the Swedish and Dutch settlements already there and strengthen the English grip on the commerce of the entire American seaboard. Second, putting a proprietor in charge kept the colony off the government's books. Third, awarding the province to Penn ensured a friendly and peaceable neighbor for New York, whose proprietor was his patron, the Duke of York (and future King James II).

Penn attracted investments from wealthy Quaker merchants, one of whom was Thomas Holme, who surveyed the rectangular grid of streets between the Delaware and Schuylkill rivers where Penn imagined his City of Brotherly Love becoming a "green country town." Penn sailed over in 1682 with an armada of eighteen large ships loaded with abundant supplies and the vanguard of 11,000 skilled settlers who emigrated during the first decade alone. Penn's agents in Wales, Ireland, France, and the Rhineland aggressively marketed the fertile soil and water, the "sylvania" of timber, and the "holy experiment" in religious tolerance and political liberty. They sold half a million acres in their first year alone.

Penn was a disciple of the political theorist Algernon Sydney, who believed that government should be free of coercion, ensure equal opportunity, and be blind to differences of birth, background, and faith. But the Frame of Government contained in Penn's charter required that settlers give total obedience to the proprietor, who in turn owed obedience to the crown. Sydney was appalled: "The Turk is not more absolute!" he cried. What happened was that Penn bowed to the wishes of the Duke of York, who was insisting on the same authoritarian arrangement drafted for the new Carolina colony by the philosopher John Locke.

Not surprisingly, Quaker settlers passively resisted Penn's proprietorship in the name of his own principles. They scoffed at quit-rents and taxes, smuggled at will, and accused Penn of abandoning his colony during the fifteen years he spent back in England fighting various lawsuits. During those years his friend the Duke had become King James II only to be deposed in Parliament's Glorious Revolution of 1688. So it was that Penn lost royal patronage. To make a long story short, he was obliged in 1701 to grant his colonists a new Charter of Privileges, which empowered their elected assembly to make its own laws and in fact exercise more freedom than any other in America (much to the frustration of James Logan, whom Penn had left behind to manage the colony). The great seal of Philadelphia dates from this event, a shield depicting a handshake, sheaf of grain, scales of justice, and a merchant ship. By then Philadelphia was already America's second city: a bustling port of 5,000 people who shipped flour, meat, and lumber to the West Indies and speculated on real estate. People even sub-migrated from other colonies because Pennsylvania quickly acquired a reputation as "the best poor man's country."

By then the proprietor himself had been mugged by his own colonists, swindled by various business partners, suffered a stroke, gradually lost his memory and—despite being the biggest landlord in the Atlantic world—died in poverty in 1718. But he was not remembered as a tragic figure at all thanks to his legacy, lovingly described by biographer Mary Maples Dunn: "William Penn conceived of and actually established a tolerant, pacific society blessed with true freedom of religion, a criminal code humane beyond anything known in England, a written constitution, and a bill of rights.... Penn's greatness was greater than the sum of his parts."

Indeed, liberty and equality were more on display in Pennsylvania than anywhere else in America save, perhaps, quirky Rhode Island. But as Pennsylvanians became more diverse they ceased to advance Quaker principles. To be sure, the Quaker party still clung to a slim majority in the Assembly during King George's War (War of Austrian Succession), and refused to contribute to military defense from 1739–48. But the valleys west of Philadelphia were filling with Lutheran Germans, who in fact invented the famed Pennsylvania rifle, and Presbyterian Scots-Irish, who were downright belligerent. When a French sloop was sighted in Delaware Bay in 1747, the transplanted Bostonian Benjamin Franklin published *Plain Truth*, which argued against pacifism on Biblical and practical grounds, and Philadelphians responded by founding a militia association, symbolically ending the era of Quaker control.

Franklin first visited Philadelphia in 1723, settled there permanently in 1726, and set up as a printer in 1728. During his adopted town's prodigious growth he founded among other things its first fire and police patrols, lending library, college, philosophical society, post office, masonic lodge, and publishing industry. Meanwhile, the town's population rose to 13,000 people by 1740, 20,000 by 1760 (thereby surpassing Boston), and nearly 40,000 by 1776. To be sure, that is only half the size of present-day Camden, New Jersey, but in the eighteenth century Philadelphia was the largest English-speaking city on earth save for London. What is more, Penn's "green country town" became highly urbanized because it was much cheaper to subdivide urban lots or build up rather than out. So Franklin's Philadelphia reached inland only so far as Eighth Street. Nevertheless, European visitors, of which at least twenty-two penned travelogues, wrote mostly glowing descriptions. Lord Adam Gordon thought it "one of the wonders of the world, if you consider its size, the number of inhabitants, the regularity of its streets…their spacious publick and private buildings, Quays, and Docks…one will not hesitate to Call it the first Town in America, but one that bids fair to rival almost any in Europe."

Not surprisingly, the diversity, freedom, and close quarters made for contentious politics among pro- and anti-proprietary parties, the Quakers, Presbyterians, Anglicans, and Germans. Franklin was a party of one. He damned the "stiff rumped" Quakers, feared the swarming Germans, and had little use for the others. But he made friends in every camp and devoted himself to unity among the bickering factions within Pennsylvania, between Pennsylvania and the other colonies, and between America and Britain. A great exponent of Enlightenment reason often considered a Deist, Franklin even befriended the charismatic evangelist George Whitefield, who made eight visits to Philadelphia during the religious revival historians call the Great Awakening. Its enthusiastic, evangelical, individualistic faith split every Protestant denomination and severed ties between Americans and European church authorities, thus helping to lay the basis for a revolutionary alliance between the Awakened and the Enlightened.

As Pennsylvania matured it was said even of Quakers that the values of the counting house had eclipsed those of the meeting house. But Philadelphians combined materialism with an idealism which never characterized New York, a toleration which never characterized New England, and an egalitarianism which never characterized Virginia. Moreover, their ability to broadcast a diversity of opinion was as fecund as their freedom to do so because William Bradford's first printing press dated from 1686, just three years after Philadelphia was founded (Boston, by comparison, waited eighteen years). Between 1740 and 1776 no fewer than forty-two printers plied their trade in the city.

Most important—and contrary to Philadelphia's image today—most of the city's elite came from somewhere else: 30 percent from other colonies and 25 percent from Europe. Moreover, since Quakers back then discouraged higher education the College of Philadelphia (University of Pennsylvania) founded by Whitefield and Franklin drew only 5 percent of its students between 1757 and 1800 from wealthy locals. Indeed, the WASP elite we associate with the city really dates from the post–Civil War industrial era, notwithstanding the reputation of Whartons, Mifflins, Rittenhouses, Biddles, and merchants like Robert Morris and Stephen Girard. The colonial city lacked what sociologists called a hegemonic or homogeneous elite such as prevailed in the plantation colonies, Hudson Valley, or Boston, where just 4 percent of the wealthy were born abroad.

Finally, Philadelphia was better equipped than other towns in the colonies with boarding houses, taverns, and public buildings, especially the lavish State House designed by Andrew Hamilton and Edmund Woolley, where a sizeable convention could meet in relative comfort. If there was any location where disparate delegations might contrive to make "thirteen clocks strike as one" (in John Adams's words) it was Philadelphia . . . except that Adams and other zealots from New England and Virginia still associated the city with Quaker passivity, so they came to the First Continental Congress in 1774 determined *not* to let the venue decide the outcome.

It seemed Adams had a point. Even after nine years of escalating tensions—years during which John Dickinson gained fame as the author of *Letters from a Farmer in Pennsylvania*—Penn's colony still remained notorious for its conservatism. But Patriots from elsewhere were wrong to think Philadelphia's culture a barrier to bold action. First, it was essential that Pennsylvania serve as anchor on the American ship of state so that when at last it did set sail all except diehard Tories were satisfied that the colonies had patiently and prudently gone the extra mile. That is, if *even* Philadelphia acquiesced in a declaration of independence then a critical mass of Americans everywhere could be counted upon. Second, it turned out Adams was mistaken about the temper of Philadelphians because their very hostility to authority and tradition and openness to new people and ideas created space for a powerful populist faction to undertake revolutionary action despite the opposition of "stiff-rumped" Quakers in the colonial assembly.

The first inkling of that came in 1774, when the Boston Committee of Correspondence, desperate for support against the Intolerable Acts, sent Paul Revere on his first famous ride to beg Philadelphia merchants to join an embargo of British trade. He was welcomed by a mass rally at the City Tavern that attracted merchants, but scores of artisans and mechanics as well. They persuaded John Dickinson to draft an invitation to "a general Congress of Deputies from the different Colonies, clearly to state what we conceive our rights and to make claim or petition of them to his Majesty, in firm, but decent and dutiful terms." Proprietor John Penn, who now served as governor, forbade the assembly to participate, whereupon the popular party staged an extra-legal convention to choose delegates.[2] When the congress convened in September, John Adams also persuaded it to spurn the Pennsylvania State House with its Quaker associations in favor of Carpenter's Hall.

Back in 1765 a Stamp Act Congress had been held in New York. That befit the word's eighteenth-century connotation of a body of representatives from separate polities coming together to concert their action for a specific purpose. The Philadelphia body was not really a "congress" in that sense because it gradually assumed the powers of an ad hoc legislature. Indeed, this First Continental Congress, by denying Parliament's right to legislate, rejecting the Galloway Plan, and urging the colonies to prepare for armed resistance, implied that its ultimate *raison d'être* was self-government.

The authors of a classic 1884 history of the city were not exaggerating when they claimed, "To write a complete history of Philadelphia during the war of American independence would be, in effect, to write the history of that revolution from its beginning until the adoption of the Constitution.... Philadelphia was the fulcrum which turned a long lever." Indeed, Philadelphia provided not only a central locus and conducive atmosphere but also a critical mass of leaders, including Dickinson, Morris, Charles Humphreys, Charles Thomson, John Morton, and James Wilson, many of whom were transplants to the city.

For instance, how many people have heard of Charles Thomson, the *éminence grise* of the American Revolution? Born in Northern Ireland he arrived in America an eleven-year-old orphan in 1740 and seemed condemned to life as a blacksmith's apprentice. But Thomson ran away and got lucky. Charitable benefactors placed him in schools, first in Maryland and then Philadelphia, where he apprenticed in a merchant house, grew modestly rich, and married into the family that owned the Harriton Plantation in Lower Merion township. His first public service was in 1757 as shorthand recorder for the Quakers' council with the famous Indian sachem Teedyuscung, who even gave Thomson a nickname, the Lenape word for "truth-teller." During the crisis with Britain John Adams gave him another: "the Sam Adams of Philadelphia." In 1765 he served as Secretary to the Stamp Act Congress and then, beginning in 1774, Confidential Secretary of the Continental Congress, in which post Thomson quietly stage-managed American politics for the next fourteen years. He corresponded with Thomas Jefferson, George Washington, Benjamin Franklin, and every member of Congress. He knew their jealousies and ambitions and where all the bodies were buried. He had personal charge of intelligence operations and ran networks of spies at home and abroad. Yet Thomson somehow made no personal enemies thanks to his humility, patriotism, and scruples.

The Second Continental Congress convened in Philadelphia in May 1775, a month after fighting broke out on Lexington Green. There was no assurance that the other colonies would permit the hot-headed New Englanders to drag them into treason and war. But a sea change had occurred in Philadelphia, where the formation of extra-legal committees to bypass the proprietor's assembly had quickly become a habit. As one historian put it, Pennsylvania in spring 1774 was still governed by an oligarchy based on a restricted electorate, but in just two years turned into the most vibrant participatory democracy *in the world*. That radical, militant populism was the basis for the historian Carl Becker's claim that the American revolution was not about "home rule, but about who would rule at home," a claim later revived by the Marxist historian Gary Nash. But the important point was that Patriots in the congress were greatly encouraged by what was occurring in Philadelphia's streets.

The populist movement climaxed in the formation of militia committees that made the willingness to bear arms the measure of patriotism, in defiance of Quakers, who still made up 15 percent of the city's population. Thousands of militiamen marched, drilled, and in effect governed in defiance of the Assembly, psychologically preparing a critical mass of the populace for armed resistance.

Accordingly, the Second Continental Congress began to function as an American government a year before it declared independence.[3] On June 14, 1775, it founded the Continental Army and placed George Washington in command. John Adams was the wise head who nominated the "gentleman from Virginia," thereby cementing an alliance between New England and the South. But it is hard to imagine his unanimous selection had Congress met anywhere else but on Philadelphia's neutral ground. October 13, 1775, was the birthday of the United States Navy and November 10 that of the Marine Corps. Still, opinions were sharply divided over the prospect of independence, which the Pennsylvania delegates Dickinson, his legal protégé Wilson, and the businessman Morris considered risky and at best premature. So Congress decided to send an "Olive Branch Petition" to the King even as it approved a plan to invade Canada thirteen months *before* the Declaration of Independence.

Finally, in November 1775, another sojourner (who had sailed for America on the advice of Franklin) wrote a pamphlet that was quickly printed and disseminated throughout all thirteen colonies. Tom Paine's *Common Sense* evangelized Americans with a republican gospel, which in turn emboldened Virginia Congressman Richard Henry Lee to call the question on June 3, 1776. "Our enemies," he cried, "are determined upon the absolute conquest and sub-duction of North America. It is not choice then but necessity that calls for Independence, as the only means by which *foreign Alliances* can be obtained; and a proper Confederation by which internal peace and union can be secured." Eleven days later extra-legal militias surrounded the State House and goaded Pennsylvania's assembly into "forming further compacts between the united colonies, concluding such treaties with foreign kingdoms and States, and in adopting such other measures as... shall be judged necessary for promoting the liberty, safety, and interests of America."

Lee's motion was hotly debated until July 1, when it was brought to a vote. Nine colonies voted aye, but New York's delegation, pleading no instructions, abstained; Delaware divided 1 to 1 because Patriot Caesar Rodney was absent; and South Carolina and Pennsylvania split narrowly against. The tension was electric because the British were on the verge of invading New York. Hundreds of sails had already been sighted off Long Island. Was this the best time to vote independence or the worst? If the Pennsylvania delegation continued to hang back, chances were Delaware, New Jersey, and New York would also balk and the edifice collapse for want of its keystone.

Then something happened which historians to this day cannot fully explain. When a second vote was called on July 2, Morris and Dickinson retreated "behind the bar" and sat with the gallery. That left Pennsylvania's decision up to Franklin and John Morton, who were in favor of independence; Thomas Willing and Charles Humphreys, who were opposed; and Wilson, who reluctantly broke with his mentor Dickinson and cast the decisive vote for independence. He did so, he said, because the people of Philadelphia had made their will clear in the "recent dramatic events." As for Morris, he explained that while he still hoped for negotiations he refused to break the unity on which the colonies' leverage depended. Morris later signed the Declaration. Dickinson never did, even though he knew it would turn his popularity into calumny. "I have so much of the spirit of Martyrdom in me, that I have been conscientiously compelled to endure in my political Capacity the Fires & Faggots of persecution."

New York still abstained, but when the Delaware and South Carolina delegations fell into line, Congress pronounced the Declaration unanimous. On July 3 Philadelphia's militia committee chose its own slate of revolutionaries for Pennsylvania's constitutional convention.[4] On July 4 Congress approved Jefferson's redacted draft. On July 6 crowds of Philadelphians tore the royal coat of arms from the State House façade.

The historians Carl and Jessica Bridenbaugh summed up the unique metamorphosis of the city. "Between 1760 and 1775 Philadelphia came of age and was now spiritually prepared to go its way alone. Silently and for the most part unconsciously, it had undergone an intellectual revolution; it had shaken off its early allegiance to Old World standards and conventions and had chosen for itself the democratic direction.... This process, effected in the short span of thirty-five years by hundreds of eager, able, intelligent Philadelphians, produced upon the banks of the Delaware a city owning the first broadly democratic society of modern times."

To suggest the Philadelphia factor was equally indispensable to the outcome of the War of Independence would be a stretch. Even British occupation of the city in 1777–78 (during which Congress fled to York, Pennsylvania, and Washington's army shivered at Valley Forge) had no strategic impact. But two Philadelphians, Franklin and Morris, played indispensable roles as chief diplomat and chief financier of the American cause.

David Hackett Fischer's encyclopedic history *Albion's Seed* describes the four cradle cultures that British colonists planted in North America: the Puritans of New England, the Quakers of the Delaware Valley, the Cavaliers of the Chesapeake, and the Scots-Irish Bordermen of the Allegheny frontier. Fischer imagined the War of Independence a sequence of conflicts fought by those four cradle cultures. Phase one was the Puritans' War, waged by New England militias egged on by their Congregational clergy. Phase two was the Cavaliers' War, in which regular armies led by gentlemen fought conventional battles. Phase three was the Bordermen's War waged by bush-whacking partisans in the southern back-country. Phase four was, if not the Quakers' war (which would have been a contradiction in terms), then a political struggle waged by civilians from the Middle Colonies.

In fact, all four phases occurred simultaneously, and success depended on all of them, not least the civilians' war. For the most decisive event in the eight-year conflict occurred in late March 1778, when King Louis XVI of France received Franklin at Versailles and concluded a full-fledged military alliance with the United States. Thus did Franklin fulfill the principal purpose of the Declaration of Independence, which was to enable Congress to solicit foreign assistance. The Declaration was first and foremost a war measure.

As early as November 1775 Congress had named a Secret Committee of Correspondence to seek ties with foreign powers, and after the Fourth of July 1776 the committee persuaded the seventy-year-old Franklin to head the American delegation. While serving as the colony's agent in London for twenty-odd years he had visited Paris on several occasions and was renowned there as a scientist, statesman, philosopher, and rustic wit: roles he reprised to perfection. Franklin's experience had taught him the Machiavellian lesson that the sure way to *fail* in politics and diplomacy was to be forthright, direct, and impatient, whereas deception, indirection, and patience at least gave a chance of success. Congress knew none of that when it asked John Adams to draft the so-called Model Treaty of 1776, a simple pact of friendship and commerce, expecting that was enough to win foreign recognition. Franklin did not waste the time of Louis XVI's Foreign Minister, Charles Gravier le Comte de Vergennes, with such expressions of American idealism. Instead, he wooed and tempted the French court while engaging in duplicitous correspondence designed to confound British spies. But most of all he waited for some battlefield victory that might persuade Vergennes the American cause was for real. The Battle of Saratoga did the trick, and on February 6, 1778, Bourbon France concluded a military alliance with the U.S. Congress and pledged to make war and peace together. In fact, the Americans got a bonus prize when Vergennes persuaded the Bourbon king of Spain to join the anti-British alliance.

How critical were those alliances to American victory? Suffice to say that Washington won the climactic 1781 battle of Yorktown thanks to an entirely French army commanded by Jean-Baptiste, le Duc de Rochambeau, a mostly American army commanded by Marie-Joseph, le Marquis de Lafayette, a French fleet commanded by François-Joseph le Comte de Grasse, and a campaign plan drafted by Francisco Saavedra de Sangronis, the Spanish governor in Havana!

To be sure, the French court hardly waged war out of sympathy for a revolutionary republic. It waged war to avenge its prior defeat at the hands of the British and perhaps to regain a foothold in the New World. What is more, Vergennes betrayed signs of wanting to make the United States a client state as well as restrict its territorial growth. That is why, when the British offered to talk peace after Yorktown, Franklin double-crossed Vergennes and negotiated separately with the British. John Jay and John Adams, whom Congress appointed to the peace delegation, were shocked and confused by Franklin's duplicity. But they were happy to share the credit for the generous terms Franklin obtained in the Peace of Paris of September 3, 1783 (the real, international, birthday of the United States). "We were better diplomats than we imagined," boasted Adams in retrospect.

What most textbooks do not tell you is that arms alone cannot win wars and that wars rarely pay for themselves. In 1781, the year Franco-American arms triumphed at Yorktown, Congress was broke and already $25 million in debt. But that was the moment Robert Morris placed his personal fortune at the disposal of the new nation. A grateful Congress broke its own habit of working through committees when it created an executive office for Morris, Superintendent of Finance, which he held for the duration.

Morris would later be accused of wielding dictatorial powers, lining his own pockets, and indulging in reckless speculations of the sort that would later land him in debtor's prison. What he really displayed, however, was the American penchant for hustling and creative corruption in the public interest. More than anyone else he deserved the sobriquet "financier of the Revolution."

Morris was raised in Liverpool, England, to age thirteen, at which point his father set up as a tobacco broker in Maryland. He sent young Robert to apprentice in Thomas Willing's Philadelphia merchant house, where he became partner at the tender age of twenty. Having made a fortune in foreign trade he had been reluctant to support independence in 1776. But once that step was taken he threw himself into the cause. "I am not one of those politicians that run testy when my own plans are not adopted," he said. "I think it is the duty of a good citizen to follow when he cannot lead."

During 1776 and 1777 Morris exhorted Philadelphia merchants to join him in the purchase of supplies for the Continental Army and issued "Morris notes" backed by his own money. In the new state assembly he worked to establish checks and balances and to overturn religious tests for office that Presbyterians had been applying to exclude Quakers, Mennonites, and Jews. He also assisted Wilson in his legal defense of Haym Salomon, another patriotic financier accused of profiteering. His contributions climaxed in 1781 when he helped to underwrite Washington's victorious Yorktown campaign. The British continued to hope that the war of *bullets* might turn into a war of *bottom lines* which the United States seemed likely to lose. But thanks to Morris's Bank of North America Washington's army staggered across the finish line.

Of course, American financial woes were far from over, as proven by the 1783 Newburgh Conspiracy. Officers led by General Alexander McDougall threatened to march their soldiers on Philadelphia if Congress did not guarantee their pay and pensions. General

Washington's authority and eloquence ended that revolt, but imagine if it had occurred while the war was still in doubt. Suffice to say, Washington became a close friend of Morris and indeed was his house guest from May to September 1787.

Those were the months when the Constitutional Convention designed the federal government, working what the author Catherine Drinker Bowen famously called "The Miracle at Philadelphia." But this time the venue was not a sure thing. In June 1783, two months after Newburgh, a contingent of soldiers did march on Congress, and the Philadelphia city council dared not call up its local militiamen for fear they might join the insurgents. So Congress, damning the "unhealthful & dangerous atmosphere" created by the city's mob rule, departed for Princeton and then for New York. Philadelphians, having hosted the Congress for nine years, bade good riddance to an institution which, Dr. Benjamin Rush now recorded, had come to be "abused, laughed at, pitied & cursed in every Company."

Indeed, after the war Congress atrophied under the Articles of Confederation to the point where it often failed to attract a quorum. As the New York socialite Eliza House Trist quipped in 1786: "Every now and then we hear of some Honorable Member getting a wife—else we should not know there exists such a Body as Congress." It became painfully clear how badly the new nation needed an executive branch to oversee commerce, defense, and foreign affairs. That is why the Annapolis Convention of 1786, where five states sent delegations to discuss standardizing their commercial laws, called for a national convention to revise the Articles of Confederation. Did it matter that they once more chose Philadelphia as the venue? I put that question to my late colleague Richard Beeman, author of a book on the Constitutional Convention, who replied: "I believe that with the rule of secrecy being so faithfully observed by the delegates, they could have been meeting in a barn in western Georgia and the outcome might well have been the same. On the other hand, if the convention were held in western Georgia it probably would have attracted only a handful of delegates."

Perhaps. But one cannot but think it mattered a great deal that the convention was held in Philadelphia, where independence had been declared and the new nation forged. All the features that had favored the city in 1774 applied even more thirteen years later. Its population was 60 percent larger than New York's and just as cosmopolitan. Its docks were loaded with goods from all over the world. Indeed, Morris and the French-born Philadelphia merchant Stephen Girard had just initiated America's China trade. The city's well-earned reputation for enlightenment was further enhanced by the Repository for Natural Curiosities, otherwise known as Peale's Museum. Another native of Maryland, Charles Willson Peale at age twenty-five was attracted to Philadelphia precisely because of its revolutionary politics. But he gained national fame as an artist (who painted five portraits of Washington), scientist, inventor, and entrepreneur. All the convention's delegates visited his museum, which one European visitor praised as a "Temple of God! Here is nothing but Truth and Reason!"

Almost all historians concur that Philadelphia's atmospherics deserve much of the credit for inspiring what Beeman called the "plain, honest men" in 1787. The city streets stank. The heat and humidity that summer were oppressive. But the convention delegates roomed, dined, and drank together at the City Tavern, Indian Queen, and London Coffee House. They exchanged ideas and opinions, fears and doubts at the bi-weekly market fairs on Front Street. Together they enjoyed walking in gardens graced with hummingbirds by day and fireflies by night. In short, they bonded, which helps to explain how thirty-nine of the fifty-five delegates, at least, brought the convention to a successful conclusion in just four months. Not the least influential were the extraordinary delegates representing Pennsylvania.[5]

Why James Wilson remains obscure to this day is a mystery. The brilliant Scotsman emigrated to Philadelphia at age twenty-four and quickly built a successful law practice. He served in both Continental Congresses and cast the decisive vote for independence. In the 1790s he would become the first professor of law at the University of Pennsylvania and one of the first Supreme Court justices appointed by President Washington. But Wilson's most lasting contributions were made at the Constitutional Convention, where he argued for "a republic or democracy, where the people at large retain the supreme power." He advocated popular election of the members of the House and Senate, proposed the three-fifths compromise on Congressional representation between the northern and southern (slave) states, and contributed more than anyone to the clauses defining the office of President of the United States.

Robert Morris, another Pennsylvania delegate, was the one who nominated Washington to become chairman of the Constitutional Convention, then worked to ensure that its clauses on taxation and commerce were flexible and confined to "essential principles only." He even recommended that Gouverneur Morris, known to be an elegant wordsmith, serve as the principal draftsman. Pennsylvania delegate Benjamin Franklin, now eighty-one, performed his final service as a member of the ad hoc committee appointed to break the deadlock between large and small states. Franklin's endorsement of the Connecticut Plan for equal representation in the Senate and proportional representation in the House proved decisive in good part because the crucial swing vote was cast by delegates from North Carolina who had previously voted with the other large states. Why did the Tarheels change their minds? Because their most eloquent delegate was Dr. Hugh Williamson, a protégé of Franklin who grew up in Chester, Pennsylvania, before relocating to North Carolina and serving as that state's surgeon-general.

Finally, nobody understood better than Wilson how vital it was that the Constitution be ratified in a timely manner and without amendment. So he proposed rules whereby states would vote in special conventions and only nine ratifications were required. Wilson left nothing to chance. On September 18, 1787, just one day after the signing of the Constitution, Federalists in the Pennsylvania assembly moved to stage a convention just two months hence. But the assembly was short of a quorum, so sergeants-at-arms were ordered to find two absent assemblymen—who happened to be anti-Federalists—and drag them to the State House so the guffawing majority could get its way. Over the next sixty days Wilson conducted an intensive campaign of public relations which triumphed when the Pennsylvania convention ratified the Constitution 46 to 23. To be sure, Delaware had done so six days earlier, hence its claim to be "the first state." But the Pennsylvania vote created the big-state momentum that soon carried the Massachusetts, New York, and Virginia conventions. Yet again, the United States of America was fashioned in good part by Philadelphians.

Remember Charles Thomson, Secretary to the Continental Congress, spy master, and *éminence grise* of the American Revolution? Legend has it that he exchanged letters with President Washington in the 1790s suggesting that they write their memoirs since no one knew better than they what really had happened throughout the years of the national founding. Washington dismissed the idea because he wished neither to lie to the American people nor disillusion them with the truth. He suggested instead that they humbly give all the credit to Providence. Evidently Thomson agreed. He burned his secret archives and devoted the rest of his life to a new translation of the Hebrew Bible.

So does Philadelphia own the Fourth of July?

It certainly did on July 4, 1788, when the city celebrated ratification of the Constitution by the ninth state, New Hampshire.

The festivities began at sunrise when church bells rang out and the Liberty Bell pealed in reply. Then gun ships on the Delaware River fired salutes as five thousand people representing the city's arts, sciences, trades, escorted by the resplendent First City Troop, formed a parade that stretched one and half miles from Penn's Landing to a country estate at Bush Hill at what is now Seventeenth Street and Spring Garden. The *pièce de résistance* was Charles Willson Peale's Grand Federal Edifice, a float which allegorized the Constitution. Wilson delivered the victory speech after which the throng repaired to a giant circle of tables groaning with refreshments. There Francis Hopkinson, the master of ceremonies (and designer of the flag sewn by Betsy Ross) proudly decreed that no *imported* wines or spirits be served; only good American porter, beer, and hard cider. Renowned as a statesman, lawyer, artist, composer, inventor, and poet, Hopkinson also composed an ode to this Fourth of July, likening the ratified Constitution to an elegant garment:

> "Oh! For a muse of fire to mount the skies,
> And to a listening world proclaim:
> Behold! Behold an empire rise!
> . . .
> My sons for freedom fought, nor fought in vain,
> But found a naked goddess was their gain;
> Good government alone can show the maid
> In robes of social happiness arrayed.
> Hail to the Festival! All hail the day!
> Columbia's standard on her roof display!
> And let the people's motto ever be,
> United thus, and, thus united, free!"

I rest my case.

★ 4 ★

THE AMAZING CAREER OF STEPHEN GIRARD, PHILADELPHIA TYCOON AND PHILANTHROPIST[1]

On May 20, 1750, in the French town of Bordeaux, Madame Anne Girard gave birth to a singular child. During gestation the fetus had grown a deformed right eyeball, in fact a grotesque walleye with a larger than normal socket and a blackened iris. It was blind and inoperable. His parents did their best to raise the child normally, but other children inevitably teased or taunted the boy, with the result that he grew up shy and reserved. By his teenage years a layer of skin had grown over the eye, which rendered his visage less macabre, but still—in the words of a contemporary—"severe or harsh." Yet the youth's personality was neither severe nor harsh because his parents encouraged him to turn his deformity into a source of motivation for himself and charity toward others with handicaps. That was the first and greatest challenge Stephen Girard overcame during his extraordinary life.

His home town, the center of the famous wine region, was also the largest seaport in southwestern France. Both sides of his family had hailed from the countryside sixty-five miles inland, but Stephen's grandparents had migrated to Bordeaux, where his father, Pierre, became a prosperous merchant. Pierre had gone to sea at the age of thirteen and by his mid-twenties was already captaining ships. During France's wars against Britain in the 1740s Pierre had served gallantly in the navy and received a medal from King Louis XV himself. Not surprisingly, he was a hero and role model for his son. But Stephen also cherished his mother, who dutifully suffered nine pregnancies in as many years and gave birth to eight children. Anne and her husband homeschooled them all, with Pierre teaching his sons geometry, bookkeeping, accounting, and navigation as well as reading, writing, and arithmetic. Stephen also read literature and philosophy, including—much to his pious mother's distress—such blasphemous authors as Voltaire and Rousseau. Although Stephen never formally renounced the Catholic faith, he did display a lifelong antipathy toward clergy.

In 1762, when Stephen was eleven, his mother died. She was just thirty-six, but must have been weakened by the sheer stress of childbearing and motherhood. That event marked the end of Stephen's childhood. Two years later he went to sea under his father's instruction as a *pilotin* (captain's apprentice) and sailed on a merchant ship bound for the West Indies. No sooner had the vessel embarked on the choppy Bay of Biscay than the boy suffered from *mal de mer*—seasickness. But eventually he found his sea legs and began his education as a sailor. In those days that meant learning to perform every task from climbing the rigging to setting the sails and handling the rudder—in his case with just one functional eye. When he was rated able seaman his father began to teach him the duties of an officer, including celestial navigation, financial accounting, and procedures for acquiring naval stores and supplies. His father taught Stephen commercial skills such as how to purchase, transport, and sell cargoes and handle the customs agents, port authorities, and quarantine officials in their regular ports of call. Finally, of course, a young skipper needed to learn how to command respect and sometimes discipline salty old sailors.

No fewer than six of Stephen's teenage voyages took him to the French colony of Saint-Domingue, or modern-day Haiti, a fetid, disease-ridden, but exceptionally fertile island where sugar plantations were worked by enslaved Africans. His father would put in at Port-au-Prince, exchange European manufactures for sugar and molasses, and sail back to France the following year. Soon his father or the firm's other captains promoted Stephen to supercargo, first mate, and finally commander when his captain was detained in a legal dispute in Port-au-Prince. Upon his return to Bordeaux in 1783 Girard was awarded his license as a full-fledged master in the French merchant marine. He was just twenty-three.

That February he boarded another ship bound for the Caribbean... and never returned. Nor would he see his father and siblings (save for one brother years later) ever again. By a series of twists of fate it turned out Stephen Girard's destiny was to become an American, a *British* North American.

The initial twist of fate was his failure—for the first time—to find buyers for his cargo, which included fine hats, parasols, and handkerchiefs for the ladies, plus saddles and whips for the overseers of the sugar plantations, because the market for such goods was temporarily glutted. That was a problem because Stephen had borrowed heavily in Bordeaux to purchase the cargo. So he determined to stiff his creditors for the time being and wait for something to turn up. Soon an opportunity too good to refuse presented itself. Another merchant was fixing to sail for New York with a cargo of sugar and coffee, but lacked a first mate. He offered the post to Girard and even granted him space in his hold for any personal cargo he might wish to transport. Girard promptly sold his French products at a loss and used the proceeds to purchase some sugar and coffee on his own account. He arrived in New York in July 1774 to discover rebellion was in the air. Tensions had been building up between the British government and the thirteen colonies ever since Parliament's attempt to impose the Stamp Act nine years before, and by the time Girard arrived the colonists were preparing to send delegates to a Continental Congress in Philadelphia two months hence.

Girard was not displeased by the American agitation since Frenchmen had no love for Britons. But he had only just arrived in New York, spoke little English as yet, and needed somehow to earn a living 3,500 miles from home. So he hung around the docks and taverns where the merchants convened, learned what products Americans sold in the Caribbean, and eventually became a partner of Thomas Randall, a merchant and shipowner who traded with New Orleans. Though Louisiana was currently Spanish, it had formerly been a French colony and Randall needed a native French speaker in his company. So Girard agreed to serve as first mate until—on May 14, 1776—he learned while in New Orleans that fighting had broken out and the American Congress was debating whether to declare independence. Moreover, the Royal Navy had already begun to blockade American ports and capture foreign merchant ships on the high seas. So Girard falsified his ship's papers to declare her real destination was the islands of Saint-Pierre and Miquelon off the Canadian coast. But the ship sailed into terrible weather off of dangerous Cape Hatteras. High seas washed over the decks, spoiling the fresh water casks, and the winds carried one of the masts by the board. Sure enough, a British warship encountered the derelict vessel. But thanks to his false papers and real excuse—the need to replenish the water supply—the British skipper released his ship. Girard studied his charts and—since their location was just fifty miles off of Delaware Bay—decided to make safe haven in Philadelphia. So it was that he arrived on the docks, half a mile from Independence Hall, on June 6, 1776.

Girard then began a new life in America's leading metropolis, a city of 35,000 renowned for its many brick buildings, churches, and 165 inns and taverns. Girard made straight for the London Coffee House, where merchants, agents, and captains swapped news, closed deals, and socialized. A lively slave market operated across the street because Philadelphia's population included some five hundred enslaved Africans, most of them in domestic service.

For the time being Girard opened a small shop on Water Street where he bought and sold groceries and dry goods. But the Declaration of Independence approved the following month would sooner or later oblige him to choose between returning to France or remaining in Philadelphia. He chose the latter in part because he still owed that tidy sum to his creditors in Bordeaux. But he also made the shrewd calculation that in the event the Americans won independence, unlimited commercial opportunities would open up in their new nation. During the fall of 1776 he braved another voyage to St. Domingue, managing to elude the British blockade. That was the last business trip he would ever make. Instead, he expanded his shop and counting house on Water Street and began to invest in the overland trade, purchasing commodities in Lancaster County and carting them to the city.

Girard, now twenty-seven, continued to work as passionately as he had since the age of thirteen. But it must be said he also had a passion for the opposite sex. What affairs and escapades he might have enjoyed while in foreign ports is unknown. But a great deal is known about his love life in Philadelphia, as you may be abashed to hear. It began during the spring of 1777, when he fell in love with an eighteen-year-old boardinghouse maid named Mary Lum. She was, as a Girard biographer wrote, "an enchanting brunette . . . with luxuriant locks curling and clustering about her neck. As she tripped along with bare feet and empty pail, in airy and unconscious grace, the saucy, titillating Mary simply captivated the susceptible Frenchman." Girard wooed her daily in the kitchen where she worked and soon won her hand. Mary might have been put off by his deformed eye, but might also have guessed he would become a rich man. Characteristically, Girard's honeymoon came first because the couple enjoyed a weekend tryst at a rural inn prior to exchanging their vows in St. Paul's Episcopal Church on June 6, a year to the day after Girard had arrived in Philadelphia.

Rumors to the effect that the British meant to occupy Philadelphia convinced Girard, who was after all a foreign national of dubious status, that he must not fall into the hands of the enemy. So he purchased a second residence twenty miles outside of town in Mount Holly, New Jersey. That house, which cost $1,407 in 1777, still stands today at 211 Mill Street. They escaped just in time because the British army, following its victories in the battles of Brandywine, Paoli, and Germantown, forced George Washington's Continentals into winter quarters at Valley Forge. Philadelphia was occupied by the Redcoats on September 26.

Exiled though he was in New Jersey, Girard established a makeshift store in his basement and soon did a bustling business in whiskey, wine, cigars, and coffee. Men from all over the county frequented the store, if only to flirt with the comely Mary Girard.

The winter of 1777–78 was the first turning point in the War of Independence because the defeats around Philadelphia were followed in October by the stunning American victory at Saratoga, New York. When news of that battle reached Paris, Benjamin Franklin, the diplomat Congress had posted to France, persuaded the ministers of Louis XVI that the American cause was for real. The French government not only recognized the United States but concluded a full-fledged military alliance with Congress in February 1778. And when news of that crossed the Atlantic the exultant French expatriate devoted himself wholeheartedly to the American cause.

Girard briefly exulted again when the British evacuated Philadelphia in June 1778, only to learn that their line of retreat was to run through Mount Holly. So the Girards dropped out of sight until October, when they returned to Philadelphia. Ready now to declare his new loyalty, Stephen swore an oath of allegiance to the Commonwealth of Pennsylvania, in effect becoming an American citizen. No doubt he did so in part to exploit the fact that Pennsylvanians got preferential tax rates and the privilege of filing civil suits against debtors—obvious advantages for an aspiring merchant—but there is also no doubt that his patriotism was genuine.

Even as the War for Independence continued to rage, Girard's commercial firm prospered. By 1780 he accumulated enough capital to invest in cargoes and soon in ships as well, which substantially increased his profits. But so, too, did risks increase: risks of piracy, confiscation, and shipwreck. Yet unlike some plunging merchants (and no doubt remembering his first failed voyage) Girard did all he could to minimize risk and ensure that his solvency would never depend on the successful voyage of one or two ships. In 1783, for example, he learned that one of his schooners, which he had christened the *Mary*, was wrecked on the shoals of Maryland during her maiden voyage. The loss barely dented his bottom line. But it did prove to be a terrible omen because Mary herself was about to be wrecked on the shoals of insanity.

The years 1781 to 1783 had been the happiest of their lives. To begin with, the American cause triumphed after the Battle of Yorktown where a French fleet and army had reinforced the Continental Army and helped Washington capture Lord Cornwallis's entire command. That defeat felled Lord North's cabinet and caused the new British government to initiate peace talks, which culminated in American independence in September 1783. On a personal note, Stephen was reunited that autumn with his brother Jean, who had also become a merchant and arrived in Philadelphia with a cargo from Saint-Domingue. Jean stayed several months with Stephen, but it was during his visit that Mary became unhinged. It seemed that Jean's entourage included an enslaved woman in her twenties named Hannah, and she in turn had a light-skinned daughter in tow who bore a striking resemblance to Jean: obviously his illegitimate child. What is more, Jean hastily decided to marry a nineteen-year-old Irish indentured servant he had met in Philadelphia, and not wanting Hannah around to complicate matters Jean simply gave her and her mulatto child to Stephen. No wonder Mary grew outraged at the presence of an adulterous slave and her child, whom she knew to be Stephen's own niece. Whether for that or some other reason she never calmed down. Over the following months her erratic temperament eventually degenerated into lunacy. A Girard biographer described it this way:

> She had spells of irrational behavior such as sudden mood changes followed by tantrums. She would be jolly one minute and sullen the next. Then she would start screaming, smash dishes, and topple furniture. If she was outdoors when a seizure came upon her she might bang her head repeatedly against a tree. Sometimes she would stay up all night shrieking and thumping on anything that would make noise. Her frightful condition deteriorated until doctors pronounced her not only insane but incurable.

She was just twenty-six. Stephen did not know what to do.

During the eighteenth century the usual treatment for violence-prone mentally ill people was to keep them fettered in chains lest they harm themselves or others. Girard found such treatment appalling. So instead of committing Mary to an asylum he moved her to the house in Mount Holly and hired her own mother and sister as nurses. Three long years passed during which Mary showed no improvement. At length Stephen decided he could no longer remain celibate and "hired" Sally Bickham, an eighteen-year-old seamstress, to be his resident housekeeper and surrogate wife. Her beauty was so stunning that Stephen hired an artist to paint her portrait—something he had never done for Mary.

During the summer of 1787 Philadelphia was again the center of the new nation's attention because the Constitutional Convention was meeting to design a new federal government. Girard was keenly interested in its deliberations because one of its purposes was to draft uniform commercial law for the states. It did so, with the result that ratification of the Constitution realized Alexander Hamilton's dream of a rapidly growing continental empire brimming with opportunity. That was what Girard had bet his future on back in 1776 when he decided to make Philadelphia his permanent home, and by 1787 his ships were trading in ports all over Europe, the Caribbean, and South America.

That very December a consortium of Philadelphians, including Girard and Robert Morris, the "financier of the American Revolution," initiated American commerce with China. Their ship departed with a cargo of ginseng, an aphrodisiac much valued in China, and returned the following year stuffed with porcelain, silks, and tea worth *sixty times* what the ginseng had cost. That was also the year when Girard himself embarked on his first voyage in a decade. Leaving his business in the able hands of his brother Jean, who was again visiting Philadelphia, Stephen sailed back to his native France. Only his destination was not Bordeaux, where he feared his ship might be impounded by his angry creditors, but rather Marseille. He spent seven pleasant months in the South of France, departing the country in January 1789, just six months before the French Revolution. It was during that sojourn that he learned his father had died, and the settlement of his father's estate finally compelled him to pay off the creditors in Bordeaux. Why it took Girard sixteen years to pay off that debt is a mystery given the magnanimity he displayed with most other people throughout his life.

Upon returning to Philadelphia he found Mary still mad, while her mother and sister had nearly gone mad dealing with her. So in August 1790 Girard had her examined again by two of the city's leading physicians, who diagnosed her as incurable. Only then did he reluctantly commit her to the insanity ward of the Pennsylvania Hospital. Yet another heartache gripped Girard when—just six months later—Mary gave birth! As it happened the child died in infancy, but how had she gotten pregnant in the first place? It was extremely unlikely to have been Girard himself because she had never conceived over eight years of randy intercourse prior to her mental breakdown, and so far as we know Girard never did sire a child during his entire life.

In any event, he never abandoned his wife. In years to come he would visit her frequently and was consoled by the fact that the Pennsylvania Hospital was the most humane and comfortable facility in the New World.

By that time Girard had lived with Sally for six years and according to the gossip enjoyed daily intimacy with her as well. The rest of his days, and often evenings, were consumed by business, and his business continued to grow. So life seemed to be an even keel until, in 1793, calamity struck Philadelphia; in fact, the first of two emergencies that would earn Stephen Girard a measure of immortality.

News of the French Revolution and its revolutionary triptych "Liberty, Equality, Fraternity" had reached the ears of enslaved Africans in the colony of Saint-Domingue. By 1791 the bloody race war known today as the Haitian Revolution erupted. Terrified planters and their families fled in terror, many to the United States. In 1793 one of their refugee ships docked in Philadelphia with a deadly stowaway on board. In the West Indies it was known as black vomit, but Europeans and Americans knew it as yellow jack or yellow fever. In the heat and humidity of the Philadelphia summer an epidemic spread like wildfire. More than a third of the city's population of 48,000 fled to the countryside while one-sixth of those who remained—about 5,000 people—perished from the disease. Contemporaries called it "the most appalling collective disaster that has ever overtaken an American city." Dr. Benjamin Rush, the famous signer of the Declaration of Independence, and Drs. Hugh Hodge and John Foulke, the two who had examined Mary, diagnosed yellow jack, but nobody knew what caused it. Indeed, not until the end of the nineteenth century would medical science prove that mosquitoes transmitted the virus. Instead, Philadelphians in 1793 blamed miasma of the air or water, hence their primitive preventive measures such as the setting of fires in the streets to cleanse the air or the wearing of masks dipped in vinegar or camphor. Doctors made matters worse by bleeding and purging infectious patients. One journalist recorded that the demand for purges of calomel and jalap (a drug derived from jalapeño peppers) was so great that apothecaries did not take time to measure out discrete doses, with the result that patients often got overdoses, sometimes with fatal consequences.

Meanwhile, Philadelphians fled from each other's presence in what we now call social distancing, while people dressed in mourning clothes (indicating a death in their family) were literally "avoided like the plague." People stopped shaking hands or even talking one to another. Courtesy, charity, civil order disappeared.

Philadelphia had served as the U.S. capital city since December 1790, but due to the yellow fever epidemic the federal government just melted away. Everyone from George and Martha Washington to cabinet members to officials and clerks evacuated the city. (Treasury Secretary Alexander Hamilton and his wife even contracted the fever.) But Philadelphia's dutiful mayor, Matthew Clarkson, remained at his post and founded a body with a name as big as the emergency: the Committee to Attend to and Alleviate the Sufferings of the Afflicted with the Malignant Fever. He also issued urgent pleas for volunteers to help the committee serve the stricken community in this hour of need.

Needless to say, wealthy residents could relocate easily, and almost all of them did. Stephen Girard did not. In an act of courage and public spirit he not only answered the mayor's call for volunteers but assumed a leadership role in the fight against yellow fever. After consulting with the mayor's committee he selected a bucolic site for a sanatorium on Bush Hill, which today is located at Sixteenth and Spring Garden streets. But the first time Girard made the two mile trip to inspect operations he found the facility so overwhelmed as to be worse than useless. Beds, linen, medicine, even food were in short supply. The floors were littered with 150 feverish victims shivering in their own vomit or excrement, seemingly left for dead.

Girard began at once to cleanse the Augean Stables. He executed a whole series of procedural reforms, saw to the purchase of sufficient numbers of beds and supplies, and hired nurses and competent staff, mostly at his own expense. He fired the four part-time physicians who had presided over the sanatorium and replaced them with competent doctors, all with the blessing and gratitude of the mayor's committee. As a result the fatality rate among patients treated at Bush Hill fell to just 10 percent. A doctor's diary recorded that Girard put in long hours dosing, feeding, and washing invalids, even those who spewed black vomit on him.

During the months of summer and fall when the epidemic was at its height Girard suspended his commercial affairs. To a partner in Baltimore he wrote: "The deplorable situation to which fright and sickness have reduced the inhabitants of our city demands succor from those who do not fear death.... This will occupy me for some time, and if I have the misfortune to succumb, I will at least have the satisfaction of having performed a duty we all owe to each other."

The epidemic peaked on October 11, when 119 people died—or the equivalent of 6,000 per day during the pandemic year of 2020—

then gradually tailed off as the weather cooled and the mosquitoes disappeared. Residents who had fled began to trickle back into town and were told by those who had remained about Girard's remarkable charity. Already a celebrity because of his wealth, he was now a civic hero as well.

No sooner did Girard throw himself back into business than American merchants began to fret about new assaults on their shipping. The wars of the French Revolution—vicious ideological wars that would last over twenty years—had just broken out, and the navies of Britain and France, especially, began to capture neutral ships suspected of trading with the enemy. Moreover, corsairs from North Africa—the infamous Barbary Pirates—were preying on everyone's commerce. When President Washington declared American neutrality in 1793 (despite the fact that the Franco-American alliance was nominally in force) Girard was disheartened. But he regretted far more the fact that the president and Congress had neglected to build any warships to protect American merchantmen. So he placed himself in the forefront of a naval movement, chairing meetings of merchants and shippers, drafting petitions, and leading protests which attracted as many as 6,000 people to Independence Square. In a matter of months the movement persuaded Congress to pass and the president to sign the Naval Act of 1794, which authorized construction of six forty-four-gun frigates. Washington also dispatched John Jay to London, where he negotiated a treaty in 1794 in which he British agreed to concessions on American trade and freedom of the seas. Later on during the 1790s President John Adams's administration successfully deployed the new frigates in the undeclared Quasi-War against the French Republic, and under President Thomas Jefferson the frigates punished the Barbary Pirates. Throughout that era the federal government also constructed fortresses defending the Atlantic seaboard, of which the most notable was Baltimore's Fort McHenry of War of 1812 fame.

For awhile, therefore, American merchants made windfall profits by selling goods to both sides in the wars of the French Revolution.

That decade marked a surprising transition in Girard's personal life as well. He had a larger brick building constructed on Water Street (now buried, alas, beneath Interstate 95) which doubled as an elegant town house and counting house sufficient for his rapidly growing commercial empire, whose value surpassed a quarter of a million dollars. But his household had barely moved in to the new building when Sally announced she was leaving Girard after nine years in order to marry another. Evidently she had given up hope that Girard's mentally ill wife would die or else that he might obtain a court-ordered divorce. Girard was dismayed, but wished her well and gifted the couple with all the furnishings they would need for their new home.

Characteristically, Stephen hired another surrogate wife in short order, a twenty-year-old laundress named Polly Kenton. No image of her survives, but a contemporary described her as "robust, buxom, happy, and competent." Like Sally before her she was happy to serve as the live-in mistress of a wealthy, affectionate man and to manage his domestic affairs. Girard's first biographer, who had been a personal acquaintance, was surprisingly candid about his friend's libido. He reported that throughout his long life Girard "drew exceptional solace from female intercourse and generously reciprocated with jewelry and other gifts for his wife or mistresses. His was a life of serial monogamy."

Finally, Girard took up an avocation in the 1790s reminiscent of his forebears' rural roots in the French province of Guyenne: he bought a working farm and kept adding to until it sprawled over 567 acres around what is now Girard Park on the banks of the Schuylkill River. He still spent most of his workdays in the office penning endless instructions, poring over accounts, assessing commodities markets in the ports of four continents, and arranging to buy and sell cargoes. But for the rest of his life the farm became a refuge where he could dig his hands in the soil, prune and weed, plow and harrow, and improve the strains and yields of his crops. All told, a biographer reports, Girard "greeted the dawn of the nineteenth century in a spirit of *joie de vivre*. He was under full sail, with a favorable wind at his back."

What was the secret of his success? Why did he keep working so hard given that he no longer needed the money and was so fond of his mistress and farm? The only explanation is that Girard enjoyed the art of the deal like a gambler craving the action. His voluminous private papers contain numerous nuggets about politics, war, and daily life, but by far the bulk of them consist of correspondence with captains, supercargos, factors, and agents. Merchants in that pre-industrial age had to rely on scanty and often outdated information, so attempting to manipulate markets must have been an intellectual game Girard loved to play. Over the years his success made him one of the three or four wealthiest Americans, on a par with New York's John Jacob Astor. But upon reaching middle age—beginning, perhaps, with the courage and charity he displayed during the epidemic—he was increasingly drawn to philanthropy. Girard had never been a church-goer and in fact had recently joined the Freemasons. Yet he began to make large donations to Catholic building funds and other charities. He likewise gave back to his native countrymen by lending generously to French people exiled by the Revolution, never expecting to be repaid. He also took a keen interest in the South American independence movements that sprang up following Napoleon's invasion of Spain in 1808. Girard ordered his captains to make contact with the Latin juntas and even shipped arms and ammunition to Simón Bolívar.

During the first decade of the nineteenth century Girard also began to invest in new industries such as coal-burning stoves, which were beginning to replace the Franklin stoves in houses and public buildings. He was among the first to promote the use of hot-burning, un-smoky anthracite coal, deposits of which abounded in northeastern Pennsylvania. But by 1807, about the time Girard became one of America's first millionaires, more trouble was brewing. The British naval victory at Trafalgar and the French military victory at Austerlitz, both of which had occurred in 1806, made the Napoleonic Wars a stalemate between the proverbial Elephant and the Whale. That is, the French army was invincible on the continent but Britannia ruled the waves, with the result that both empires began to wage aggressive economic warfare through reciprocal blockades. The British cabinet approved the so-called Orders in Council, which prohibited neutral ships to trade with the continent, while Napoléon's Continental System forbade Europeans from importing British goods no matter what flag their ships flew. Consequently American merchants, so recently flush, now traded with Europeans at their peril.

Girard had always been a supporter of the Francophile Thomas Jefferson and his Democratic Republican Party. But as president Jefferson resorted to desperate measures even more ruinous to trade than the European blockades. In 1808 he instructed his Democratic-Republican majority in Congress to pass a draconian Embargo Act, which simply forbade Americans to engage in foreign trade, period. The economic calamity that caused cannot be exaggerated. Merchants, the shipping industry, and all sectors of the economy that depended on exports were temporarily ruined. In 1813, after Jefferson left office, Congress repealed the embargo, but his protégé and successor, James Madison, replaced it with a so-called "Non-Intercourse Act," which forbade commerce with Britain or France so long as their blockades remained in force. Not surprisingly, merchants and captains routinely smuggled cargoes into and out of lesser ports on the Atlantic seaboard, accepting the risk of ruinous fines if customs officials proved they had engaged in illegal trade.

On June 11, 1812, the U.S. Treasury filed suit against Girard on the basis of evidence that one of his ships had carried a British cargo, and asked the court to forfeit the cargo and impose a punitive fine. Just a week later the Democratic Republicans in the Congress defiantly declared war on Britain by votes of 79 to 49 in the House and 19 to 13 in the Senate. Suddenly prosecution of a lawsuit against Girard's firm became the Treasury's lowest priority, which meant that the dispute would drag on for the duration.

In fact, however, that War of 1812 turned out to be the second emergency which would earn Girard a measure of immortality. Why? Because the Democratic Republicans in Congress had wrecked the federal government's only institution for financing a war when they rescinded the charter for the First United Bank, that had been founded by Alexander Hamilton in 1791. Girard had owned shares in the bank and had strongly favored renewal, but now his own party had killed it. So Girard did the next best thing: he purchased the bank's elegant Corinthian temple on South Third Street in Philadelphia for $115,000 and re-opened it as a private bank. That explains why Treasury Secretary Albert Gallatin took a carriage to Philadelphia and begged Girard to lend the government half a million dollars *even as his own department was prosecuting his firm*. Yet Girard agreed on condition that the government deposit a portion of the funds in his bank. Gallatin refused, and so no loan was made.

In February 1813 Congress authorized the Treasury to sell $16 million in war bonds, hoping to attract broad participation. But the truth was the Federalists had all voted against the war, while most rural supporters of the war were unable or unwilling to subscribe. So Gallatin appealed to rich Americans, notably Girard and Astor, to make large contributions of their own and to market the bonds to smaller investors. Girard pledged $100,000 and promised to raise the whole $16 million if, again, the Treasury patronized his bank on an equal footing. Two anxious months followed, but this time, reported Secretary of State James Monroe, the president "readily assented to the measure proposed by [Girard]."

Still, public subscriptions fell woefully short—just $6 million was pledged. Worse, the British were poised to invade the United States by land and sea. So Gallatin returned to Philadelphia and begged again for the mercy of its wealthiest citizen. Girard held all the cards and might at least have insisted the Treasury drop its lawsuit against him. He did not. He promised to subscribe to the missing $10 million himself. That patriotic act primed the pump. Public confidence in Girard (not the U.S. government) was such that his bank sold $4.6 million of government bonds in just ten days.

It proved to be the turning point of the war because it bought time for the American civilian and military leadership to reboot their war efforts and overcome the reverses they had suffered on the northern, southern, and western frontiers. The War of 1812 is usually said to have ended in a draw because the Treaty of Ghent merely restored the *status quo ante bellum*. But a draw was a victory for a callow republic waging in effect a second war of independence. It also gave American frontier militias under leaders such as William Henry Harrison and Andrew Jackson the chance to defeat hostile Native American tribes allied with the British and thus to remove the last obstacles to the frontier expansion of American pioneers.

When news of the Treaty of Ghent reached Philadelphia in February 1815 huge crowds turned out in frigid weather to celebrate. An eyewitness recorded, "The town is in a a great bustle and joy sparkles in every countenance." What is more, the Democratic-Republicans, having learned their lesson, promptly created the Second Bank of the United States, whose elegant Doric temple still stands on Chestnut Street across from the Museum of the American Revolution. What about that Treasury lawsuit? It dragged on until 1819, when Girard's lawyers settled for a fine of $50,000.

During that victorious year of 1815 the long-standing conjugal thorn in Girard's side was finally removed. His wife, Mary, died at the age of fifty-six, twenty-five years after being committed to the hospital. One of his firm's captains who attended her funeral wrote this: "I shall never forget the last and closing scene when we all witnessed Mr. Girard, filled with emotion, step forward and kiss his wife's coffin, his cheeks moistened by tears."

His current mistress, Polly, must have hoped that Girard would now marry her and make her a very rich woman. But that was evidently the reason he never proposed. Under Pennsylvania law she would be entitled to most of her husband's estate, and Girard feared that her greedy relatives would soon squander his fortune. So Polly remained his surrogate wife for another twelve years until advanced age and declining health caused her to "retire" in 1827. Girard, now seventy-seven years old, found an instant replacement in Emeline Keaton, Polly's eighteen-year-old niece.

Girard himself never considered retirement. "When death comes for me he will find me busy, unless I am asleep in bed" was one of his adages. "If I thought I was going to die tomorrow, nevertheless I should plant a tree today" was another. "To rest is to rust" was a third. So he maintained his frenetic schedule in the office and on the farm, expanded his coal mines, and leapt into another revolutionary technology: railroads.

Finally, Girard performed another public service when the Commonwealth of Pennsylvania, like many state governments that overinvested in internal improvements, defaulted in 1829. "The last cent of its credit, as well as its resources, has been expended," wrote an associate. "Public works projects stood still. Interest on state loans went unpaid...and alarm overspread the public." So the Governor of Pennsylvania John Shulze traveled from Harrisburg to Philadelphia in hopes of a bailout. Girard loaned the Commonwealth $100,000 with little expectation it would be repaid. Such altruism caused a friend to write what could serve as an epitaph: "No man in this town has more pleasure than yourself... [because] your enjoyments are in accomplishing lasting good to mankind."

Late in the afternoon of December 21, 1830—the shortest day of the year—dusk was settling over the city when Girard stepped into Market Street and was struck by a horse-drawn wagon. One of the wheels ran over his face, lacerating his cheek and ear and causing a serious loss of blood. Nevertheless, he struggled to his feet and hobbled the two blocks to home. The accident was likely caused by the fact that Girard, blind from birth in one eye, was now gradually losing sight in the other. After several months confined to his bed he was relieved to be permitted to get back to work. But the following December a virulent influenza epidemic plagued Philadelphia, and this time Girard was infected. Suffering fevers, nausea, and insomnia, he grew gradually weaker. Friends took turns standing vigil over his bed until one day he sprang suddenly up, walked across the room, and exclaimed in his native tongue: "*à quel point ce trouble est violent; comme c'est extraordinaire*—how violent is this disorder; how extraordinary it is!" He lingered a few more hours before passing away in the company of his mistress, a few friends... and Hannah. Remember Hannah, that enslaved woman from Saint-Domingue whom his brother Jean had given to Stephen thirty-eight years before? She had served him faithfully all that time and was the first beneficiary named in his will.

The city fathers declared Girard's funeral a municipal holiday and grand memorial. Philadelphians had seen nothing like it since they laid Benjamin Franklin to rest in 1790. But the lasting epilogue to Girard's biography was that will.

He and his lawyers had drafted a long document, which included a philosophical essay and discourses on architecture, education, and urban planning, in addition to meticulous instructions about his bequests. Hannah, Emeline, Sally, and Polly all received comfortable lifetime annuities, as did his servants in Philadelphia, Mount Holly, and the farm, plus the indentured servants and apprentices employed by his firm. Girard's ship captains received lump sums, as did various relatives back in France. But all those bequests amounted to just 2 percent of his $7.7 million estate. He also endowed trust funds benefiting the Pennsylvania Hospital and other institutes serving the poor and needy, sick and suffering, aged and infirm. He gave the City of Philadelphia $500,000 with instructions to "pull down and remove all wooden buildings within the city limits and replace them with brick or stone" and to beautify boulevards, parks, and buildings on the Delaware River waterfront. He gave the Commonwealth of Pennsylvania another grant to expand its roads and canals. But he also set aside a sizeable trust fund for future investment, with the result that the Girard Estate today is worth about $300 million.

Far and away his largest bequest endowed a boarding school for "poor, white, male orphans" on a forty-five-acre tract a mile north of the city. He called it Girard College, but it was really a prep school for pupils in grades 1 through 12. The architecture was to be Greek Revival and the centerpiece a grand Founders Hall. The trustees later decided to make the hall's most prominent feature a sarcophagus for Girard's body, which they had translated from its original grave in the cemetery of Holy Trinity Catholic Church.

Interestingly, Girard's will specified "that no ecclesiastic, missionary, or minister of any sect whatsoever shall ever hold or exercise any station or duty whatever in the said College; nor shall any such person ever be admitted for any purpose, or as a visitor, within the premises.... I do not mean to cast any reflection upon any sect or person whatsoever; but, as there is such a multitude of sects, and such a diversity of opinion among them, I desire to keep the tender minds of the orphans, who are to derive advantage from this bequest, free from the excitement which clashing doctrines and sectarian controversy are so apt to produce...." He enjoined the administrators and teachers to instill into the minds of the scholars "the purest principles of morality," but not to confound them with dogma.

Thanks to Girard's legacy, therefore, the ideals of the eighteenth-century French Enlightenment were revived in an American school founded in the fourth decade of the nineteenth century.

Various litigants hoped to overturn Girard's will on their own behalf and imagined his religious restriction might be grounds for disallowing the bequest. They fought the will all the way from the local Orphan's Court to the U.S. Supreme Court, where they hired Senator Daniel Webster to argue their case. But the High Court ruled in Girard's favor in 1844. Note that nobody challenged the will for discriminating on the basis of race or sex. Indeed, not until 1968 did the Supreme Court declare the whites-only clause unconstitutional and not until 1984 did Girard College admit girls. But from its inception the school has always been praised for its academic rigor, and its 30,000 graduates over 180 years might be considered the children Girard himself never sired.

The one-eyed mariner from southwestern France was truly a man in full. To be sure, a series of fluky adventures washed him up on American shores. But his own daring, determination, decency, courage, and humanity were the qualities that propelled the career he made in his adopted country and defined what came to be known as the American Dream. Stephen Girard surely worked intensely to promote himself, whether as a sailor, merchant, banker, farmer, or investor. But he worked just as intensely to promote the interests of Philadelphians, Pennsylvanians, and Americans, with the epidemic of 1793 and the War of 1812 surely his finest hours.

★ 5 ★

THE GRAND STRATEGIC CONSEQUENCES OF THE ALLEGEDLY FOOLISH WAR OF 1812[1]

"Britain and the United States are destined to become . . . the dominant nations of Christendom. . . . Each an incumbrance to the other when united, their severance seems to have been the signal for unequalled progress, and boundless prospects to each; not only in material dominion but also the glory of broadening the empire of rational thought throughout the world." So wrote Richard Rush, the American minister to London, in 1820, and so the historian Bradford Perkins began his account of the origins of the War of 1812. According to Perkins the cause of that conflict was simply that "America chose to be neutral while Britain struggled for her life against Napoleon."

The wars against the French Revolution and Napoleon were an existential struggle which lasted twenty-three years, claimed 300,000 British lives, and cost the British exchequer a billion pounds sterling. At various stages in these wars Britain variously allied with the Austrian and Russian empires and kingdoms of Prussia and Spain, organized and subsidized seven coalitions, and in the end needed to defeat Napoleon not once but twice because his escape from exile on the island of Elba in 1815 sparked another military campaign that ended at the Battle of Waterloo.

But during the climactic years of this world war the British found themselves in another war that would decide the future not of Europe but of North America. Yet U.S. historians, who tend to focus myopically on their own country and rarely think systemically, often fail to understand this War of 1812. If the conflict is still taught in our schools at all, it is usually dismissed as a mistake because Congress declared war only after the British cabinet had rescinded its ostensible *casus belli*, then was fought to a draw, then ended in an anodyne treaty simply restoring the *status quo ante bellum*, then anti-climaxed in the Battle of New Orleans fought two weeks after the peace treaty was signed. In short, a war so devoid of meaning that it deserved to be named for nothing but the year in which it began.

Indeed, Theodore Roosevelt, who at age twenty-three wrote a history of the war, expressed that conventional wisdom when he wrote, "the Battle of New Orleans was a perfectly useless shedding of blood, since peace had already been declared." That so-called wisdom is still conventional today, as demonstrated by a survey of the many books published around the war's bicentennial. But the most erroneous feature of the historiography is that so few authors have posed the simple counterfactual question: what if the British had won the Battle of New Orleans?

In a previous lecture we addressed the remarkable career of Stephen Girard, the Philadelphia merchant, philanthropist, and patriot whose financial support enabled President James Madison's administration to wage the War of 1812. But that lecture had little to say about the diplomatic and military history of what was—contrary to all the myths—a critical event for America and Britain alike.

The place to begin the story which climaxed on the bayous of New Orleans is 1789, the year President George Washington was inaugurated and the year the French Revolution erupted. When that revolution eventuated in total, ideological warfare in Europe

Washington wisely proclaimed neutrality in 1793. But the United States could hardly be unaffected for the simple reason that the new nation was by no means isolated.

The British ruled Canada, the Spaniards Florida and Mexico, various European states had colonies in the Caribbean, and the British, French, and Spanish navies contested the Atlantic. What is more, domestic politics came quickly to be shaped by the wars because Thomas Jefferson's Democratic-Republican Party favored the French and despised the British, whereas Alexander Hamilton's Federalist Party abhorred the French and hoped to replicate British institutions in America.

Washington did his best to hold these rival factions together while maneuvering prudently in foreign affairs. In 1793, at the height of the French Reign of Terror, "Citizen" Edmond-Charles Genêt arrived in America on a mission to propagandize on behalf of the revolution and to conspire so brazenly against U.S. neutrality that Washington demanded his recall. The following year, when French and British warships began to interfere with neutral merchantmen bound for Europe, Washington dispatched John Jay to London to negotiate a treaty ensuring Americans freedom to trade. That prompted Democratic-Republican opposition and stalled Senate ratification until a British ship captured documents suggesting that Secretary of State Edmond Randolph, a prominent Jeffersonian, was betraying American secrets to the French Republic.

Such domestic discord and foreign meddling in American politics inspired Washington's Farewell Address in 1796, in which he warned against "the insidious wiles of foreign influence," undue sympathy or antipathy toward any foreign country, and the wisdom of steering clear of all foreign alliances except in emergencies.

Following Jay's treaty with Britain the French Republic escalated its commerce raiding, capturing 316 American merchant ships by 1797. That obliged Federalist John Adams, Washington's successor, to wage a so-called Quasi-War by arming merchant ships and deploying the U.S. Navy against the French. That American riposte soon obliged French Foreign Minister Talleyrand to seek a truce.

The resulting Convention of Mortefontaine of September 1800 ended the Quasi-War and terminated the old 1778 Franco-American alliance still on the books from the War of American Independence.

But unbeknownst to the Americans, the duplicitous Talleyrand was laying the groundwork for a much more ambitious scheme. Napoleon Bonaparte, who by then presided over the French Republic, meant to acquire the vast Louisiana Territory west of the Mississippi River. Now, French explorers had claimed the wilderness for Louis XIV in the seventeenth century. But Louisiana had been awarded to Spain in the peace that ended the last French and Indian War in 1763. Napoleon and Talleyrand were determined to take it back. The very next day after the Convention of Mortefontaine was signed Talleyrand inked the Treaty of San Ildefonso, in which Napoleonic France cajoled Spain's King Carlos IV to retrocede Louisiana and receive in return a (sublime) consolation prize, the Italian province of Tuscany.

That same fall Thomas Jefferson was made president by the House of Representatives after the election of 1800 ended in a tie. His magnificent Inaugural Address called Americans to unity with the cry "We are all Federalists; we are all Republicans" and reaffirmed Washington's Great Rule with the famous phrase "No entangling alliances." But as the first Democratic-Republican president Jefferson meant to promote his vision of America as an agricultural nation with commerce and the trades as its handmaidens. Spurning concentrations of power, Jefferson favored small government, low taxes, free trade, and a token military establishment. Albeit the retrocession of Louisiana troubled him greatly. In April 1802 he wrote to the U.S. Minister in Paris, Robert Livingston, that "every eye in the United States is now fixed on this affair of Louisiana. Perhaps nothing since the revolutionary war has produced more uneasy sensations through the body of the nation." The prospect of having Napoleon as a neighbor was so alarming that Jefferson even feared for a time that the United States might need to make an alliance with Britain.

The plot thickened later that year when France and Britain concluded the Peace of Amiens, the only truce during their twenty-three years of warfare. Napoleon took advantage by dispatching a fleet and army to the Caribbean colony of Saint-Domingue (present-day Haiti). His purpose was to crush a revolt of enslaved Africans on the island, then use it as a base for the colonization of New Orleans. President Jefferson wrote again that "France possessing itself of Louisiana... is the embryo of a tornado which will burst on the countries on both shores of the Atlantic" and that "every eye in the United States is now fixed on this affair of Louisiana."

Luckily for the president the French campaign aborted when a yellow fever epidemic devastated their expeditionary force in Haiti even as Napoleon's continued mischief in Europe provoked the British into resuming the war. So it was, on April 10, 1803, that Napoleon flipped Talleyrand's script. Better to sell Louisiana to the grasping Americans than to let the Royal Navy seize New Orleans and the Mississippi: "I know the full value of Louisiana and have been desirous of repairing the fault of the French negotiators who lost it in 1763... but now I must expect to lose it again.... [The English] already have twenty ships of the line in the Gulf of Mexico. The conquest of Louisiana would be easy [for them].... But they shall not have the Mississippi which they covet."

The same thought occurred to Jefferson, who dispatched envoys James Monroe and Robert Livingston to France in hopes that they might purchase New Orleans. Imagine their surprise when Talleyand offered to sell them all of Louisiana! Monroe and Livingston eagerly exceeded their instructions and drafted a treaty that ceded 828,000 square miles to the United States in exchange for just $15 million. The Senate ratified the treaty 24 to 7, but the appropriation of money in the House of Representatives passed by only two votes because some Republicans and all Federalists thought the whole business rotten and possibly unconstitutional. That Louisiana Purchase doubled the size of the United States.

The French retreat from America might have pleased the British government if it had not harbored its own ambitions for Louisiana in hopes of containing the United States. The official position taken by London was that Napoleon had coerced the Spaniards to cede Louisiana, which in turn made America a "receiver of stolen goods." But with total war resuming in Europe there was nothing they could do about it for the foreseeable future. As early as 1812 the U.S. Congress would confer statehood on the southern portion of Louisiana despite the fact that its total white population in 1810 was just 34,311.

Jefferson's luck held throughout his first term because American merchants were making windfall profits selling to all sides in the European war. Indeed, the U.S. merchant fleet doubled in size between 1793 and 1807 and its volume of trade sextupled. The United States was fast becoming the principal challenger to Britain's commercial supremacy on the high seas and, worse still, aiding and abetting the Napoleonic empire.

That is why—beginning without warning in 1805—the Royal Navy began seizing American ships by the hundreds and putting an end to the era of Yankee war profiteering. Adding insult to injury, the British also boarded American ships to impress sailors suspected of having deserted or dodged duty in the Royal Navy, a practice John Quincy Adams denounced as "authorized kidnaping." As a result, Jefferson's second term as president proved a disaster.

The year 1805 also confirmed that the Napoleonic Wars had become a stalemated struggle between a Whale and an Elephant. In October Admiral Horatio Nelson's British fleet destroyed the

French and Spanish navies in the Battle of Trafalgar. In December Napoleon's army defeated the Austrian and Russian armies in the Battle of Austerlitz. With the military conflict thus stalemated, both the French and the British resorted to economic warfare. Napoleon issued the Berlin Decrees, which strictly forbade continental Europeans from importing British goods no matter which nation's ships carried them. The British retaliated with its Orders in Council forbidding neutral nations from trading with Napoleon's empire.

An especially humiliating incident resulting from Britain's new resolve occurred in June 1807 when the *H.M.S. Leopard* fired on the *U.S.S. Chesapeake*, a Navy frigate, killing three sailors and wounding eighteen. The British then boarded the ship and impressed several sailors. Members of Congress howled for vengeance, but Jefferson loathed war and—since he had moth-balled the navy and reduced the army to a few frontier forts—could not have waged war in any event. Still, the president had to defend American sovereignty. So he and Secretary of State James Madison, recalling how effective the colonies' Non-Importation Acts had been in the run-up to 1776, reckoned that a cut-off of American trade with Britain would bring pressure to bear on its powerful merchant class and by extension the Parliament. Accordingly, Jefferson ordered his pliant majority in Congress to pass the Embargo Act of December 1807.

Thus began what Federalists had always feared: a Democratic-Republican reign of terror against property. Imagine yourself a farmer; horse breeder; planter of tobacco, rice, or cotton; forester; fisherman; merchant; sailor; chandler; or anyone who provided goods and services to any of the above. Suddenly your own government is telling you it is illegal for you to make a living dependent in any way on foreign markets, even as the resulting oversupply of commodities drives domestic prices through the floor. Yankee traders were ruined. Pennsylvania farmers saw the price of grain fall by half. Southern tobacco and cotton piled up on the wharves, but planters still had to feed their 400,000 slaves. Not surprisingly, many Americans cheated. Merchants smuggled wagons into Canada. Ship captains sneaked out of port under cover of night, or else claimed they were bound for domestic ports-of-call. So the angry president rammed through Congress more laws granting him power to enforce the embargo by force. One irate Yankee wrote the White House: "Thomas Jefferson, you are the God-damndest dog God ever made. God damn you!"

The late-nineteenth-century historian Henry Adams (grandson of John Quincy Adams) judged that Americans' personal liberties and property rights were more directly curtailed by the embargo than by the British blockade, while the presidential exercise of arbitrary powers probably violated the Fourth Amendment's ban on "unreasonable search and seizure." But Henry Adams also observed that no episode in American history was "more touching than the devotion with which Virginians... drained the poison which their own President held obstinately to her lips."

So the embargo failed and Jefferson departed the White House under a cloud. But so well-oiled was his Democratic-Republican machine that Jefferson's protégé Madison won the presidency in 1808. Congress promptly repealed the "Dambargo," but substituted a Non-Intercourse Act which banned commerce with Britain and France so long as they maintained their blockades against neutral shipping. They did. By 1812 the British had seized 389 American vessels and the French 468.

Madison abhorred war as much as Jefferson did, but as American grievances multiplied the Congressional majority turned bellicose and had by 1812 even formed a self-described faction of War Hawks led by South Carolina's John C. Calhoun and Kentucky's Henry Clay. But these southern and western members of Congress had ulterior motives for promoting a war against Britain.

Native American resistance to white settlement in the Northwest was becoming intolerable, and many suspected the British army of aiding and abetting hostile tribes from its forts around the Great Lakes. The Department of Indian Affairs reported increasing incidents of violence, especially after the Shawnee chief Tecumseh and his brother the Prophet Tenskwatawa promoted an alliance of tribes. In November 1811 some five hundred warriors attacked the Indiana Territory's militia at Tippecanoe, killing or wounding 188 Americans. War Hawks figured the least the government should do was to break the Indian resistance and force the British out of their forts. The most the government might do, of course, was to exploit a war allegedly about commercial rights to annex Canada once and for all. Had not Jefferson said the conquest would "just be a matter of marching"? By the time Congress convened in 1812 the dissident Republican John Randolph of Roanoke cried that the War Hawks were motivated more by agrarian greed than by maritime rights: "We have heard one word—like the whipporwill's monotonous tone—it is Canada! Canada! Canada!"

Madison never explicitly called for a war, but his message to Congress implied that Britain was already waging war against the United States at sea and on the Canadian frontier. "We have been so long dealing in small ways of embargoes, non-intercourse, and non-importation, with menaces of war...that the British government has not believed us. [The British] prefer war to a repeal of their Orders in Council. We have nothing left therefore than to make ready for it." Then a strange turn of events occurred over in London. On May 11, 1812, the Prime Minister Spencer Perceval, the author and champion of those hated Orders in Council, was murdered. An entire month passed before the Prince Regent (the future King George IV) settled on a new government led by Robert Jenkinson, the Second Earl of Liverpool, whose very first act in office was to please British merchants and manufacturers by repealing the Orders in Council. But news of that huge British concession did not reach Washington City until August 12, six weeks after the U.S. Congress declared war on Great Britain.

American motives for the War of 1812 are still debated by historians today, because even though Madison implied that the war was about British restrictions on trade and impressment of sailors, most of the Congressmen representing the commercial states—and indeed every Federalist—voted nay! So the declaration of war was passed, 79 to 49 in the House and 19 to 13 in the Senate, solely on the strength of Democratic-Republicans, suggesting party politics must have been the primary motivation and the conquest of Canada the ulterior motive.

What happened when news of the British repeal of the Orders in Council reached America? Did Madison ask Congress to rescind its declaration of war? He did not. Nor did the Democratic-Republicans desire to do so. Even Jefferson declared that "once the sword is drawn, full justice must be done." For that matter, neither did the British Parliament call off this apparently accidental conflict. For Liverpool's cabinet had war aims of its own, including the defense of Canada and the creation of a Native American buffer state under British protection in order to contain the expansion of American pioneers. Indeed, British opinion in these latter stages of the Napoleonic Wars had turned bitter toward the United States given its seeming betrayal of Britain's crusade against the tyrant Napoleon.

So it was when the U.S. *chargé d'affaires* in London received word of the declaration of war and asked his hosts whether their two governments should restore peace, the Foreign Secretary, the Viscount Castlereagh, said no, and Prime Minister Liverpool disdained the United States, which "ought to have looked to this country as the guardian power to which she was indebted not only for her comforts, not only for her rank in the scale of civilization, but for her very existence." In short, both sides willingly accepted the coming of war.

Nevertheless, Britain's top priority was always the European war, not least because June 1812 was the month Napoleon invaded Russia. When Tsar Alexander I learned of the Anglo-American War he even offered to mediate peace talks lest the British be distracted from the European theater. President Madison, willing to sound out his options, sent envoys Albert Gallatin and James Bayard on the long voyage to St. Petersburg only to learn that the British had refused Russian mediation and in any case demanded terms "consistent with the maritime rights of the British Empire," which included impressment. Secretary of State Monroe in turn insisted the United States would negotiate only the basis of reciprocity and sovereign rights.

During the first year of Anglo-American hostilities the Royal Navy was heavily engaged in the Atlantic, Baltic, and Mediterranean seas, where its ships blockaded Napoleonic Europe and raided French shipping, and the British army was heavily engaged in Spain's Peninsular War against the French occupiers. So for the time being the British could only dispatch token forces to the American theater. They were also abashed by the victories won by the Yankees in single-ship actions such as that of the *U.S.S. Constitution* over *H.M.S. Guerrière.* Still more damaging were Yankee privateers, which captured four hundred British merchantmen in 1813 alone. But by the end of that year the Royal Navy mounted an effective blockade in American waters.

The second theater of war was around the Great Lakes, where the Americans foolishly expected to defeat British regulars with their state militias. General William Hull—uncle of Isaac Hull, who commanded the *U.S.S. Constitution*—not only failed to defeat Tecumseh's confederation supported by the British but fell back on Detroit, which he then surrendered without a fight. A similar fiasco befell the New Yorkers who tried to invade Canada via Niagara. By the end of the year American forces on the frontier had their hands full trying to prevent a British invasion of the United States.

In November 1812 Americans staged their first presidential election during wartime and Madison won handily again, so secure was the Democratic-Republican grip on national politics. But Madison began his second term by accepting the resignations of his incompetent Secretary of War and the Navy and replacing them with the able John Armstrong and William Jones. The American war effort vastly improved under their leadership.

It was during that winter of 1812–13 that Napoleon's *Grande Armée* literally perished from battle wounds, famine, frigid weather, and a typhoid epidemic. But the Emperor fled back to France, raised a new army, and fought the Allies to a draw in Germany. So the British remained fixated on Europe and deployed nearly all their armed forces there. That enabled the American forces to win their first victories around the Great Lakes. First, they soundly defeated the British and Canadians in a series of battles on and around Lake Erie, thanks in large part to the leadership of the naval commander Oliver Hazard Perry. Next, American regulars led by William Henry Harrison recaptured Detroit and invaded Upper Canada, as Ontario was then called. At the climactic Battle of the Thames Harrison's soldiers routed the British and Indians and killed Tecumseh himself.

However, the theater in which American frontiersmen and regular soldiers won their most decisive victories over hostile Indians was in the Deep South. The British had occupied forts at Pensacola, Mobile, and Biloxi, from which they supplied arms, ammunition, and encouragement to belligerent tribes, especially the Red Sticks of the Creek nation. The bloodiest predation they committed was the August 1813 massacre at Fort Mims, where some four hundred men, women, and children were scalped. The governor of Tennessee hastily called for five thousand volunteers commanded by Andrew Jackson. Over the winter of 1813–14 his Tennessee Volunteers managed to trap the Red Sticks in an oxbow on the shores of the Tallapoosa River and kill or wound over a thousand at a cost to themselves of just two hundred men. That crushing victory in March 1814 opened all of Georgia, plus the future states of Alabama and Mississippi, to white settlement.

But over those same months British armed forces were finally being freed up thanks to the victories achieved by Russia, Prussia, Austria, and Britain over France's dwindling armies. Liverpool, anticipating Napoleon's imminent downfall, sent Castlereagh to the Allies' winter quarters in eastern France to begin peace negotiations. It was he who largely inspired the March 1814 Treaty of Chaumont, which sketched the grand outlines of post-Napoleonic Europe. When the Allied armies resumed their advance, the French resistance dissolved, and Napoleon abdicated his throne on April 6.

Castlereagh remained on the continent to begin the enormous task of putting the European Humpty-Dumpty back together again, which meant Liverpool and Bathurst took charge of the American war. Bathurst was determined "to destroy and lay waste the principal towns and cities assailable either by land or land forces," specifically targeting Baltimore, Washington, Charleston, Savannah, *and New Orleans*, whose future now returned to the front burner on Britain's hot stove. Now that the war in Europe was over, Bathurst shifted British naval and military forces to the New World, including 14,000 veterans of the Peninsular Campaign. The War of 1812 ceased to be a sideshow for the British, if indeed it ever had been.

Liverpool prepared Parliament and public opinion for the campaign with some ferocious rhetoric. The Americans, he proclaimed, mean "to annihilate the British way of life. We ought to consider the United States are the wanton and bitter enemies of our existence, and treat them accordingly." He and Bathurst imagined that once in possession of the Great Lakes the British could fashion a formidable Indian confederation to blunt U.S. expansion. They imagined that once in possession of the Hudson River Valley the British might abet the sullen New Englanders, whose Federalist leaders were planning a Hartford Convention to debate whether or not to secede from the Union. They imagined that once in possession of New Orleans the British might "command all the rivers of the Mississippi valley and the [Great] Lakes" and make Americans "prisoners in their own country." Finally, the man placed in command of the American Station, Admiral Alexander Cochrane, arrived in Bermuda spitting venom. The Americans, he declared, are "a whining, canting race much like spaniels and require the same treatment." One of Cochrane's first acts was to recruit 2,000 Indians along the Gulf Coast to augment a British invasion and to "give Americans a good drubbing before peace is made."

Finally, the mood of elite opinion in London itself was expressed by *The Times* of London, which ran editorials in May 1814 bemoaning the fact that "Mr Madison's dirty, swindling maneuvers in respect to Louisiana and the Floridas remain to be punished." Britain must reduce America to "submission."

Why then did the British choose that moment to inform the State Department they were "willing to enter into discussion with the Government of the America for the conciliatory adjustment of the differences subsisting between the two States"? That peace feeler would appear to be a great contradiction except for the fact that it soon became clear that the British were in no rush to convene peace talks, much less to bring them to fruition. First, the British dithered over the site for negotiations, insisting at first that they convene in London. Eventually they agreed on a neutral site, the Flemish city of Ghent. Next, Liverpool took his own good time choosing the British delegates. Third, those diplomats were in no hurry to show up at Ghent, which is why the Americans, who either traveled from distant Russia or else sailed across the Atlantic, still had to wait weeks before the British finally showed up on August 6.

Madison's peace commissioners were a distinguished, bipartisan group including the Delaware Federalist Bayard and the Pennsylvania

Republican Gallatin, plus Massachusetts Republican Jonathan Russell, Massachusetts Federalist John Quincy Adams, and Kentucky Republican Henry Clay. They differed as to goals and tactics, but all honored their instructions from the Secretary of State; all meant to defend America's national interest; and all deeply distrusted their interlocutors. The British delegates, by contrast, were non-entities precisely because Liverpool and Bathurst meant to micro-manage negotiations themselves.

Liverpool's instructions stated the substance as follows: "Are we prepared to continue the war for territorial arrangements? If not, this is the best time to make our peace.... Or is it desirable to take the chance of the campaign, and then be governed by circumstances?" He certainly hoped for decidedly favorable "territorial arrangements" given the grand offensives already under way. Indeed, it soon became obvious to the American delegates that the British meant to obfuscate, frustrate, and otherwise delay the negotiations. Their delegates repeatedly raised new points of contention such as the rights of Indian tribes around the Great Lakes, or fishing rights off the Canadian coast, or title to the trivial Passamaquoddy Islands in the Bay of Fundy, or Britain's own claims for "territorial adjustments" favoring Canada. Those delaying tactics obliged the Americans to request new instructions from the State Department, an exchange which could take six weeks or more.

All the while British armed forces waged war *à outrance*, beginning with amphibious assaults on Washington City and Baltimore late in August. The British fleet landed soldiers who marched inland and soundly defeated a far more numerous American force at the Battle of Bladensburg, which in turn allowed the Redcoats to occupy the American capital. They were amused to find a banquet set in the deserted White House for forty guests. So the officers sat down to the feast themselves and toasted their victory with "Jimmy Madison's wine," after which they ordered their men to put the White House and Capitol to the torch. The following month the British famously failed to capture Baltimore's Fort McHenry, but it mattered little because those attacks were really diversions meant to draw American forces away from the real targets of British ambitions on the border with Canada in the north and the Gulf Coast ports in the south.

To their surprise, the British were denied the decisive victories they expected because it turned out that Americans had finally learned how to fight. In September 1814 the British invested Lake Champlain, intending to move down the Hudson River and isolate New England. But the defenders under General Alexander Macomb and Commandant Thomas Macdonough routed the British on land and sank their gunboats on the strategic lake. The following week a British naval squadron accompanied by marines failed to capture Fort Bowyer, which Jackson's men had occupied at Mobile, Alabama. But those setbacks did not discourage Bathurst or his commanders from planning a much larger naval and military campaign designed to occupy the entire Gulf Coast, whose greatest prize was the port of New Orleans. Now, the idea of a Southern offensive had first been suggested back in November 1812 by Admiral Sir John Warren, who boasted that with New Orleans in British hands the western states of Kentucky, Tennessee, and Ohio would be orphaned. Warren had also suggested the British arm Southern Indians and liberate Negro slaves. In 1814, Bathurst and Admiral Cochrane revived this ambitious scheme and deployed some 10,000 soldiers and sailors for its execution.

Meanwhile, what had transpired at Ghent? More palaver and more delays as the British delegates played for time. They pretended for weeks that the fate of American Indians was their primary concern before abruptly dropping their demand for a Great Lakes Indian Confederacy. Then, on October 8, they raised an entirely new topic: the future of the Louisiana Purchase. The British government, they declared, had never recognized the purchase on the grounds that the King of Spain had not willingly ceded the province to France, hence the subsequent American purchase was null and void. Two weeks after that they fed the Americans yet another poisoned pill. They offered to make peace on the basis of the international legal principle of *uti possidetis*, or "as you possess, thus may you possess." In other words, the British suggested a ceasefire in place, with each side retaining possession of whatever land its armies had occupied during the war. Thanks to those American victories in September the British currently occupied no significant American territory, but it was obvious they intended to do so prior to the conclusion of peace.

Indeed, that very week Liverpool and Bathurst were completing the plans for the invasion of America's Gulf Coast. They initially intended for the Duke of Wellington to take command, but he chose to accompany Castlereagh to the Congress of Vienna, where the Great Powers would hammer out the European peace. So Bathurst chose instead Major General Sir Edward Pakenham, another hero of the Peninsular War and not incidentally Wellington's brother-in-law.

On October 24 Bathurst drafted four orders for Pakenham. The first named him commander of all the soldiers on the Gulf Coast and instructed him to execute Admiral Cochrane's plans. The second instructed him to respect the lives and property of all peaceable residents in Louisiana and not to "incite the Black population to rise against their Masters." He clearly hoped the inhabitants might "peaceably acquiesce in our Possession of the Country." The fourth instructed him on how to handle booty and prizes. But the third instruction was telling: "You may possibly hear whilst engaged in active operations that the Preliminaries of Peace between His Majesty and the United States have been signed in Europe and that they have been sent to America in order to receive the Ratification of the President.... Hostilities should not be suspended until you shall have official information that The President has actually ratified the treaty and a Person will be duly authorized to apprise you of this event.... [Until then] the termination of the war must be considered as doubtful." Bathurst's concluding sentence repeated that loaded instruction: "And you will take special care not so to act under the expectation of hearing that the Treaty of Peace has been ratified."

That document certainly seems a smoking gun. Evidently the British meant to occupy New Orleans even if peace terms had already been agreed to at Ghent. Whether Liverpool made any further plans for Louisiana is unknown. But Bathurst did appoint a cohort of *civil servants* (and their families!) to accompany the military to New Orleans and presumably to administer the province.

A final clue to British intentions is the fact that their delegates at Ghent abruptly dropped the principle of *uti possidetis* on October 31 and substituted the cryptic phrase "possessions belonging to either party and taken by the other." They pretended this change had to do with two insignificant islands in Passamaquoddy Bay, Massachusetts, whose ownership Britain had disputed since 1783. But it really had to do with Louisiana inasmuch as the British claimed it had never legally belonged to the United States, hence *need not be given back*. Wellington even advised Liverpool several weeks later: "If you had territory as I hope you soon will have in New Orleans, I should prefer to insist upon the cession of that province as a separate article than upon the *uti possidetis* as a principle of negotiation." John Quincy Adams smelled a rat. "I cannot but deeply distrust their intentions. They cling to atoms involving principles."

Andrew Jackson had spent the fall of 1814 marshaling militias and small contingents of regulars for the defense of Mobile, where he judged the weight of the British invasion would likely be felt. But when he arrived there on November 11 a letter from William Claiborne, the governor of Louisiana, awaited him. Rumors had reached the governor that New Orleans, not Mobile, would be the principal British target, and he was desperate to fortify the town lest his motley civilian population of around 18,000 Frenchmen,

Spaniards, Indians, Africans, and Anglo-Americans either dissolve in panic or else defect to the enemy. Claiborne had already written to the governors of Tennessee and Kentucky, imploring them to send volunteers. Jackson also learned from his own agents that New Orleans was the main British target. So he led his soldiers on a forced march that covered 230 miles in just nine and a half days. The British fleet numbering fifty warships and transports was already at sea.

"Jackson has come! Jackson has come!" cried the jubilant residents of New Orleans on December 4. He had indeed arrived just in time and spent the next six days working from sunup to sundown to recruit men, gather firearms, scrounge shells, shot, and powder for his batteries, reconnoiter the ground, and dig earthworks. The militias were a piebald mix of ethnicities and even included the cutthroats of the Caribbean pirate Jean Lafitte. The 5,700 mostly irregular soldiers in Jackson's command were outnumbered by 8,000 British veterans. But Jackson had two things going for him: his own charismatic leadership and very favorable terrain. The southern approaches to New Orleans were so pocked by lakes and swamps that he needed only to defend a few narrow marches. In other words, the British attacks must be channeled, canceling out their manpower advantage.

Meanwhile, five thousand miles to the northeast, the British and American commissioners at Ghent began to finalize the text of a treaty. The British still tinkered with words, for instance deleting "taken by either party from the other" and inserting "belonging to either party and taken by the other," all the while intimating that what was at issue were those Passamaquoddy Islands. The rest of the treaty merely restored the *status quo ante bellum*. The commissioners signed the Treaty of Ghent on Christmas Eve, and within days the British Prince Regent ratified it. Then the treaty took ship for the United States.

Why did the British choose that moment to conclude peace? Why did they not delay for another few weeks until the Battle of New Orleans was either fought or called off?

That is another mystery historians have not been able to solve if indeed they ever asked themselves the question at all. But circumstantial evidence suggests that by December 1814 Liverpool really did want and perhaps even need to end the American war as soon as possible. One reason, which probably did not force the prime minister's hand, was the sheer war-weariness in Britain. A second reason, which might well have forced his hand, was the financial desperation bequeathed by twenty-three years of war and the likelihood that members of Parliament would protest and the public would riot if new taxes and economies were proposed. But a third reason, which most definitely forced his hand, was the appalling breakdown of Allied unity at the Congress of Vienna. It seemed a serious territorial dispute had arisen which brought the powers to the brink of war.

That issue, which came to a head in the very weeks during which the Treaty of Ghent was finalized, concerned the distribution of power in East Central Europe. The Russian Tsar, whose army after all had triggered the final European revolt against Napoleon's empire, insisted on making himself the King of Poland and annexing that whole country. Likewise, the King of Prussia, who had been the first to join the Tsar in that last coalition, insisted on annexing the entire German kingdom of Saxony. But Klemens von Metternich, representing the Austrian Empire, and Castlereagh, representing Britain, objected to those dispositions lest Russia become too strong in Europe and Prussia too strong in Germany. Moreover, the Tsar—who had offered to mediate an American peace two years before—now hoped the continuation of the Anglo-American war might distract the British and even enable Russia to make common cause with the United States.

The conflict among the victorious powers also gave Talleyrand, the wily foreign minister now representing the restored Bourbon King, the chance to restore France to equal status. He boldly offered to align his country with Austria and Britain in case the Polish–Saxon dispute should burst into war. That explains why Talleyrand cheered news of the Treaty of Ghent, calling it "a sterling peace" that would permit British forces to refocus on Europe. Likewise, Castlereagh wrote Liverpool that the Treaty of Ghent "has produced the greatest possible sensation here, and will, I have no doubt, enter into the calculation of our opponents. I wish you the joy of being released from the millstone of the American war...." Sure enough, just two weeks later the Russians and Prussians withdrew their immoderate claims and the Congress of Vienna turned copacetic again.

But of course, the war in America had not really ended because the Battle of New Orleans remained to be fought.

On December 23, 1814, the British began to land troops south of New Orleans. Jackson upset their deployments by launching a surprise nighttime attack, which inflicted nearly three hundred casualties on the surprised Redcoats. Then Jackson withdrew all his men to a series of defensive lines on a narrow neck of land situated between the Mississippi River and an impassable Cypress Swamp. There the Americans waited until January 8, 1815, when Pakenham attacked.

He ordered a frontal assault expecting to overwhelm the outnumbered defenders, but it turned out to be a suicidal blunder. For the Redcoats, hemmed in by the river and swamp, had no chance to outflank the enemy and instead had to march across open terrain while Jackson's artillery, firing grapeshot, chains, and cannon balls, raked them from two directions. As British survivors recorded, their regiments were so blinded by the billowing clouds of smoke from the American cannons that they could not see their enemy and were so deafened by the cannonades that they could not hear each other. One officer likened it to a great earthquake: "Little more than one thousand soldiers were left unscathed out of the three thousand that attacked the American lines. They fell like blades of grass beneath the scythe of the mower." In a battle that lasted just thirty minutes the British suffered 2,034 casualties to just sixty-two for the defenders.

Some old-timers may recall Johnny Horton's "The Battle of New Orleans," which was a number one song on the "top 40" charts back in 1959: *"In 1814 we took a little trip along with Colonel Jackson down the mighty Mississipp. We took a little bacon and we took a little beans and we met the bloody British in the town of New Orleans...."* The lyrics are a hilarious example of American frontier humor. But the rout they describe was real. The British soldiers retreated, licked their wounds, then boarded their ships and sailed away on January 27.

When news of Jackson's glorious victory reached the East Coast it was—in the words of an overwrought historian—"like a clap of thunder in the clear azure vault of the firmament, and traveled with electromagnetic velocity through the confines of the land." It persuaded many Americans that their country had really won the War of 1812 and perhaps even dictated the terms of the Treaty of Ghent, which finally arrived in America in February and was unanimously approved in the Senate. But Secretary of State Monroe was not alone in suspecting the British would have repudiated the treaty or otherwise claimed that its terms did not apply to Louisiana if Pakenham had prevailed at New Orleans.

As it happened the British were soon relieved to have extricated themselves from the American war because Napoleon escaped from his exile on the island of Elba on March 20, 1815, regained power in Paris, rallied his soldiers, and tried to start all over again. Those Hundred Days would culminate in the Duke of Wellington's victory at Waterloo, which helped the British people quickly forget the inglorious American war.

But the consequences for the United States of this allegedly unnecessary conflict cannot be overstated.

First, it ushered in a two decades of one-party government known as the Era of Good Feelings. That was because the Federalist Party just dissolved given its opposition to Madison's war and especially that treasonous Hartford Convention. Monroe, elected president in 1816, even boasted in his inaugural address that "discord does not belong to our system." He gave thanks to a gracious Providence which sheltered the United States, and he invoked the word "happy" twelve times. Discord did disappear in good part because Democratic-Republicans now understood the need for such Federalist institutions as a strong central bank, standing army and navy, and government support for manufactures.

Second, the nation was happy because every sector of the U.S. economy and every section of the nation boomed in the decades after the Treaty of Ghent. So did the population explode and move west in the wake of those victories over the Native Americans. Suffice to say that Indiana, Illinois, Alabama, Mississippi, and Missouri were all admitted to statehood by 1821.

Third, the war made Andrew Jackson a national hero who was destined in 1828 to become the first Westerner elected president. By the end of his second term a transportation revolution had also begun which spread canals, roads, and railroads throughout the states east of the Mississippi.

Finally, thanks to the war's outcome British and American diplomats negotiated conventions in 1817 and 1818 which settled boundary disputes along the border with Canada and demilitarized the Great Lakes, making that boundary the longest—and longest-lasting—unfortified frontier in world history.

But those agreements did not mean that the British ceased to think of the United States as a rival or caused their leaders to discard "containment strategies." On the contrary, Liverpool, still in office during the 1820s, explicitly warned that sooner or later Britain would have to confront the meteoric rise of American power and wealth. Subsequent British occasions to contain American power would come before the Mexican War in the 1840s and during the Civil War in the 1860s. But in retrospect, the first and best chance Britain had to forestall the rise of the United States was that too forgotten, allegedly mistaken war with no name declared by the Congress in 1812.

★ 6 ★

MEDITATIONS ON A HIGH HOLY DAY

The Fourth of July[1]

In September 2004 fifteen apprehensive undergraduates gathered for the first meeting of the new seminar I had decided to lead. They were not sure they wanted to enroll in the course. Indeed, they were not sure what it was even about. So imagine their discomfort when I postponed all introductory remarks and bade them sit still for thirty-two minutes while I played a videotape of the presidential inaugural ceremony from January 2001. Forget whether you favored Al Gore or George W. Bush, I admonished, and try to ignore Bill Clinton's smirks in the background. Just watch the proceedings and think about what is transpiring.

After the last ruffles and flourishes I asked the students—in a seeming *non sequitur*—what sorts of activities comprise the liturgy (that is the ceremony, I explained) of worship in a church or synagogue? Prayers, they answered, and hymns, and psalms? Did we just observe those activities on the tape, I asked? Yes, we sure did. What about a sermon or homily? Absolutely, for what is a presidential inaugural addresses but a political sermon ("an angel still rides in the whirlwind," Bush had intoned). Did we witness a solemn procession, an invocation of the Divine, and a convocation in which the congregation celebrates its shared beliefs? Yes again. How about a call to repentance and amendment of those shortcomings besetting our nation? Yes again. How about a dismissal in which the new high priest calls on the assembly to go forth in faith and serve as good citizens? Yes again. Well, I concluded, if a presidential inauguration possesses all the characteristics of a religious service, what religion does it serve? That was the mysterious subject of our semester's quest "In Search of the American Civil Religion."

The spiritual qualities of public rhetoric in American politics, courtrooms, churches, schools, and patriotic *fêtes* used to be so pervasive, familiar, and unobjectionable that most citizens just took them for granted. Our national motto is "In God We Trust." Our Pledge says we're a nation "under God." Our Congress and Supreme Court pray at the start of sessions. Presidents of all parties and persuasions have made ritual supplications that the United States might be blessed with Divine protection. The last stanza of "America" begins, "Our Father's God to Thee, Author of Liberty, to Thee we sing" and ends by naming "Great God" (not George III) "our King." The last stanza of the "Star-Spangled Banner" asks our "heaven rescued land" to "praise the Power that has made and preserved us a Nation." "America the Beautiful" bids God to "shed His grace on thee." Most Americans, even today, would likely agree with the Boston Puritans John Winthrop, John Adams, and Jonathan Mayhew; the Princeton Presbyterian John Witherspoon and his disciple James Madison; the Virginia Anglican (and Freemason) George Washington; and the Deists Thomas Jefferson and Benjamin Franklin that Americans are "called unto liberty" (a phrase from the Apostle Paul's epistle to the Galatians), that we are a new chosen people and ours a new promised land, and that our mission is to bestow liberty on all mankind, by example if not exertion. To be sure, the majority of Americans always found it easy to identify the God who watches over America with the God of their Protestant theology. But thanks to the free exercise of religion—which the law professor John Noonan called the "lustre of our country"—ensured by the First Amendment, religious minorities have been free to embrace the American Creed with equal fervor. Thus did Bishop John Carroll, founder of the American Catholic Church, "sing canticles of praise to the Lord" for granting his flock "a country now become our own and taking us into her protection." Thus did the Jewish immigrant Irving Berlin liken Americans to the Children of Israel being led through the Sinai: "God Bless America, land that I love, stand beside her and guide her through the night with a light from above." When Americans of all sects or no sect gather in civil ceremonies to praise their freedom, honor its Author, and rededicate themselves to their nation's ideals, they do not merely prove themselves a religious people; they prove the United States of America is itself a sort of religion, a *civil* religion, or, as the British philosopher G. K. Chesterton put it in 1922, "a nation with the soul of a church."

Civil religion broadly defined is a universal phenomenon. The ancient Greeks and Romans worshiped the gods and goddesses whom they believed to be patrons of their local city-states and regional empires. To chant "Great is Artemis of the Ephesians" or to burn incense to Caesar was to pay political as well spiritual obeisance. The cults of the god-kings and -emperors of Egypt, China, Korea, and Japan were civil as well as religious. Even monotheistic Judaism displayed features of a civic cult in the eras of its monarchy and two temples. In late medieval and early modern Europe the divine right of kings conflated civil and religious loyalties, while the city-states of the Italian Renaissance inspired their own patronage cults, albeit this time to saints (e.g., St. Mark in Venice). But the modern concept of civil religion was born of the Protestant Reformation's notion of civic polity as a holy covenant or social contract made by the people themselves. James Harrington, theoretician of Cromwell's Puritan Commonwealth in mid-seventeenth-century England, and Jean-Jacques Rousseau, philosopher from the Republic of Geneva, Switzerland, in the mid-eighteenth century, asked what might hold a government of the *people* together in the absence of royal or ecclesiastical hierarchy. Their answer was civil religion, a faith and commitment all the more powerful for being voluntary (not imposed), devoted to the unity and prosperity of the commonwealth (not a king or oneself), and inspired by devotion to God or Nature (rather than corrupt human authorities). Patriotic American choirs gave voice to such religiosity when they sang in 1778, "To the King they shall sing Hallelujah, and all the continent shall sing: down with this earthly King; NO KING BUT GOD."

I did not realize this nation possessed an American Civil Religion (ACR) until I began my research on the 2004 book *Freedom Just Around the Corner: A New American History 1585-1828*. Evidence of an ACR just piled up until I was obliged to make it a major theme in the story of American independence and early national growth. Then, while preparing my seminar, I learned how few Americans in the nineteenth and twentieth centuries were conscious of the religion they shared. Walt Whitman, the ACR's poet laureate, certainly was, and Whitman's hero Abraham Lincoln, the ACR's martyr and messiah. Later, when the United States got into the business of exporting its faith in the Spanish-American and First World Wars, a handful of scholars wrote books on "the American religion" and "the religion of the flag." But otherwise American statesmen, artists, teachers, and preachers disseminated the creation myth, martyrology, moral code, theology, liturgy, and eschatology of American republicanism without explicitly acknowledging its status as a transcendental creed. Indeed, not until 1967 did the Berkeley sociologist Robert N. Bellah describe in a celebrated article what he christened "the American Civil Religion." Curiously, what inspired him to think about the matter was the 1961 inauguration of the nation's first Roman Catholic president, John F. Kennedy. Prior to then intellectual scoffers usually dismissed the "God talk" permeating public life as evangelical cant pandering to Bible Belt voters. Now Bellah observed a young, hip, liberal, rich, Harvard-trained *Catholic* politician intoning "the belief that the rights of man come not from the generosity of the state but from the hand of God" and "asking His blessing and His help" in the knowledge "that here on earth God's work must truly be our own." Fascinated by the non-sectarian (or poly-sectarian) cast of this rhetoric, Bellah recalled President Dwight D. Eisenhower's observation, "Our government makes no sense unless it is founded in a deeply felt religious faith...and I don't care what it is!" Clearly there was more to this than "feel good" piety. So Bellah turned to history and found he could trace the ACR all the way back to the Founding Fathers, who had institutionalized a civil faith meant not to *replace* sectarian faiths but to stand above them in benign toleration so that a diverse people might unite and fulfill the glorious destiny allotted them by the Almighty.

Who was that God of the Founders, the God of the ACR, if not Jehovah or the Holy Trinity? He is the God with no name, but a hundred names. Benjamin Franklin called him Father of Lights and Supreme Architect; George Washington the Almighty Being, Invisible Hand, and Parent of the Human Race; John Adams the Patron of Order, Fountain of Justice, and Protector; Thomas Jefferson the Infinite Power; Madison the Being Who Regulates the Destiny of Nations; James Monroe merely Providence and the Almighty; John Quincy Adams the Ark of our Salvation and Heaven; Andrew Jackson that Power and Almighty Being Who mercifully protected the United States during its national infancy; and so on down to Abraham Lincoln. It was he who understood that Northerners and Southerners, praying as they did to the same Biblical God, must listen to "the mystic chords of memory" and indulge "the better angels of our nature." It was he who understood, four years later, that "the judgments of the Lord are true and righteous altogether" and that his people must strive to bind up their nation's wounds "with malice toward none, with charity for all, with firmness in the right as God gives us to see the right." Lincoln himself seemed never to confess Christian faith, but was himself the Christ of the ACR. Jackson posed for electoral purposes as a Presbyterian, but was in fact a fervent Freemason who believed in the God whose name is Geometry, the Master Builder and Mason whose All-Seeing Eye looks down in blessing upon the Unfinished Pyramid which appears on the reverse side of the Great Seal of the United States and our one-dollar bills even today. Likewise, Jefferson was an Enlightened philosopher who clung romantically to a faith in reason alone. Yet they, no less than devoutly Protestant presidents, swore fealty to the Providence which seemed to watch over the American people.

"Seemed to watch over" is a loaded phrase. For however much historians trace the intellectual origins of the American Creed to James Harrington's seventeenth-century republicanism, John Locke's natural rights ("life, liberty, and property"), the Scottish Enlightenment ("pursuit of happiness," "common sense," and free markets), English Common Law, Whig ideology, and the evangelical individualism of the First Great Awakening, the fact remains that the ACR derived in large part from American colonists' experience over 150 years. The Bible makes clear the fact that Jews and Christians did not invent their religions. Rather their experience of divine intercessions in history was what turned them into Jews and Christians in the first place. In like fashion, the things that *happened* to American colonists—material blessings beyond measure, deliverance from "Egyptian bondage" in the Old World, the liberty and self-governance sheer remoteness allowed, a sense of being guided for some higher purpose, not least the extraordinary series of "lucky" events that permitted thirteen ragtag, divided colonies to win independence from earth's greatest empire—invited Patriots to embrace an inchoate, but powerful faith that they, their forebears, and their descendants were actors in a play scripted by the Author of

History. Indeed, it is almost impossible to imagine the Continental Congress, comprised mostly of wealthy, well-connected men with the most to lose by rebellion, ever taking the mortal risk of declaring independence without faith in the justice and therefore divine blessing of their cause.

Blessing comes at a price. That was the message of Abraham, Moses, Jonah, Jeremiah, St. Paul, and the Revelation to St. John. It was also the message of a radical Deist who penned the pamphlet that was the immediate inspiration for the Declaration of Independence, Tom Paine.

Early in 1775 the thirteen colonies were ablaze with resistance to Britain's Intolerable Acts. In the years following the great Anglo-American victory in the last French and Indian War, the Parliament, with the blessing of the King, violated all the spirits that had set England's (and after 1709 Great Britain's) national agenda for two hundred years: rabid anti-Catholicism, militant rivalry with the French and Spanish empires, hustling capitalism both agricultural and mercantile, and self-righteous displacement of "savage" peoples who made little use of their lands such as the Irish and Native Americans. But no Briton had drunk more deeply of those four spirits than the mostly British emigrants who peopled the thirteen colonies of North America. The historian David Hackett Fischer's encyclopedic study of the American colonies' four "cradle cultures"—the Puritans in New England, the Quakers in the Delaware Valley, the Cavaliers of the Chesapeake Bay, and the wild Scots-Irish Bordermen on the Allegheny frontier—described how those cultures embraced various definitions of liberty. But all the colonists were shocked when the Crown and Parliament suddenly jettisoned the Salutary Neglect the British had displayed toward America over the previous seventy years prior to the end of the last French and Indian War in 1763. Parliament's Québec Act established the Roman Catholic church in Canada by way of appeasing the Crown's new

French-speaking subjects. The King's Proclamation Line forbade new American settlements west of the Allegheny Mountains by way of appeasing Britain's American Indian subjects. The peace treaty had broken French power in America but vastly expanded that of Catholic Spain, which was awarded the west bank of the Mississippi River and entire province of Louisiana. Most egregious, Parliament began to impose a whole series of taxes, commercial restrictions, and monopolies that, if enforced, would have choked the colonies' economic growth. The British were violating all four of their own imperial spirits. They had become, in effect, heretics in their own church! No wonder Patriots such as John Dickinson spied in Parliament's acts a plot to reduce the colonists to the status of *slavery*.

The Stamp Act Congress of 1765 and Continental Congress in 1774 urged colonists to unite, resist, and make themselves worthy of divine protection by boycotting English luxuries and staging days of fasting and prayer. The British were equally determined to punish colonial impudence in the fear that their whole empire might unravel if they did not. Accordingly, after the infamous Boston Tea Party, the Royal Navy blockaded the port and Redcoats patrolled its streets. In Philadelphia Congress urged solidarity with Massachusetts lest all the colonies lose their liberties. Down in Richmond, Virginia, Patrick Henry preached a fiery sermon whose stirring climax—"Give me liberty or give me death!"—was in fact preceded by these assurances: "We shall not fight our battles alone. There is a just God who presides over the destinies of nations, and who will raise up friends to fight our battles for us.... The war is inevitable—and let it come! I repeat it, sir, let it come."

The war came in April 1775, beginning on Lexington Green. Yet the colonies' representatives shrank for over a year from severing their ties to the crown. Many New Englanders and Virginians might have been eager to train their rhetorical muskets and cannons, so recently aimed at the French crown and Catholic church, on the

English crown and Anglican church. But many New Yorkers, Rhode Islanders, and South Carolinians looked to their trade, which was bound to suffer gravely in war, while the Quakers in the Middle Colonies were pacifist on principle. Several colonies counted as many Loyalists (Tories) as Patriots. How was it then, in the words of John Adams, that thirteen clocks at last struck as one?

Tom Paine was a thirty-seven-year-old ne'er-do-well when he landed in Philadelphia in November 1774. The rudely educated son of a Quaker father and Anglican mother, he had failed in two marriages and numerous jobs ranging from corset-maker to collector of taxes on tobacco and liquor. His sole achievement in life was a broadside exposing corruption among excise officials, which he blamed on the low wages they received. But by chance (or Providence) the colonial agent in London, Benjamin Franklin, advised Paine to seek his fortune in America. Armed with Franklin's recommendation Paine published a series of articles for *Pennsylvania Magazine* which caught the eye of Dr. Benjamin Rush, who suggested that Paine write an essay weighing the arguments for and against independence. He even suggested the title. But Paine's *Common Sense* did much more than weigh arguments. His choleric fifty-page indictment of British oppression targeted the King himself, not misguided ministers or members of Parliament. He took as his text the Old Testament prophet Samuel, who rebuked the Israelites for demanding a king when they had the Lord and His prophets and judges to govern them. He invited Americans to heed Samuel's godly admonition and liberate themselves and mankind from three millennia of oppression. He reminded Americans how they were uniquely blessed with self-government in a new world. He described the stark choice faced by the colonists as one between acquiescing in their own enslavement, which amounted to rebellion against God's purpose for man, and claiming their freedom, which amounted to rebellion against the Crown. Indeed, Paine accused colonists who *shrank* from a declaration of independence of lacking not only common sense but virtue and manhood itself.

Published in January 1776, *Common Sense* went through so many printings that 150,000 copies were in circulation by spring, most of them read or heard by multiple people. In Washington's estimation the "unanswerable" tract worked a magnificent change in the minds of men and women. With brilliant intuition, Paine tapped both vocabularies—Enlightenment philosophy and moral evangelism—that resonated with Americans eager to know their destiny. He demanded the colonies separate from Britain before they themselves were corrupted beyond redemption. His sublime aphorisms, exhortations, and jeremiads thrilled and horrified. Paine did in print what Patrick Henry did with his voice.

Yet liberty comes at a price, which Paine was not sure Americans were willing to pay. So *Common Sense* also echoed Moses's farewell address in Deuteronomy in which he promises the children of Israel every blessing if they hearken to the law of the Lord, but warns they would be cast out and become a byword among nations if they reject the Lord and the law. Thus did Paine foresee a continental union of limitless potential arising in North America, yet warned that union might prove as fragile as glass. He damned governmental authority, yet called for its relentless exercise lest the American cause abort. He told Americans they were like Noah's family, free to begin the world over again, yet feared they might lack the virtue that calling required. He preached liberty, yet called on Patriots to repress enemies in their midst. He extolled equality, yet feared "the mind of the multitude." He foresaw unimagined prosperity, yet warned that materialism bored and corrupted. He praised Americans' rebelliousness, yet chided them for their lawlessness. He pleaded for reason, yet played on a keyboard of emotions ranging from hatred, anger, and vengeance to fear, self-love, and self-doubt. In fact, the pamphlet's demagogic style and "democratical" implications moved

John Adams to write a hasty rebuttal. But Paine, after just one year in America, understood the colonists' temper better than Adams did. Paine preached a *civil religion* in language that appealed to Americans of all persuasions. Congregationalists, Presbyterians, and Baptists nodded in agreement when Paine labeled vice the solvent of liberty and established churches and monarchies the symptoms of sin, not its correctives. Deists and skeptics nodded in agreement when Paine employed Biblical allusions to make secular political points. "Ye that oppose independence now, ye know not what ye do" made independence itself the Messiah and faint-hearted colonists the Roman soldiers on Calvary. In sum, Christians reading *Common Sense* found in it the God of the Bible and a politics derived from religion. Deists found in the pamphlet the God of Nature and a religion derived from politics. Paine even foresaw the three ways by which the colonists might achieve nationhood: "by the legal voice of the people in Congress; by a military power; or by a mob." He hoped for a combination of all three, which is precisely what Pennsylvania, Virginia, and Massachusetts proceeded to make.

Paine's remarkable pamphlet cemented the alliance between the Awakened and the Enlightened, summoned them to a just war, and promised a kind of heaven on earth if they won. That is why some historians miss the point when they denigrate the role of religion in the American rebellion. The American cause was profoundly religious for Theists and Deists alike because both identified America's future with a providential design, both entertained millenarian hopes, and both placed their cosmologies at the service of an overarching civil religion. Thus did Paine, like Paul the Apostle, become "all things to all men" and craft a template for all American political rhetoric to come. He made unity the first and greatest civic virtue and did unite most Americans in hatred and fear of external oppressors and internal dissenters. Paine implied that to be lukewarm or cold toward the glorious cause was sacrilege. Paine invited—nay, commanded—colonists to become part of his ubiquitous "*we*," adding always the not-so-veiled threat that "*we*" will get all who do not. As for devising a new form of government—"the noblest, purest constitution on the face of the "earth"—that could wait. The first task was to wrest power away from corrupt British lords. That could only be done by winning the war, and that could only be done by declaring independence. Only then would Americans be forced to hang together lest they be hanged as traitors. Only then could Americans gain the foreign alliances needed to prevail in the war, and so enlist monarchies such as France and Spain in their own holy war against monarchy.

During the months *Common Sense* swept up and down the Atlantic seaboard two wars of nerves played themselves out. The first was in Paris, where the court of Louis XVI balked from aiding the English colonies before being assured of their commitment to independence. The second was in Philadelphia, where the Continental Congress balked from declaring independence before being assured of French aid. The logjam began to break on May 2, 1776, when King Louis approved clandestine shipments of money and arms to the colonial rebels. The American logjam broke on May 15 when Congress, riding the storm stirred up by Paine, instructed the thirteen colonies to suppress royal authority and organize themselves as autonomous states. Most colonies already had conventions or committees at work designing provisional governments. They justified their acts with local declarations of independence that borrowed freely from each other's language and displayed remarkable similarities. Almost all cited the King's use of foreign mercenaries (the Hessians) as the last straw, justified separation by appeal to natural law or Providence, and named as their purpose the preservation of liberties. Jefferson described preservation of liberty as "the whole object of the present controversy" and rued having to go to Philadelphia because it meant he would miss Virginia's constitutional convention.

Patriots knew the survival of their thirteen new sovereignties depended on the success of a people acting "in Congress." Hence the May 15 resolution called on colonies to fashion governments which were "sufficient to the exigencies of their affairs" and could provide "for defense of lives, liberties, and properties against the hostile invasions and cruel depredations of their enemies." Congress thereby proclaimed the existence of a new people and nation, lurched into republicanism, and echoed Paine's call for vigilance against Tories, traitors, and pacifists as well as Britain's Redcoats. Some delegates protested the haste, but on the same day down in Richmond Edmund Randolph authorized Virginia's delegation to propose that Congress declare the colonies "free and independent states" so they could make foreign alliances. The Carolinas and Georgia, menaced by British invasion, likewise instructed their delegations to pursue all measures necessary to defend America and win foreign allies.

On June 7, Richard Henry Lee moved that Congress declare independence and unite under a constitution. Such audacious steps would be worse than useless if not unanimous, but foot-draggers argued the Middle colonies were still undecided. Proponents retorted "the people" of the Middle colonies were in fact pro-independence even if some of their delegates frustrated popular will. So Congress agreed to postpone a vote until July 1, which gave both sides three weeks to bully, bribe, cajole, or persuade undecided delegates. Meanwhile, a committee chaired by John Adams was charged with preparing a text. Since the other members, notably Franklin, had what they considered to be *more* important chores to perform, they asked Jefferson, their cerebral thirty-three-year-old colleague, to scribble a first draft.

"American Scripture" is the epithet the historian Pauline Maier attached to the Declaration of Independence, and rightly so, for it would become holy writ and is still revered by most Americans in the twenty-first century. But it did not begin in apotheosis. Jefferson himself confessed that he took up the quill in his parlor on Market Street not to discover "new principles, or new arguments" but simply to state "the common sense of the subject." What is more, most of the original passages in Jefferson's draft were not very good, while the good ones were not very original. The text's lofty philosophical introduction, bill of particulars against King George, and syllogistic conclusion calling for independence were a pastiche of phrases lifted from *Common Sense*, from the "little declarations" issued by colonies, and from Virginia's Declaration of Rights, composed by George Mason and published in Philadelphia on June 12. It was Mason who based Virginia's government on the premise that all men are "born equally free and independent." It was Mason who listed the rights of man as the "enjoyment of Life and Liberty, with the Means of acquiring and possessing Property, and pursuing and obtaining Happiness." It was Mason who traced those rights to "God and Nature, vested in, and consequently derived from the People." It was Mason who called for abolition of privilege, separation of powers, an independent judiciary, a bill of rights, a free press, and "the fullest Toleration in the Exercise of Religion."

Jefferson did compose the elegant preamble "When in the course of human events. . . ." He did tighten Mason's natural rights to "life, liberty, and the pursuit of happiness." He did compose the Declaration's moving conclusion, which pledged "our lives, fortunes, and sacred honor." But in between those majestic heights lay a murky swamp of complaints that stick to a reader's boots even today. One that especially troubled Congress was Jefferson's diatribe against the British *people*, whom he accused of being "deaf to the voice of justice and consanguinity" despite "our former love for them" and necessitating "our everlasting Adieu!" Its romantic and false sentimentality aside, that passage shifted the focus of Americans' anger away from the Crown while gratuitously insulting the British subjects whom Congress hoped might pressure Parliament to change course. More bizarre still, Jefferson exonerated American slave-traders and southern planters by blaming the British Crown for African slavery. Since he cannot possibly have believed this canard he must have been groping for some way to square the persistence of slavery with his postulate "all men are created equal." Congress retained the latter phrase for its ring, but otherwise saw the wisdom in taking its stand on particular abuses, not universal principles. So Congress deleted a full fourth of Jefferson's draft, tweaked the rest, and appealed to Providence at the end—all to good effect. Nevertheless, Jefferson maintained his text had been "mangled" and went into a funk that lasted all summer. But as Richard Henry Lee put it, so long as the declaration did no harm its wording was less important than "the Thing itself."

Still, "the Thing itself" was far from certain during the days Jefferson worked on the draft. The New England–Virginia alliance appeared to hold firm, but South Carolinians expressed doubts about independence while delegates from New York, a Tory stronghold, pleaded a lack of instructions. Most anxious were delegates from the Delaware Valley, where the stakes were gigantic. For if Pennsylvania's Quakers, pietist Germans, and Tories carried a "nay" on independence, chances were the American edifice would collapse for want of its keystone. Exactly how that was forestalled will never be known, but the story began in 1774 when Proprietary Governor John Penn forbade the Pennsylvania assembly to send delegates to the First Continental Congress. Dickinson defied Penn by calling an ad hoc convention that met in the same Carpenter's Hall as the congress. Penn hastily summoned the regular assembly into session to restore his authority, with the result that Pennsylvania now had two legislatures speaking in the name of the people. As late as spring 1776 a majority of Penn's assemblymen opposed independence. That suggests the May 15 call from Congress to suppress authority "under the crown" might have been an invitation to local Patriots to disperse Penn's assembly by force. Pennsylvania's militiamen did not go that far, but in mid-June they resolved to ignore any orders issuing from the assembly. The atmosphere in steamy Philadelphia could hardly have been more electric.

War news also weighed on wafflers in Congress. Back in autumn 1775 a militia force under Richard Montgomery struck north via Lake Champlain in hopes of conquering Lower Canada. Washington supported him with a second detachment under Benedict Arnold. But a winter campaign in Québec was madness: the two columns lost half their men before reaching the citadel on the St. Lawrence River. Still, Arnold and Montgomery hurled their thousand frigid soldiers into Québec's lower town in the midst of a blizzard on New Year's Eve. A melee ensued in which Montgomery was killed, Arnold was wounded, and young Aaron Burr was heroic. But the garrison held, and when reinforcements arrived in the spring the Redcoats pushed south to menace New England with invasion. Elsewhere, the news seemed better. In North Carolina Patriots routed a band of Scots Loyalists at Moore's Creek in February 1776. In New England Redcoats under General William Howe evacuated Boston by sea on March 17. In Charleston, South Carolina, militias led by Christopher Gadsden and William Moultrie defeated a premature naval assault from palmetto forts. But even good news portended bad. Yes, those crazy Highlanders were cut down, but they proved how easily Tory militias might organize in the Patriots' rear. Yes, Howe had left Boston, but was free to return in greater force at a time and place of his choosing. Yes, Charleston had humiliated some British tars, but what vengeance might the proud Royal Navy exact elsewhere?

Indeed, by July 1, 1776, when Congress resumed debate on Lee's motions, hundreds of sails had already been sighted at sea off Long Island. Would a clean break with King George end equivocation, energize the war effort, and secure an alliance with France?

Or would it unleash civil wars in the states, steel British resolve, and condemn Congressmen to the gallows? Dickinson suspected the latter. He told of the folly of tearing down one's house in winter before a replacement was built, warned that the British lion had barely begun to roar, and imagined Indian scalping parties rampaging down Market and Wall streets. John Adams turned no magic phrases, but made a sincere and logical case that no alternative to independence remained and freedom was worth any risk. The vote was a letdown for both. Nine colonies favored independence, Pennsylvania and South Carolina split narrowly against it, Delaware deadlocked (with one member absent), and New York abstained. What happened next is uncertain except that many comings and goings were made that thunderous summer evening. Caesar Rodney, the missing Delaware delegate, rode all night through rain and lightning to cast an exhausted, asthmatic "aye" on July 2. The South Carolinians were probably brought into line by Virginians. Most decisively, two Pennsylvanian dissenters, Dickinson and Robert Morris, failed to vote in the caucus the following day, enabling the commonwealth's delegation to divide 3 to 2 in favor of independence instead of 4 to 3 against. New York still abstained, but Congress proclaimed the vote unanimous on July 2, 1776.

All that happened on the Fourth was official approval of the *text* of the Declaration. It was printed, widely distributed, read publically on parade grounds, tavern steps, and village greens, cheered... and forgotten. Patriots had more pressing concerns. Already on July 3 General Howe began to land an army of 32,000 Redcoats and Hessians on Staten Island, just sixty miles from Philadelphia. No wonder Congress suppressed distribution of *signed* copies of its treasonous Declaration until the military situation improved somewhat in January 1777.

Like all great religions, the ACR only gradually developed its creeds, canonized its scriptures, inspired its hymns and liturgies, blessed its martyrs, commemorated its heroes, and sanctified its holidays. Indeed, Jefferson's principal contributions to the ACR were made when he founded the Democratic-Republican political party and served as third president of the United States, hence the high priest of the civil religion. His 1801 inaugural address, following an especially contentious election campaign, was a brilliant summation of the creed and catechism of the republic. The first principle, as always, was unity, hence Jefferson assured his national congregation that "We are all Federalists, we are all Republicans." Next, he pronounced us a people "acknowledging and adoring an overruling Providence, which by all its dispensations proves that it delights in the happiness of man here and his greater happiness hereafter." Next, he told Americans what they revered: "Equal and exact justice to all men, of whatever state or persuasion, religious or political; peace, commerce, and honest friendship with all nations, entangling alliances with none; the support of the State governments in all their rights…; the preservation of the General Government in its whole constitutional vigor…; a jealous care of the right of election by the people; absolute acquiescence in the decisions of the majority…; a well-disciplined militia…; the supremacy of the civil over the military authority; economy in public expense…; the honest payment of our debts…; encouragement of agriculture, and of commerce as its handmaid…; freedom of religion; freedom of the press, and freedom of person under the protection of the habeas corpus and trial by juries impartially selected." All these "should be the creed of our political faith."

The Banquo's Ghost in that republican creed was, of course, slavery, which belied Jefferson's principle of equal justice and persisted because of Jefferson's devotion to states' rights. Americans both north and south were conscious of that scandal, yet chose to ignore it in the name of their highest principle, unity. For without unity there would be no "church" at all and surely no continental and global destiny under Providence. So Americans formed a conspiracy of silence over slavery that would last sixty years, long enough for the United States to annex Florida and Texas, occupy Oregon, and conquer California and New Mexico in the Mexican War of 1846–48. During those decades of expansion and "Jacksonian Democracy" the iconography of the ACR reflected both the flimsiness and mighty ambitions of the Union. As yet no official holidays were celebrated and the only ones unofficially celebrated were the Fourth of July and Washington's Birthday (a republican version of the King's Birthday). However, New England Puritans, who otherwise eschewed "popish" feasts such as Christmas and Easter, contributed four precocious examples of *civil* religious observance: Election Day (honoring the polity), Training Day (honoring the militia), Graduation Day (honoring education), and Thanksgiving Day (honoring the Lord's blessings on America). As yet the only members of an American pantheon were Washington and Franklin. The "Star-Spangled Banner," composed in 1814, grew popular, but another century would pass before it became the armed forces' anthem in 1916 and the national anthem by act of Congress in 1931. Nor was Old Glory, the flag "dyed in the blood of our forefathers," especially revered prior to its going abroad for the first time during the Mexican War. What did fire early Americans' imaginations was the iconography of ACR. Illustrations, works of art, and patriotic displays invariably focused on symbols of liberty and liberty's fruits, which were peace and prosperity. The eagle and goddess of liberty were especially ubiquitous, the former always protecting the latter. But by the 1830s liberty was being increasingly joined or even eclipsed by material images of boundless frontiers, bountiful crops, bustling ports, busy canals, boisterous machinery, booming exports, and boasts of more for generations yet unborn. In other words, ACR's balance between God and Mammon began to tilt ominously in the direction of Mammon.

No wonder the Constitution, a compromise contract which preserved national unity but which abided slavery, became the lodestone for Southerners and Northerners, Democrats and Whigs in the run-up to the Civil War, while the Declaration of Independence was squirreled away and largely ignored. The actual document was nearly lost several times and nearly destroyed in the British sack of Washington City in 1814. In the aftermath of that war the document sat for years in the archives of the State Department until 1841, when it was put on modest display in the Patent Office. Only the great schism in ACR over slavery, secession, and Civil War resurrected the Declaration of Independence and caused Americans north and south to revere the primary statement of the American Creed. At Gettysburg Lincoln reminded the American people of what had happened "Four score and seven years ago" (1863 – 1776 = 87), trumped the Constitution's states' rights with "all men are created equal," and bade Americans midwife "a new birth of freedom."

Nevertheless, the document itself remained obscure except for a cameo appearance at the 1876 Centennial Exhibition in Philadelphia. By then the original parchment was frayed and faded. Only in 1921 did the Library of Congress fashion a shrine for the Declaration of Independence and study scientific means to preserve it. Only after 1941 did the U.S. government truly beatify the Declaration (and Constitution). Obviously, Americans during the Second World War and Cold War needed more than ever to recall what their nation stood for. So at last was the "American Scripture" proudly displayed in a chemically, climatically controlled tabernacle in the foyer of the National Archives building on the mall in Washington, D.C. It is ringed by a chancel rail over which endless queues of tourists (perhaps pilgrims) squint in reverence.

Scoffers and cynics have drawn analogies to the embalmed bodies of Vladimir Lenin and Josef Stalin which used to be on display in Moscow's Red Square. If the Spirit of 1776 still lived in Americans' hearts, they surmised, it would not be necessary to idolize a piece of paper. But the analogy is a faulty one. Communism was born of faith in an idea which the Soviets pretended was still alive by embalming dead human beings. Americanism was born of faith in human beings who prove that faith by "embalming" their sacred ideas.

By the end of the twentieth century ACR's church calendar had grown to a veritable cycle of commemorations of those citizens in the past and present who kindled and especially defended America's faith. Beginning in January, the calendar includes Martin Luther King Day, Presidents' Day, Army Day, VE Day, Armed Forces Day, Memorial Day, Flag Day, Air Force Day, Coast Guard Day, VJ Day, Labor Day, Constitution Day, Columbus Day, Navy Day, Election Day, Marine Corps Day, Veterans Day, and not least Thanksgiving Day. Indeed, if there is a second candidate for high holy honors in the ACR it is surely the Pilgrims' original feast. For on Thanksgiving all Americans, whatever their sectarian creed, comfortably praise whatever they choose to name God for bearing their immigrant ancestors across the sea, forging them into a nation dedicated to propositions, and blessing them with unprecedented prosperity.

But the highest of all holy days is still the Fourth of July. After the Civil War it gained even more prominence because Independence Day called Southerners and Northerners back to what unified them in the first place: their faith in themselves, in God's special providence, in their ancestors' courage and sacrifice, and the life, liberty, and happiness a unified federal republic made possible. Should the Fourth of July ever cease to be a day "set apart" for joy, pride, and community, then the text approved on that day will turn as cold as the body in Lenin's tomb. But so, too, may it perish if the Fourth of July becomes nothing but a day of self-congratulation and pride. It is a day when Americans, especially young ones, need to reflect on how supremely *implausible* the birth of this nation was, how often its survival hung by a thread, and how its Founders were emboldened because—be they Protestants, Catholics, Jews, Deists, or Freemasons—they believed the Author of History meant for this to happen.

★ 7 ★

THE MADNESS OF SAINT WOODROW

Or, What If the United States Had Stayed Out of the Great War?[1]

On April 2, 1917, Woodrow Wilson rose before a joint session of Congress to make the case for a declaration of war on Germany. Summoning his considerable eloquence, Wilson intoned such phrases as "the right is more precious than peace"; "make the world safe for democracy"; "a universal dominion of right by a concert of free peoples"; "America is privileged to spend her blood"; and in a conscious echo of the Protestant reformer Martin Luther, "God helping her, she can do no other."

But the sentence that really proclaimed a global crusade was this: "Neutrality is no longer feasible or desirable where the peace of the world is involved and the freedom of its peoples, and the menace to that peace and freedom lies in the existence of autocratic governments backed by organized force which is controlled wholly by their will, not by the will of their people." The 1947 Truman Doctrine promulgated at the start of the Cold War was moderate by comparison.

During the Senate's cursory two-day debate, William J. Stone (D-Mo.), chairman of the Foreign Relations Committee, warned that to enter this war would be "the greatest national blunder in history." George W. Norris (R-Neb.) rejected Wilson's rhetoric as moral gloss obscuring financial interests, declaring, "We are putting the dollar sign on the American flag." The noted Wisconsin Independent Robert "Fighting Bob" La Follette rebutted the President's arguments in a tearful address lasting four hours. If, as Wilson said, Germany was waging a war against all of humanity, how come the United States was the only neutral nation to object? If, as Wilson said, this was a war to make the world safe for democracy, how come the British refused to bestow it on the peoples of Ireland, India, and Egypt? If, as Wilson said, the United States meant to wage war on a militaristic government rather than the German people themselves, how come more Germans supported their Kaiser than Americans had voted for Wilson in 1916? Nevertheless, the Congress had bowed to the White House on issues of war and peace ever since 1812 and did so again. The Senate voted 82 to 6 in favor of war on April 4, and the House approved the war resolution 373 to 50 two days later. But British Ambassador Cecil Spring-Rice cabled to London that in his judgment the Americans had gone to war "with the greatest reluctance."[2]

Historians today conventionally speak of a "short twentieth century" extending from 1914 to 1991—bracketing, in other words, the unspeakably violent and ideological era that included World War I, World War II, and the Cold War. Historians invariably trace the origins of the latter two horrors to the human, economic, social, and cultural destruction of the first, the Great War, because it shattered the liberal myth of progress and the balance of power which had prevailed for a century before 1914. The carnage of the Great War hurled its disoriented survivors into a moral vacuum that totalitarian movements such as communism and fascism exploited. Mix in the effects of an economic cataclysm, the Great Depression beginning in 1929, which enervated the democracies even as it energized the dictatorships, and the coming of a Second World War in 1939 was just a matter of time. That crescendo of violence was what gave birth in turn to a bipolar world dominated by rival empires, each with its own universal ideology and each armed with nuclear weapons.

The trends of the twentieth century can be made to appear inevitable such that humanity was doomed to its cruel fate. But what if we err to think it can all be traced back to 1914? What if the subsequent calamities really trace back to 1917 and the foolish American decision to enter the Great War?

One of the gems of historiography in my lifetime was written in 1999 by the brilliant Scottish professor Niall Ferguson. He edited a fat volume of essays called *Virtual History: Alternatives and Counterfactuals*, which examined what might have occurred if plausible contingencies had differed at various times. Such counterfactual history served as the very "antidote to determinism."[3] Ferguson opened the book with a ninety-page introduction examining the legitimacy of virtual history from the standpoints of thirty writers ranging from Augustine of Hippo to Bertrand Russell. Most of the historians he cited argued against virtual history or even dismissed it as a mere parlor game. To them history was shaped either by the hand of a providential God or by universal laws such those postulated by Karl Marx, John Stuart Mill, and Arnold J. Toynbee. Indeed, the whole notion of accident was abhorrent to believers in religion and science alike. Chance disconnects cause and effect, seeming to rob history of meaning as if it really were Shakespeare's tale told by an idiot. Thus did the German philosopher Georg W. F. Hegel write, "The sole aim of philosophical inquiry is to eliminate the contingent."

Ferguson gave a patient hearing to all those negative views before arriving at a positive argument based on chaos theory, which concerns the stochastic (seemingly random) behavior that occurs in systems otherwise governed by natural laws (for example, biology or meteorology). Thus the ubiquity of chance occurrences in history does not necessarily prove that natural laws do not exist, but rather that they are too numerous and complex to sort out even in hindsight. The way to reconcile causation with contingency, wrote Ferguson, is precisely to do virtual history, drawing distinctions between what happened and what might plausibly have happened based on alternative choices which the actors really considered. His own contribution was a fifty-two-page speculation entitled "The Kaiser's European Union: What If Great Britain Had 'Stood Aside' in August 1914?" It cogently argued that if Britain had not gone to war or else limited itself to a naval war of defense—options seriously considered by the cabinet of Prime Minister Herbert Asquith in 1914—the result would have been a German victory, but one the still-mighty British Empire could have lived with. A German-dominated *Mitteleuropa* under the Kaiser's constitutional monarchy would not, Ferguson speculated, have differed so much from today's European Union, while the Soviet Union and Nazi Germany would never have existed at all.

Let that serve as a model for our own (much briefer) inquiry into Woodrow Wilson's decision to lead the United States into the Great War. For President Wilson not only considered, but really made, "alternative choices" for two and a half years before changing his mind and with it the whole course of American, European, and world history in the "short twentieth century."

Wilson was a High Progressive who, as one of the earliest participants in the then-new discipline of political science, cheered America's rise to world power because he believed that vigorous foreign policies would empower the presidency. He was also a liberal Presbyterian whose modern theology imagined Jesus Christ a social reformer who called followers to build heaven right here on earth.

The diplomatic implications of his Progressive Social Gospel, which could hardly have been more profound, gave rise to a heresy in American civil religion. For a century after 1796 Americans had deemed sacred the veritable Mosaic commandments laid down in George Washington's Farewell Address in that year. He exhorted his countrymen to cultivate religion and republican virtue; to practice unilateralism, neutrality, reciprocity, peace, and commerce with all nations; to harbor no inveterate sympathies or antipathies toward foreign countries; and to husband the public credit. But during the Progressive Era at the end of the nineteenth century the nation's elites turned those principles upside down. Both secular and religious leaders imagined that government staffed by credentialed experts and endowed with centralized power could literally perfect society at home and abroad. Virtue, humility, and prudence in foreign relations gave way to power, glory, and pride.

The transition can be precisely timed. Contrast President William McKinley's first inaugural address of 1897, in which he pledged to uphold traditional American values, with his second inaugural address of 1901, in which he praised as God's will the Spanish–American War, annexation of colonies, and bloody suppression of the Filipino independence movement. "Our institutions will not deteriorate by extension, and our sense of justice will not abate under tropic suns in distant seas," predicted McKinley, none too accurately. Hence, Wilson was by no means out of the mainstream when he lectured in 1911 that when nations take up arms to defend liberty, "there is something sacred and holy in the warfare. I will not cry 'Peace' so long as there is sin and injustice in the world."[4] The following year he was elected president in spite of his candidacy being a fluke, his campaign a fraud, and his landslide a fable.

The Democratic convention nominated him on its forty-sixth ballot thanks to a deal brokered by an eccentric Texan named Edward M. House, the author of a fantasy novel (*Philip Dru, Administrator: A Story of Tomorrow*, 1912) which extolled a Progressive dictator whose authoritarian rule prevents a second American civil war. By contrast, Wilson's platform, called "The New Freedom," disingenuously promised to fight such concentrations of power. What got him elected to the Oval Office was the third-party candidacy of former

President Theodore Roosevelt, which split the Republican Party and enabled Wilson to win with just 42 percent of the popular vote.

In 1821, Secretary of State John Quincy Adams had lectured Congress that "America goes not abroad in search of monsters of destroy," for if it did the "maxims of her policy would insensibly change from liberty to force" and "she would be no longer the ruler of her own spirit." As president, Wilson asserted the opposite. He told a convention of businessmen in 1913 that it is "a very perilous thing to determine the foreign policy of a nation in terms of material interest" and that Americans were climbing a moral mountain toward "those great heights where there shines unobstructed the light of the justice of God." In response to a British diplomat's inquiry he defined his foreign policy toward the Mexican revolution this way: "I am going to teach the South American republics to elect good men." The following year, his graduation address at the U.S. Naval Academy proclaimed that the very "idea of America is to serve humanity."

Thus did a scholar recently conclude: "Wilson's optimism concerning the power of humankind to do good hailed not from his Reformed heritage but from liberal theology, the Social Gospel, progressivism, and, ultimately, the romantic spiritualization of religion." The doctrine of total depravity, Calvin's equivalent for original sin, was nowhere to be found in Wilson's Presbyterianism. Indeed, his rhetoric implied that America—and by implication himself—had a messianic destiny.[5]

To be sure, when the Great War erupted, Wilson proclaimed neutrality and clung to it for thirty-one months. But his policies were neutral in name only given that the president, an avid and lifelong Anglophile, allowed private Americans to extend "all aid short of war" to Great Britain twenty-five years before Franklin Roosevelt coined that phrase. By the end of Wilson's first term, the British and French were importing 40 percent of their war materiel from the United States and borrowing heavily to finance it. World

War I thus reversed trans-Atlantic capital flows and crowned Wall Street king. The Wilson administration also complied with Britain's surface blockade of German-occupied lands even as he protested Germany's submarine blockade of Britain.

Neutrality was also good politics. The vast majority of Americans wanted no part of the bloodbath in the trenches.[6] But no sooner had Wilson, who posed as the peace candidate, narrowly won re-election in 1916 than he received some very bad news. The British secretly let on that their exchequer was broke and their larder depleted. They would be unable to prosecute for another year without the massive assistance U.S. belligerence would provide. When Germany resumed unrestricted submarine warfare later that winter the British were bitterly disappointed that it failed to tip the American public opinion toward intervention. So British intelligence, in late February 1917, leaked to the U.S. government an intercepted cable—the infamous Zimmermann Telegram—in which Germany offered Mexico a war alliance in case of American belligerence. The British were bitterly disappointed again. Contrary to the conventional wisdom, even that failed to outrage American opinion.[7]

Over those weeks Wilson famously agonized until, by the end of March, he made up his mind to wage war. For all the historical debate over the issue, "one incontrovertible fact remains: the United States entered World War I because Woodrow Wilson decided to take the country in."[8] Moreover, he made that personal, unforced choice to preach a crusade for liberal internationalism under the worst possible circumstances.

By spring 1917 Wilson knew (or should have known) that prominent senators led by Henry Cabot Lodge (R-Mass.) were hostile to his League of Nations idea. He knew (or should have known) that the Allied powers led by Britain and France were hostile to most of the liberal principles he would espouse in his Fourteen Points. He knew (or should have known) that most of the points, not least national self-determination, were inapplicable in much of Europe, where ethnic groups were hopelessly mixed and in the colonial world, whose rulers—the British, French, Italians, and Japanese—were now Wilson's comrades-in-arms. He knew (or should have known) that the vast majority of Germans, however war-weary, remained loyal to their emperor. He knew (or should have known) that to maximize his leverage at the peace conference the United States must wage a total ground war, not a limited naval war. He also knew (because he said as much) that war would undermine his domestic agenda, violate civil liberties, and unleash Americans' most bigoted instincts.

Nevertheless, Wilson chose to flip Washington's biggest "Thou shalt not" (meddle in Europe's broils) into a "Thou must," and to insist under threat of imprisonment that all American citizens fall into line.[9] Most damning of all, Wilson knew well, unlike the over-confident Europeans in 1914, exactly how hellish modern, industrial, total war had proven to be.[10]

The president had four options by spring 1917:

1. He could have kept the United States neutral, accepting the risk of a German victory.
2. He could have justified total war, but on the realistic grounds of preserving the European balance of power and thus U.S. security.
3. He could have gone to war over neutral rights, as in 1812, and waged a naval campaign rather than shipping an army to France.
4. He could preach a crusade, a holy "war to end all war," enthrall Americans with that fantastic mission, and then hope to persuade or cajole Europeans to convert to it, too.

Ferguson and others have speculated that the first option might have been best. Kaiser Wilhelm II was no Adolf Hitler, and after their sacrifices in a total war the Germans themselves would likely have demanded democratic reforms. Moreover, a German victory might likely have meant no totalitarian dictators, no World War II, no Holocaust, and no Cold War.

Henry Kissinger and others have speculated that the second option (which was Theodore Roosevelt's preference) might have been best, with Americans helping to restore a balance of power on terms the Allies, the Germans, and the U.S. Senate might grudgingly have accepted.

Scholars such as myself have speculated that the third choice might have been best since a naval war would have been far cheaper in money, blood, and damage to civic values, would have given both sides a powerful new incentive to end the carnage, and would have left it to Europe's Great Powers to hammer out a compromise peace.[11]

Wilson of course chose the fourth option, presumably because he had persuaded himself that God was calling America to redeem the horrible war by turning it into a "war for righteousness." Liberal Protestant clergy, previously divided over the war, turned zealous. The celebrity pastor Lyman Abbott thought it "more than a coincidence" that the Senate went to war on Good Friday. He called Germany heathen, America righteous, and the war the climactic chapter in God's plan for human redemption. The dean of Yale's divinity school asked, "May we not believe that this country, strong and brave, generous and hopeful is called of God to be in its own way a Messianic nation?" The evangelist Billy Sunday cried, "Christianity and Patriotism are synonymous terms, and hell and traitors are synonymous." The cross all but disappeared behind the American flag.

A good reason for Wilson to encourage the mania was that he meant to do the unthinkable: to conscript, train, and deploy a million-man army "over there." He even praised the "singular insight" of a Social Gospeler who declared the President's goal to be nothing less than the kingdom of God.[12]

With what results? Suffice to say that the Wilson administration's war mobilization was what inspired the philosopher Randolph Bourne's ironic comment that "War is the health of the state." The executive branch accumulated enormous power. The national debt exploded from 2.5 percent of GNP to more than 30 percent. The War Industries Board turned the most laissez-faire society in the world into a command economy and made the military-industrial complex a permanent feature of life. The butcher's bill numbered 53,000 combat deaths (in just five months), 116,000 lives overall, and twice that many wounded. The anti-German hysteria generated by George Creel's propaganda agency, the Committee on Public Information, belied Wilson's claim that America was not waging war against the German people, while inflaming nativism and encouraging persecution of German-Americans. The CPI employed every medium to propagate what Creel called the "gospel of Americanism," including a feature film that heralded the doughboys in France as "Pershing's Crusaders." The Espionage Act of 1917, and its extension as the Sedition Act of 1918, mandated the worst violations of civil liberties in American history. In effect, the war no one had wanted became overnight the war it was illegal to question.

Overseas, the Great War, the Russian and Chinese revolutions, and Japanese imperialism sowed unfathomable chaos from one end of Eurasia to the other. So the President of the United States can scarcely be faulted for not getting all of his policies right. But Wilson arguably got nothing right. When on October 5, 1918, the Germans secretly contacted the president in hopes of negotiating an armistice on the basis of the Fourteen Points, Washington exchanged notes with Berlin for several weeks without even informing the Allies. When Wilson did consult the (furious) British and French, they understandably insisted on harsh terms that would render the enemy harmless and clearly signaled their intention to impose a victor's peace. Their cruelest condition was maintenance of the food blockade after the war so they could present the peace treaty on a "sign-it-or-starve" basis.

The worst blunder made by Wilson might have been his demand for regime change. *Kaiser Wilhelm must abdicate* before he would agree to an armistice. Hence the Germans who ended up getting blamed for their army's "stab in the back" on November 11—and later for ratifying the draconian Versailles Treaty—were the left-center politicians in Germany's Reichstag, not the "militaristic regime" that preceded them. Moreover, the legitimacy of the treaty was undermined when Wilson's moralistic pretensions were exposed as naive, if not hypocritical. He had promised open covenants openly arrived at, but the treaty was a *Diktat* hammered out by the British, French, and Americans and foisted on the Germans.

The infamous war-guilt clause, inserted at the beginning of the treaty's section on German reparations, was inspired by American legalism, which required that damages be awarded as if in a civil tort case. As a result, Germany's new democracy, soon to be known as the Weimar Republic, was obliged to bear all the responsibility for the outbreak of war in 1914. That not only crippled German democracy but undermined the legitimacy of the treaty once revisionist historians began to argue that all the European Great Powers shared more or less guilt for the outbreak of the war. The other principles promised by Wilson, such as disarmament, economic opportunity, freedom of the seas, and self-determination, were either ignored or else denied to Germany alone. Wilson's sole consolation was that all these grievances might be resolved peacefully through the League of Nations his precious treaty created.

Wilson should not have gone to Paris with the American peace delegation since his participation in the daily bickering and compromise frittered away his prestige. He should not have appointed a delegation composed exclusively of Democrats which made peacemaking appear to be a partisan rather than patriotic exercise. He should not have promised an impossible new world order certain to disillusion public opinion, not least among his own avid supporters, who predictably recoiled when the harsh peace terms were published in May 1919. The *Nation* editorialized that the "one-time idol of democracy stands today discredited and condemned," proving again that "wherever liberalism strikes hands with war it inevitably goes down." The *New Republic* wrote: "The Treaty of Versailles subjects all liberalism and particularly that kind of liberalism which breathes the Christian spirit to a decisive test. If a war which was supposed to put an end to war culminates without strenuous protest by humane men and women in a treaty of peace which renders peace impossible, the liberalism which preached this meaning for the war will have committed suicide."[13]

Having been forced to make serial concessions to British, French, Italian, and Japanese nationalists, Wilson refused to accommodate American nationalists. When Senator Lodge introduced twelve reservations to the Treaty of Versailles before the Senate as conditions for its advice and consent, the president rejected them and insisted that Democratic senators do likewise. In Wilson's mind, the League Covenant had become the Ark of the Covenant, a holy thing that belonged not to him or the Senate but to God. To his way of thinking the League justified the war's suffering, justified Wilson's decision to lead America into it, and promised to lift humanity to those glorious heights where shines the light of the justice of God. So he launched a national tour to stump for the League, during which he collapsed, suffered a stroke, and lived out his term an invalid.

Wilson did not make the world safe for democracy. It might even be argued that his hapless policies toward Russia made the world safe for communism.[14] Surely the disillusionment caused by his diplomatic malpractice contributed not a little to the later isolationist pall which descended over Americans of all nearly all persuasions during the 1930s and thus helped to enable fascist aggression.

The historian Michael Kazin recently published a book on the antiwar movement betrayed by President Wilson in 1917. In a *New York Times* editorial on the centenary of the U.S. declaration of war he pointedly asked how the war might have ended had America stayed out. "If the Allies, led by France and Britain, had not won a total victory," he wrote, "there would have been no punitive peace like that completed at Versailles, no stab-in-the-back allegations by resentful Germans, and thus no rise, much less triumph, of Hitler and the Nazis. The next world war, with its 50 million deaths, would probably not have occurred."[15]

Why then, has Wilson's Progressive civil religion—a heresy from the perspective of George Washington's classical creed—remained the "default position" of U.S. foreign policy almost ever since? Perhaps the historian Richard Gamble is correct in suggesting that "Righteous interventionism appeals to our national vanity and piety. We have to face the fact that there is something deeply and authentically American about Wilsonianism."[16] After the Soviet Union went poof, our elites even imagined the United States to be a benevolent hegemon policing a new world order through militarism and globalization.[17] That crusade also aborted when Presidents Bill Clinton and George W. Bush pursued wildly ambitious policies toward the former Soviet bloc, the violent Balkans, and especially the wasting wars in Iraq and Afghanistan following the 9/11 terrorist attacks. One result was the surprising election of President Donald Trump. But I predict the Trump phenomenon will be ephemeral because he will prove no more able than Barack Obama to break the spell cast by Woodrow Wilson one hundred years ago.

Is it possible to distill that incantation down to its essence? Rereading an old book of essays on religion and history I recently stumbled on the following passage:

> Man is not content merely to study history. The ego will not be satisfied with this, because the ego in its unredeemed or natural state is not able to see history apart from itself.[18]

Thus wrote Arthur Link, the Princeton professor who devoted his whole career to the sanctification and beatification of Thomas Woodrow Wilson.

★ 8 ★

THE ECSTASY AND THE AGONY OF OUR ROMANCE WITH FLIGHT

A Meditation on the Centennial of the Wright Brothers' Triumph[1]

THE HUNGER

I believe it was 1979. While researching what would become my Pulitzer Prize–winning history of the dawn of the Space Age in Washington, D.C., I frequently visited the Smithsonian Institution's National Air and Space Museum. It had recently installed a two-story high IMAX movie theater and crowds routinely flocked in to view its inaugural film, *To Fly!* A paean to the romance of human flight, its cinematography was thrilling. But for me the magic began even before the lights dimmed. The speakers played beautiful music. Music which did not still the chatter of children, but which reduced most adults to silence, then wonder. It was the Canon in D Major by the seventeenth-century Lutheran organist Johann Pachelbel. The composition's sublime and strangely bittersweet melody put into sound the feelings of a mortal race capable of imagining heavenly things always just out of reach. Alas, Hollywood spoiled Pachelbel's magic the following year by using the Canon as the theme for the film *Ordinary People*, after which it devolved into muzak. But I shall always associate Pachelbel with the sweetest of human yearnings: *To Fly!*

The story of human flight is rightly called a romance, both in the sense of a romantic affair full of joy and anguish and in the grander sense of Romanticism, that cultural mood which expresses the human psyche's disillusionment with its rational efforts to endow our short lives with meaning. To the Romantic wild Nature is a temptress who beckons mankind to possess her only to turn all of our dreams into nightmares. Youth is soon vanquished, callow hopes dashed, until we succumb to what Germans called *Weltschmerz* (world-grief) or *Lebensmüdigkeit* (life-weariness). But no portion of Nature conjures our hopes and fears more than the sky. Who has not dreamed in their sleep they could fly like Superman over the houses and trees in the neighborhood? Who has not envied the birds? Who has not imagined that if heaven exists surely we shall be able to fly there, like angels? The dream of breaking the chains of gravity and escaping our two-dimensional life seems to be part of what makes us human.

Our fairy tales tell of magic carpet rides, the pixie dust in *Peter Pan*, and the plaintive lament of Dorothy in *The Wizard of Oz* ("birds fly over the rainbow, why then, O why can't I?"). But abundant evidence suggests that all civilizations have imagined flight a privilege reserved only to the gods, whose abodes are in "high places." The Greeks placed their pantheon on Mt. Olympus and warned of the hubris mere mortals displayed in attempting to trespass on their preserve. Thus, Icarus soared on the waxy wings crafted by Daedalus until he dared to approach the Sun, melted the wax, and fell to his death. Thus, Bellerophon was permitted to ride the wingèd horse Pegasus in order to slay the monster Chimera, but was cast down the moment he tried to ascend Mt. Olympus. He should have remembered that Pegasus was born of the blood of the hideous gorgon Medusa and his destiny was to serve as Zeus's courier, "air-mailing" his thunderbolts. Hindu, Buddhist, and Chinese mythologies contain similar cautionary tales about human efforts to fly. In Hebrew texts the Lord was "up there," appearing as a pillar of cloud or light, leading His Chosen People on their Exodus. He met with Moses on the top of Mt. Sinai, showed Jacob a vision of angels ascending and descending from heaven, and carried Elijah on high in a flaming chariot. In Christian texts the Holy Spirit descended like a dove upon Jesus, who in turn ascended into heaven after the resurrection. Likewise, the Bible offered the sternest of warnings to the heathen who built the Tower of Babel and tried to reach heaven through artifice. Wrath—be it divine or evil—invariably came from above. The Chinese version of nemesis was the fire-breathing dragon. Christians named Satan the Prince of the Power of the Air. Many civilizations endowed ravens, cranes, albatrosses, and eagles with transcendent powers. After all, birds can fly and we cannot, hence they must somehow share in the godhead. Finally, the human hunger to fly has often been distinctly erotic. The pagan Romans made that explicit in myths about maidens abducted by deities often disguised as birds. They sculpted intricate pendants of phalluses with wings. To fly! It must be, the ancients imagined, "like sex with gods!"

THE HUNT

Birds inspired the first technological efforts to realize humanity's primordial lust. As a boy, Leonardo da Vinci dreamed that a swooping hawk brushed his mouth with its feathers. As an adult, da Vinci observed how birds manipulated their tail and wing feathers to regulate attitude and lift: the basic principle behind rudders and ailerons. But the ornithopters he and later inventors sketched were based on the assumption that a flying machine would need to have wings which flapped. The source of aerodynamic lift was a mystery until Daniel Bernoulli, an eighteenth-century Dutch mathematician, discovered the principle of fluid mechanics. As the speed of a liquid or gas moving across a body increases, its internal pressure decreases. The brilliant English scientist Sir George Cayley applied that principle to aerodynamics. A curved and tapered wing (airfoil) would force air to pass more quickly over the top than under the bottom, thus creating a "low-pressure center" that sucked the wing up. By 1800 he identified thrust, lift, drag, and gravity as the forces in need of control and imagined the first true airplane with fuselage, cockpit, wings, and a tail. Suffice to say the Wright brothers said that "Cayley carried the science of flying to a point which it had never reached before and which it scarcely reached again during the last century."

By then human beings were already aloft in balloons. In "the astonishing year" of 1783 the paper-making Montgolfier brothers and scientist Jacques A. C. Charles kicked off a frenzy in Paris with their ornately painted egg-shaped balloons inflated with hydrogen. But as thrilling as ballooning could be (Thomas Jefferson wrote of those "endeavoring to learn us the way to heaven on wings of our own"), it was not really *flying* but rather drifting at the mercy of winds. Not until 1884 did French aeronauts construct the first lighter-than-air "dirigible" boasting a propellor driven by an electric motor and an elevator and sliding weights for steering. That was humanity's first controlled, powered flight, and it sparked the imagination of the retired general Ferdinand Graf von Zeppelin. His LZ-1, a gigantic cigar loaded with 400,000 cubic feet of hydrogen, first flew in 1900, giving birth to the brief and ultimately tragic era of luxurious, earth-circling zeppelins. But "bird-men" believed the future belonged to wings, if someone could just figure out how to keep a heavier-than-air craft aloft and under control.

The most charismatic "bird-man" was another German, Otto Lilienthal. Suspended beneath two bowed gossamer wings he leapt from heights and glided for long distances, controlling his flight by shifting his weight. He was more of an "aerial gymnast" than a scientist, and even if he had succeeded in perfecting hang-gliding as we know it today, his methods were useless to those trying to design airplanes. Still, Lilienthal's Icarus-like death in 1896 inspired others, not least the Wright brothers, to realize his dream through meticulous observation of the behavior of gliders.

No one contributed more technocratic optimism and acumen to the United States than the dapper Parisian-born Octave Chanute. Brought to America by his immigrant father, a history professor, Chanute became a builder of railroads, bridges, and the great stockyards of Chicago and Kansas City. He grew rich and famous and was honored with the presidency of the American Society of Civil Engineers until, in 1883, he gave it all up to pursue his real dream: to fly! He imported all the aeronautical texts he could find over in Europe, consulted with Thomas Edison, the physicist Albert F. Zahm, and the engine designer F. A. Pratt (later of Pratt & Whitney). He staged conferences to share information and ideas, experimented with trusses to stabilize wings, and taught Americans scientific flight-testing. Scoffers denied the possibility of heavier-than-air flight. But Chanute gave bird-men reason to persevere, not least Samuel Langley. If anyone could conquer the air, he believed, it was he. A distinguished scientist and president of the Smithsonian, he enjoyed the patronage of Theodore Roosevelt and Alexander Graham Bell, and won grants totaling $73,000 (nearly $2 million today) from the Army, the Smithsonian, and private donors. Langley proceeded methodically for seventeen years, experimenting with scale models of flying machines he called aerodromes. He hired crack engineers, expanded his staff, and at length built a full-size fabric-winged flyer powered by a 52 horsepower gasoline engine. Confident of success, Langley launched a publicity campaign that fixed all eyes on his Great Aerodrome moored in the Potomac River. On October 7, 1903, rockets and horns signaled the moment of an apotheosis. Whereupon the machine snagged on its launcher and "slid into the water like a handful of mortar." So much for big government R&D. But even if Langley had succeeded, his Aerodrome was a turkey. It needed to be catapulted into motion and lacked control mechanisms, landing gear, and a cockpit. Had the plane reached its planned cruising speed of 50 miles per hour, the pilot would have been doomed!

Unbeknownst to the crowds on the Potomac, the venerable Smithsonian Institution housed in its recondite castle on Washington's Mall had already made a far quieter contribution that proved nothing less than decisive. It happened on June 2, 1899, when an obscure bureaucrat named Richard Rathbun perused a letter from a humble citizen asking if the Smithsonian might send him materials to assist his "systematic study" of flight. Rathbun, a paleontologist, might have discarded the letter or considered its author a crank. Instead, he bade his office assemble the best available scholarship for Mr. Wilbur Wright of Dayton, Ohio.

The Wrights were middle-class, Middle West foliage of a family tree nourished by English, Dutch, and German roots. Their father, in good Yankee fashion, sired seven children, and served as a bishop in the Church of the United Brethren. The boys Wilbur, born 1867, and Orville (nickname "Bubbo"), born 1871, grew up behaving in ways the next century's psychologists would term obsessive-compulsive. They stuck close to home, were very shy, especially around females, and devoted all their free time to private projects of various kinds. When a fad for bicycle racing swept the nation they went into that business in 1892. Then news of Lilienthal's death reminded the brothers of their fascination with a toy their father had given them way back in 1878. It was a rubber band–driven whirligig that "flew" around the room when released. The boys tried to fashion bigger versions without success. But by 1899, when the Wright brothers took up their quest for powered flight, they had become master mechanics, self-taught mathematicians, residents of one of America's "high-tech" cities, and possessed—thanks to Rathbun—

of the best current data. Not least, they adopted a method known today as systems integration. Uppermost in their minds was the challenge of mastering attitude, pitch, and yaw, because getting an airplane into the air would be suicidal if it could not be controlled. That in turn obliged the brothers to mesh several new or improved technologies, including an engine/propellor, handles and pedals, and a sturdy airframe. As any reader of Robert Pirsig's classic *Zen and the Art of Motorcycle Maintenance* knows, acquiring the "feel" of a complex machine is an art as much as a science. Third, the Wrights engaged in dogged research, development, and testing, first with gliders and models in a makeshift wind tunnel, then prototype flyers. Their temperaments suited them to such careful, repetitive, empirical work. Thanks to the principles established by Cayley, Chanute, and others, the negative examples of Lilienthal and Langley, their own trial-and-error adjustments, and a light 12 horsepower aluminum engine with magneto ignition, the Wrights made remarkable progress in just a few years, spending just $1,000 of their own money.

After the disaster on the Potomac, Orville wrote Chanute, "I see that Langley has had his fling, and failed. It seems to be our turn to throw now, and I wonder what our luck will be." A month later, the "Whopper Flying Machine," as the brothers called their minimalist box of fabric and struts, was assembled at breezy Kill Devil Hills near Kitty Hawk on North Carolina's Outer Banks. On December 12, 1903, they placed the craft on a slight downward slope thinking to help it gain speed. But that only forced Wilbur (who had won a coin toss to go first) to lean too much on the elevator. The craft stalled, then fell gently to the sand. So it was on December 17, a date which would live in ecstasy, that the brothers tried again from a level surface. Orville reclined at the controls, warmed up the engine, then broke the tether holding the airplane in place. The headwind plus the velocity generated by the propellor sufficed to lift the biplane while Orville, learning the pilot's trade "on the wing," kept it aloft and stable for twelve seconds and 120 feet. On their fourth trial that morning Wilbur stayed in "thin air" for just under a minute and covered almost three football fields. A small group of locals witnessed the historic event, of whom young Johnny Moore was most eloquent: "They done did it, they done it, damned if they ain't flew!" The brothers, collected as always, shared a lunch basket then walked casually down to the coastal lifesaving station where they scribbled a telegram to their father in Dayton:

> SUCCESS FOUR FLIGHTS THURSDAY MORNING ALL AGAINST TWENTY-ONE MILE WIND STARTED FROM LEVEL WITH ENGINE POWER PLANE AVERAGE SPEED THROUGH AIR THIRTY-ONE MILES LONGEST 57 SECONDS INFORM PRESS HOME CHRISTMAS.

THE HONEYMOON

Invention of the airplane did not kick off a frenzy. The Wrights did not want it to. Indeed, they spent several years dodging publicity while conducting private test flights and awaiting approval of patents. So most Americans did not know, understand, or believe what had happened at Kitty Hawk until September 1908, when the Army Signal Corps asked Orville to perform at Fort Myer, Virginia. The brass wanted to know if this alleged "aeroplane" might have some military utility. News spread by newspaper and word of mouth until 5,000 civilians crowded the fort on Labor Day in what came to resemble a religious revival. Some people said it was "inhuman" or even "occult" for man to take flight. Most just cried, "My God, my God," and called it a miracle. The Wrights went on tour, charging $5,000 per exhibition, and performed their wonders before entire towns. They opened a school to train pilots, who competed to top each other's dare-devil loops and rolls. Dozens of copycat mechanics and bird-men soon built variations on the Wright flyer and taught themselves to pilot them. William Randolph Hearst put up prize money for the first person to fly across the United States. Calbraith Rodgers did it in forty-nine days in 1911 and was greeted in Pasadena by 20,000 screaming fans. Women leapt at the chance to soar above the confines of terrestrial society, truly "equal in the eyes of God." Air races were front-page news, as well as each "first," such as the first scheduled passenger service in 1914 and first airmail service in 1918. A new age of limitless, if ineffable potential seemed to have dawned. Aviators were gods, aviation a secular religion.

The sole sour note was played by the motorcyclist Glenn Curtiss, who founded the second U.S. aircraft manufacturing company and viciously challenged the Wrights' patents. When the courts ruled against him Curtiss conspired with Smithsonian officials to cobble a case suggesting Langley's aerodrome deserved legal priority! In 1929 the issue became moot when the Curtiss and Wright firms merged. But Wilbur died unvindicated of yellow fever in 1912, and it took the Smithsonian until 1942 to apologize to Orville and display a replica of his flyer in its castle.

Not even World War I troubled the honeymoon of America and the airplane. Aviation advanced rapidly under the impress of war. The Packard auto company designed the V-12 Liberty engine with Delco ignition that powered the Curtiss Jennies on which hundreds of military pilots trained. They returned home eager to own planes and either barnstorm or fly for airlines serving the post office. Even aerial combat seemed pristine and chivalric by comparison to the barbaric slaughter in the trenches below. Hollywood rode the craze with films featuring fighter pilots and stunt men. The public thrilled as the earth shrank. In 1919 the six-man crew of a U.S. Navy "flying boat" crossed the Atlantic. In 1923 two Army pilots made the first non-stop coast-to-coast flight in just twenty-seven hours. In 1924, four Army crews flying Douglas World Cruisers took off from Seattle bound for…Seattle! Clinging to coastlines and hopping islands, two of the aircraft circled the globe in 175 days. A quarter of a million people cheered their return. In 1926 Commander Richard E. Byrd flew over the North Pole.

The federal government promoted aviation, but with a light hand. The National Advisory Committee for Aeronautics (1915) was nothing like the NASA behemoth it would become in 1958. It consisted only of a modest assemblage of scientists with a meager budget and a few wind tunnels. It nonetheless did a great deal to advance airfoil design, avionics, and navigation. The Kelly Air Mail Act (1925) fostered free enterprise by authorizing the Postmaster General to contract with airlines and establish a national grid of lighted airports, emergency runways, and meteorological radio stations. The Air Commerce Act (1926) provided for the licensing of pilots and federal safety regulations. Hence, far from setting up government-owned airlines as most other countries did, the United States subsidized private competition. That is what gave a lease on life to entrepreneurs such as Clement Keys (North American), Malcolm and Allan Loughead (Lockheed), Pop Hanshue (TWA), Juan Trippe (Pan American), Erle Halliburton (Delta), Donald Douglas, William Boeing, Glenn Martin, Jack Northrop, Jerry Vultee, Chance Vought, Tom Braniff, Clyde Cessna, Curtiss, and Wright.

The only threat to public ownership of airplanes and airlines was Franklin D. Roosevelt's New Deal. In 1934 the president, Postmaster General James Farley, and Alabama Senator Hugo Black claimed the former Republican postmasters had been "dictators" whose choice of airmail contracts in "spoils conferences" spelled death for some airlines and windfall profits for others. Roosevelt ordered the Army Air Corps to start delivering mail. But due to penurious budgets the corps's obsolete aircraft and fledgling pilots were so inadequate to the task that a dozen crewmen and planes were lost in three weeks. Roosevelt repented of socialism. He did, however, press Congress to create the Civil Aeronautics Board to regulate airlines and approve routes and rates (thereby granting himself the same powers he claimed Republicans had abused).

"Our gaze drew upward—from the skies you taught, Man is divine, and meant by God to soar!" So did a poet express what "air-minded" Americans took on faith in the interwar years. First thousands, then hundreds of thousands of people were born again as disciples of the "winged gospel." If flying was reserved for gods, then human beings must themselves be, or on the way to becoming, gods. Aviation, said its ecstatic proponents, promised to end war for all time, either by making neighbors and partners of all nations through cultural contact and trade or by making war so horrible no sane person would wage it. Aviation, said its proponents, promised to liberate people from their sooty cities and tenements, mundane jobs and impediments, indeed from each other. As Henry Ford put an automobile within reach of each working man, soon every family would own its own airplane and commute from rustic retreats. Most of all, the "air-minded" testified to the spiritual high of soaring through the skies under one's own control. To look down on the world from high above made instantly clear how base and petty was the earthly rat race for money, power, prestige.

Believers in the "winged gospel" formed myriad clubs and gathered at air shows. They took their air circuses on the road to woo converts. They made shrines of the Wrights' bicycle shop and Kitty Hawk. The very site chosen by the Wrights—Kill Devil Hills—seemed inspired. They made December 17 a holy day, a sort of technologists' Christmas, and gathered to hear the gospel read anew from the Wrights' journals. Tracts, posters, models, statuary, futuristic artistry depicting the transformation of society through aviation: all were employed to spread the "good news," especially to children. But evangelization, however pervasive, would not have moved so many American hearts were it not for a lone eagle named Lindbergh.

In 1919 a prize of $25,000 was offered to the first pilot to leap the Atlantic Ocean non-stop. By 1927 aircraft of sufficient size and power were coming on line, and three French aces from the Great War plus three famous American pilots were determined to win. But two of the Frenchmen perished in the attempt, while the other four were scratched due to accidents or injuries. Against all odds, the prize was still up for grabs when Charles "Slim" Lindbergh, a handsome tow-headed barnstormer from Minnesota, arrived in New York in his single-engine Ryan NYP monoplane. When he announced his intention to cross the ocean alone through uncertain weather just days after the Frenchmen disappeared, people called him "The Flying Fool." But all Americans held their breath when the *Spirit of St. Louis* took to the air on May 19. The next morning Lindbergh landed at Le Bourget Aerodrome, Paris, exhausted and utterly unaware of what he had become in the hearts and minds of his countrymen. "He is US personified," wrote the *New Republic*. "He is the United States." Lindy "is the dream that is in our hearts," wrote the *North American Review*. He taught America "to lift up its eyes to Heaven," said the *New York World*. He was Lucky Lindy, the Lone Eagle, the new Daniel Boone calling America back to its pioneer virtues. He was welcomed back to New York by four million people, and millions more turned out in all forty-eight states, which he toured in the Ryan. What did it mean? Did Lindbergh's solo flight thrill Americans who instinctively felt that modern, industrial, urban life ground down individuals and left no room for heroism? Not quite, because, as President Coolidge noted, Lindy's "silent partner" was American industry. "I am told that more than 100 separate companies furnished material, parts or service" to the airplane. Lindbergh himself honored his "partner" by naming his memoir *WE*. *We* did it: my Ryan and I. What Lindbergh and the winged gospelers hallowed was the marriage of man *and* machine, rugged individualism *and* modern science. U.S. Ambassador Myron Herrick, Lindy's host in Paris, had no doubt as to the source of his luck: "He was the instrument of a great ideal, and one need not be fanatically religious to see in his success the guiding hand of Providence."

Many more such flights in the 1920s and 1930s rekindled Americans' faith. But with the possible exception of Amelia Earhart's feats all subsequent aerial "firsts" were like routine visits to church by contrast to the thrill of their initial conversions. From the Wright brothers Americans learned that Yankee pluck and know-how still trumped big money and organization. From Lindbergh they learned that Ralph Waldo Emerson was wrong when he wrote, "Machines are in the saddle and ride mankind." Self-reliant Americans were still in the saddle, and through their machines could make magic.

Anne Morrow Lindbergh, the aviatrix who married Charles, put it exactly that way. Gazing down from 10,000 feet she thought the busy, bothered old earth looked frozen in form, as if a glaze were put over life: "And if flying, like a glass-bottomed bucket, can give you that vision, that seeing eye, which peers down to the still world below the choppy waves, it will always remain magic." Pilot John Magee, Jr., looked up not down, so to him magic became mystique. "I have slipped the surly bonds of earth..." he wrote, "and touched the face of God."

THE HEARTBREAK

When and why did the honeymoon end and heartbreak ensue? The answer most likely to leap to mind is December 7, 1941, when Americans awoke to the truth of what various Jeremiahs had prophesied about fire and death from above. As early as 1908 H. G. Wells predicted in *The War in the Air* that the twentieth century would witness urban conflagrations of Biblical proportions. The Allied powers' spring

1919 offensive against Germany would have inaugurated massive, if primitive bombing behind enemy lines had the Armistice not intervened. In the 1920s, the Italian strategist Giulio Douhet wrote in *The Command of the Air* that future wars would be won in a matter of days by whichever side boasted the superior air force. America's own prophet of doom was the naval pilot and war hero Billy Mitchell. He lectured incessantly on the potentially decisive impact of naval air power and proved it in 1921 by demonstrating how a few lightly armed airplanes could sink a Dreadnought-class battleship. In 1924 he even described in a secret report how the Japanese were planning to build aircraft carriers and initiate a Pacific War by launching air raids against American bases in the Philippine and Hawaiian Islands. Mitchell was ignored, derided, and reprimanded to the point that he accused the War and Navy departments of "incompetency, criminal negligence, and almost treasonable administration." That earned him a court martial.

By the 1930s dictators made abundantly clear how the winged gospel might be perverted. Benito Mussolini, Adolf Hitler, and Josef Stalin patronized aviation to advertise their high-tech futuristic regimes. Italian designers and pilots like Italo Balbo won numerous air races. Hitler made the *Luftwaffe* (air force) a Nazi showpiece and put Hermann Goering, a World War I air ace, in command of it. Visitors such as Lindbergh were impressed by the evident superiority of fascist regimes to promote air power. The Soviets called their pilots "Stalin's Eagles" and plastered cities with placards crowing over their international triumphs. The most frightened nation were the British because aerial bombing seemed likely to nullify their centuries-old advantage as an insular country. Even before the Nazis took power Prime Minister Stanley Baldwin lamented, "Whatever people may tell [the man on the street], the bomber will always get through." By 1935, when Hitler lied that the *Luftwaffe* already enjoyed superiority, Englishmen feared London might be destroyed on the first day of a war. Baldwin confessed, "I wish for many reasons flying had never been invented.... Somehow we have got to Christianize it." Evidently, the winged gospel needed the old gospel to realize its promise. When war did come to Spain, China, and Europe, Americans shuddered at newsreel footage of the bombing of Guernica, Shanghai, and London. Still, the horror seemed oceans away until Pearl Harbor brought it home to Americans. Right?

Wrong. Americans' romance with flight continued in spite and *because of* the war. The principal reason was undoubtedly the fact that the American mainland was spared from attacks such as those which destroyed cities in Europe and Asia. Americans even considered it their bounden duty in a total war to pay the enemy back for his "fascist way of war" by incinerating German and Japanese cities with napalm delivered by armadas of bombers. At the same time, World War II was the occasion to educate average Americans about the wonders of flight. During the war several million servicemen and thousands of civilians took their first ride on an airplane. Thousands of male pilots and hundreds of Women's Airforce Service Pilots (WASP) ferried aircraft all over the world. The technology leapt forward, from the Lockheed P-38 Lightning to the Grumman F-4-F Hellcat, from the Boeing B-17 Flying Fortress to the B-29 Superfortress. No airplane was more beloved than the sturdy Douglas DC-3 (C-47 transport plane), of which 11,000 were manufactured. Far from repenting of what aviation had wrought, Americans honored their brave bomber crews wreaking havoc over their enemies' cities. Walt Disney Studios promised "Victory Through Air Power" in a stunning animation depicting waves of American bombers crossing the Pacific Ocean and morphing into angry eagles who tear at Japan's vitals with their talons. Even the crescendos of horror, the atomic bombings of Hiroshima and Nagasaki, were cheered wildly by a million servicemen who were suddenly spared a bloody invasion of Japan. In any event, the United

States enjoyed an atomic monopoly. Some clergymen even suggested God Almighty had bestowed the bomb on the United States in the interest of perpetual peace. World War II, far from disillusioning the "air-minded" evangelists, seemed only to hasten the day when the full promise of aviation would be fulfilled.

Polls conducted near the end of World War II showed hopes far outpacing fears. No less than 85 percent of Army Air Force pilots said they intended to own their own planes after the war. Some 43 percent of businessmen and professionals expected their firms to own planes after the war. Almost a third of *all* American civilians confessed to wanting a private plane, while 39 percent of the readers of *Women's Home Companion* intended to take flying lessons! In 1946 alone, civilians purchased 33,254 private planes and back-ordered so many more that new manufacturers leaped into business. Even Macy's department store peddled a line of aircraft.

Then the novelty began to wear off. Other consumer goals ranging from homes to automobiles and appliances soaked up Americans' cash. Not least, the Soviets tested an A-bomb in 1949 and boasted they would soon deploy transcontinental bombers. So if one had to pick a date and say with the country song "that's when the heartaches begin," the year 1950 is as good as any. The Cold War turned hot in Korea, where North American's F-86 Saber jet fighters dueled Soviet MiGs nearly equal in prowess. The military again monopolized aviation technology and personnel. The most symbolic of sad events might have been the recall of the beloved baseball slugger Ted Williams to duty as a fighter pilot despite his already having lost four years to World War II. In the mid-1950s Congress investigated an alleged "bomber gap," suggesting that the sort of armageddon visited upon other continents might next time visit North America. The Dwight Eisenhower administration built the Distant Early Warning (DEW) line of radar stations in Canada and convened secret scientific committees predicting imminent Soviet parity in strategic weapons. Most shocking, the launch of Sputnik

1 in 1957 seemed to prove the Soviet Union had grabbed a lead in the race to control outer space and possessed an intercontinental ballistic missile sufficient to hurtle nuclear warheads over the North Pole and on to America's cities. Suddenly the sky became as scary as it had been to the ancients. Men could fly, even rocket through space, but they were still men—some evil, all flawed, and none gods.

Civilian aviation continued to excite the postwar American public. During the 1950s Americans put on their Sunday best when boarding commercial airliners and were assured by elegant stewardesses there was nothing to fear. The advent of jet travel began with the Boeing 707 and DC-8 airliners in 1957. (Jet aviation enabled Major League Baseball to expand to the West Coast as the Brooklyn Dodgers moved to Los Angeles and the New York Giants to San Francisco in 1958). But during the decades that followed the very success of the now-routine, coast-to-coast airliners drained the experience of its former excitement. None other than Anne Morrow Lindbergh had foreseen the disillusionment in her 1938 memoir *Listen! The Wind.* "As time passes," she prophesied, "the perfection of machinery tends to insulate man from contact with the elements in which he lives. The 'stratosphere' planes of the future will cross the ocean without any sense of the water below. Like a train tunneling through a mountain, they will be aloof from both the problems and beauty of the earth's surface. Only the vibration of the engines will impress the senses of the traveler with his movement through the air. Wind and heat and moonlight take-offs will be of no concern to the transatlantic passenger. His only contact will these elements will lie in accounts such as this book contains."

Once upon a time people dreamed of flying by themselves, free as birds. But the experience of late-twentieth-century travelers made sense of the poet Bob Dylan's query: "Are birds free from the *chains* of the skyways?" Instead of anticipating the thrills of flight, commercial passengers grew weary of beating their way to a remote airport, standing in line to get ticketed and check baggage, and then squeezing themselves into narrow seats where they would remain immobile for hours. Pressurization made the cabin a stale, artificial environment. Even those with window seats might see nothing but clouds. Far from being in control, white-knuckled customers felt thoroughly out of control if their aircraft encountered turbulent weather. Airplanes were certainly much faster than railroads or automobiles, but their speed annihilated the romance of travel.

Magic died for manufacturers and airlines as well. To be sure, individual engineers and pilots might still take pride in an elegant new design, a problem solved, or a feather-like landing in a cross wind. But the truth was, aerospace manufacturing and airline management were tough industries in which to make an honest dollar. The Pentagon and NASA—Eisenhower's "military industrial complex"—dominated much of the nation's research and development, forcing aerospace firms to low-ball on bids, over-promise on results, and lobby hard to win government contracts. Firms that failed to gorge at the public trough disappeared, while survivors merged into ever larger conglomerates or else diversified into other industries. The federal aviation bureaucracy became ever larger and more opaque, especially after President Lyndon Johnson subsumed it into the new Department of Transportation in 1967. Deregulation cut the legs out from under marginal carriers and invited the big carriers to push fares into the stratosphere or else offer cut-rate fares (subject to all sorts of penalties and restrictions) in order to gain market share. Airlines routinely over-booked, thus ensuring a certain number of outraged customers every flight. The "once in a lifetime" thrill turned into an all too frequent annoyance, not least for those who suffered from air sickness, jet lag, and inner ear disequilibrium.

For a few nervous years, the Space Race kept alive the memory of men and machines braving the unknown, while spaceflight enthusiasts dusted off the utopian or calamitous projections applied earlier to aviation. Americans were ecstatic with relief in 1962 when John Glenn matched Yuri Gagarin's feat by orbiting the earth in his Mercury capsule. A United States rent asunder by race riots and Vietnam War protests managed to pull together for a week in July 1969 when Apollo 11 touched the Moon and returned safely to earth. Then even Moon missions grew boring, such that Richard Nixon's administration canceled the last three Apollo flights. Even more tellingly, it canceled the U.S. program for a Supersonic Transport (SST) plane. For the first time in the air age Americans surrendered "faster, higher, longer" technology on the grounds it was too expensive, noisy, and polluting. The "sex" just wasn't good, or worthwhile, anymore.

Ironically, the mistresses which replaced aviation in the hearts of Americans, the ones which now provided the kicks they craved, were computers and the computerized special effects in Hollywood films. By the 1980s NASA's routine Space Shuttle missions paled by comparison to the "gee whiz" thrills served up by *Star Wars* movies and video games. That such experiences were not real did not matter.

THE HORROR

In 1759 Dr. Samuel Johnson wrote a satirical fantasy called *Rasselas*. It told of an Abyssinian savant who learned the secret of flight. His king was elated until told by the sage that the secret could never be shared. "If men were all virtuous," he explained, "I should with great alacrity teach them to fly. But what would be the security of the good if the bad could at pleasure invade them from the sky?"

Heartbreak turned to horror on September 11, 2001. None of us will ever purge those television images from our memories. Recently in a history seminar at the University of Pennsylvania I screened for the students the Ken Burns video on the Statue of Liberty. They enjoyed it and learned a good deal. But they also confessed to being disturbed. Why? Because it had been filmed in 1985, hence the wide-angle shots of the Statue of Liberty caught in the background the looming Twin Towers in Lower Manhattan, often with airplanes soaring above. For the 9/11 generation the very image of the Statue of Liberty had been spoiled by routine takeoffs and landings from JFK International Airport.

During President George W. Bush's Global War on Terror aviation played as large a role as it did in the Iraqi, Bosnian, and Kosovar wars of the 1990s. The Defense Department even boasted of the "Shock and Awe" its air power would visit on the helpless Afghans and Iraqis below. But the confidence placed in air power by our allegedly intelligent defense intellectuals has been mocked by reality. Insurgents in countries such as Afghanistan, Iraq, and Syria simply resorted to asymmetrical warfare and visited upon the United States defeats as costly and humiliating as the one Americans suffered in Vietnam, where U.S. armed forces dropped more bombs than all the belligerents in World War II, only to lose in the end.

We pray nothing like 9/11 will happen again. But the civilian costs Americans bear in the wake of the Al Qaeda attacks are even more annoyance and tedium due to TSA security checks and even worse service and amenities from the airlines. It calls to mind the confession of a Viet Cong guerilla who had been captured by the French in the first Indochina war. He survived cruel imprisonment by focusing his mind on the dream of a free and united Vietnam. It took twenty-four more years and another war against the United States, but when Saigon fell in 1975 it seemed his dream had been realized...until, that is, the North Vietnamese government pushed the Viet Cong aside and ruled the South with an iron fist. How I wish, wrote the guerilla in his memoirs, I could be transported back to that French prison when my dream was still alive.

Were the Wright brothers alive today perhaps they might wish to be transported back to Kitty Hawk, where they hungered only *To Fly!*

★ 9 ★

NO DISCHARGE FROM THAT WAR

The Vietnamization of America[1]

"All in all, it's a good year for war buffs," quipped the humorist Tom Lehrer about 1964–65, noting the hundredth, twentieth, and fiftieth anniversaries of the end of the Civil War and World War II and the start of World War I. Likewise in 1994–95 we commemorated the fiftieth anniversaries of the World War II victories from D-Day to VJ Day, the twenty-fifth anniversary of the first Moon landing, and the twentieth anniversary of the fall of Saigon.

What is more, it was twenty-five years ago this month that I was standing knee-deep in muddy water at a particularly nasty jungle base in South Vietnam. When the waters continued to rise we were ordered to empty all our sandbags, slog all our gear to the helicopter pad, and wait to be evacuated. Only the choppers did not come. The sun began to set. We were drenched and covered with filth. We had dismantled our defenses and packed up our weapons. We were naked if the enemy chose to attack. Few twenty-two-year-olds ever know despair, but we were all very near it when the Chinook helicopters finally roared through the rain to rescue us as darkness fell.

Darkness. Never had I experienced such utter blackness and utter silence as in the jungle on a moonless night. It even made going to the latrine an adventure, especially since, as often was the case on dark nights, the Viet Cong were up and about, somewhere out there.

I would never have guessed that a quarter century would pass before I talked about Vietnam in public or in private, or that it would finally happen at a women's prep school in suburban Philadelphia. But I think it is high time for me and all veterans, indeed all Americans of my generation, to take stock of the fact that the Vietnam War still sputters inside us—that in fact there has been no discharge from that war. All soldiers expect to get a discharge from the military sooner or later, preferably an honorable one, and then get on with their lives. But something about Vietnam does not let us go. Do I still have dreams about Vietnam, like so many other soldiers? Yes, occasionally. But mine are not flashbacks of combat. I simply dream that *I am still in Vietnam*, long after I was supposed to go home, due to some bureaucratic screw-up. Or I dream that I did go home, but that the war is still raging many years later and I have been activated from the reserves and sent back. In other words, my deep-down fear is simply that there's no discharge from that war.

In how many ways is that true of America as a whole? In how many ways were our national politics, society, and culture permanently changed by the trauma of Vietnam? Historians speak of Lyndon Johnson Americanizing the war and of Richard Nixon Vietnamizing the war. But in the end, America itself underwent Vietnamization. Later on, I shall summarize some of the ways I think that occurred. But first, I am going to do something that I have never done before. I am going to tell a few war stories.

By 1966 or 1967 I knew something was wrong with the Vietnam War because of the simple fact that the mighty United States had not won. When LBJ escalated U.S. involvement during my freshman year in college we all assumed that the war, or conflict, or police action (or whatever the government chose to call it) would be over long before we graduated. By the time our senior year arrived in 1967–68 it was clear that the war would not be over, and that we were going to be caught up. It was not a political thing for most of us. The anti-war protests did not engulf sleepy Amherst College until after my time. Indeed, what bothered me was not the fact of the war and its motives, but the fact that it had become a quagmire. Nor did I consider dodging the draft. When deferments for graduate students were abolished, I resigned myself to serving in the Army. I even had the naive idea that whether I ended up supporting or opposing the war, my voice would count for something because I had really been there. Moreover, by enlisting instead of waiting to be drafted, I could choose my combat branch and thus avoid getting stuck in the infantry. In any case, the enlistment was only for two years. I never dreamed that there would be no discharge from that war.

The Army's "Vietnam orientation" training deepened my sense that something was wrong. We soldiers were herded into a large auditorium and obliged to listen—not to some charismatic general like George S. Patton at the start of the Academy Award–winning film—but to a pot-bellied redneck sergeant. "Awright, you mens, listen up," he barked. "Y'all will now git oree-en-tated to Vit-nam which is a Confusion So-ciety where ever-body's knows their place, sorta like th' Army chain o' command!" Next, we toured a model strategic hamlet, which we were assured was Viet Cong proof. Next, we were told what to do in an ambush—don't duck for cover but charge the enemy's guns (*yeah, right*)—and were warned about booby traps such as camouflaged pits hiding razor-sharp punji stakes. Scariest for me were the sergeants' descriptions of tropical snakes, scorpions, and spiders sufficient to daunt a toxicologist. We received no pep talks, no positive reinforcement, for which by then even smug college graduates like myself were thirsting. A soldier needs reassurance before going off to war. We got none.

No wonder they locked us up in a warehouse at the Oakland, California, Army Base for forty-eight hours before our departure. Our morale was so bad they feared we would go AWOL. Outside the base protesters from Berkeley alternately appealed to us as victims of the military-industrial complex and damned us as "baby-killers." Nor did it help morale that soldiers were transported to Vietnam on chartered commercial jetliners complete with stewardesses and muzak. When the song "I'm Leavin' on a Jet Plane" played some of us started to cry. When our airplane refueled in Honolulu we were locked up again. Only when we had reached Wake Island two-thirds of the way across the Pacific Ocean did the officers relax their vigilance because we had passed the point of no return.

That something was wrong struck me again at the Philippine Islands' historic Clark Air Base, whose terminal was graced by a giant mural of General Douglas MacArthur. I stepped onto the tarmac and for the first time smelled the distinctive damp odor of Asia and gazed at the tropical rainforest on the horizon. Something did not feel right. Then I knew what: the American flag seemed so out of place. How disorienting it was to spy the Stars and Stripes waving over that alien Asian landscape.

Something else struck me as wrong when we landed in Vietnam and were bused to the giant base at Long Binh, because there nothing at all seemed alien. What we saw from the bus was a prefabricated American town stretching for miles, with paved highways and permanent, multistory buildings. It was as if the Army itself knew that victory was not going to come anytime soon. We were also struck by the relative absence of Southeast Asian faces. Here we were in Vietnam, but all one could see were American faces, save for the hooch-girls bused in each morning to work in the laundries and mess halls. The only other contact I would have with the inhabitants were the occasional messages the Viet Cong sent, by rockets and mortars, to remind us that we were on somebody else's turf.

After a week, my orders came down and I learned that by chance I had been assigned to an artillery battery of the New Hampshire National Guard called up for active duty in wake of the 1968 Tet

Offensive. Some of the guardsmen had challenged their call-up in court on the grounds that Congress had not declared war. One of those who did was severely wounded in a mortar barrage, while the captain commanding our battery, a Granite Stater of French-Canadian extraction, was later be killed while serving as a forward observer. On my own first day with the battery, I learned something else was shockingly wrong. While learning to operate our radios I occasionally heard Vietnamese chattering on our frequency, or "push." Now, my trainer was a genial fellow about thirty years old, with a family and job back in New Hampshire. He was by no means a bigot. Yet, when he heard those Vietnamese—*South* Vietnamese, mind you—he keyed his mike, gave me a wink, and said, "Ditty mow, gook! Ditty mow!" meaning, "Get lost, get off our push." I soon learned it was *de rigueur* for American soldiers—not only white, but black and Hispanic—to condescend to the "little people" or else treat Vietnamese as inferiors.

I surmised that "ditty mow" must have been a corruption of the French *dites-moi* (tell me, talk to me), but could not imagine the process by which "talk to me" turned into "shut up." Barracks French, a hangover from the First Indochina War, formed a large part of our Vietnam slang, including "boo-coo" for *beaucoup* (many) and "coo-shay" for *coucher* (going with a prostitute). More slang was based on the radio code for the alphabet: alpha, bravo, charlie, etc. Thus BS became "Bravo Sierra," and Viet Cong (VC) became "Victor Charlie," just "Charlie," or if you were feeling genial toward the enemy, "Chuck." America was "the world," civilian airliners were "freedom birds," and to be killed was to get "wasted." Everything in Vietnam was either "Number One," meaning the best, or "Number Ten," meaning the pits.

The number one commodity for many American soldiers was grass, pot, weed. I knew again that something was wrong with this war when a corporal took me into a hooch during my first week in-country and offered me a cigarette from a pack of Marlboros that looked so normal it even had an American tax stamp on the bottom. Only the cigarettes were filled not with tobacco but with prime Laotian marijuana dipped in liquid opium. I was amazed, and asked him what it cost. "Five bucks," he said. "Five bucks a joint?" I asked. "No, five bucks a pack!" Believe it or not, I had never tried pot before. But I did try it then and (unlike what Bill Clinton later would claim) I did inhale. Uncontrollable giggling ensued for an indeterminate length of time before I simply passed out. When I came to hours later the corporal was long gone and I could not remember for a minute who I was, where I was, or where I was supposed to be. Luckily, I still had my wallet. That loss of control so terrified me that I was never again tempted by drugs. But what really troubled me was the realization that a significant portion of the U.S. military in Vietnam was habitually stoned. For those who remained addicts when they returned to the States, there would truly be no discharge from that war.

Ours was known as the Jungle Battery, a special artillery unit composed of three 105 millimeter howitzers (short-barreled cannons) and three 155 millimeter howitzers. We spent half our time in base camp and half our time in the boondocks where combat engineers bulldozed little bases out of the jungle. Our artillery fired in support of the Special Forces, that is, Army Green Berets who served as officers in command of a battalion of Cambodian mercenaries. Their mission was to go on reconnaissance sweeps hoping to flush the enemy. In fact, I heard President Richard Nixon declare on the radio that we had no mercenaries in South Vietnam at the very time my life depended on them. But they also had good reason to volunteer. For these were ethnic Cambodians deemed racially inferior by Vietnamese. So rather than suffer maltreatment in a Vietnamese army unit, "the Cambods" preferred to sign up with the Yankees. We liked them but felt sorry for them. Since they refused to eat our army chow the Green Berets gave them bags of rice and live chickens, which they strangled and cooked over fires on the perimeter. Nor did they ever seem to bathe or clean up their refuse.

Most disturbing was the fact that the Cambods would not protect themselves, sometimes throwing away their heavy packs and flak jackets while on patrol. Nor could they be bothered to fill sandbags or dig trenches while guarding our base. One Cambod who knew some English told us he did not bother to entrench because his Buddha protected him. (They all wore wooden Buddha charms on strings around their necks, and when under incoming fire they would put their Buddhas in their mouths.) "Wait a minute," asked an American soldier, "how come your buddy got wasted last week if his Buddha was protecting him?" The Cambod replied, "His Buddha Number Ten Buddha. My Buddha Number One Buddha." Those were the troops who stood between us and an enemy-infested jungle.

I was lucky. My tour was relatively quiet, proving the dictum that war is 95 percent boredom punctuated by 5 percent terror. But I did get a dose of the latter. It happened at a remote location perhaps a hundred yards in diameter, called Fire-Support Base Ann. There the Special Forces got their wish when they bumped into an entire regiment of North Vietnamese Army (NVA) regulars. The Cambods got badly chewed up, and when the survivors limped into camp the Green Berets told us to prepare for a fight because they expected the fire base to be attacked after dark. Sure enough, the first rounds landed and the siren sounded about ten o'clock that evening. My shift, consisting of an officer and five artillerymen, was off duty and so had to ride out the assault in our sleeping bunker, which consisted only of a metal culvert layered with sandbags. There was barely room inside for the six canvas cots, so everyone felt trapped and helpless. There was nothing to be done but put on our helmets and flak jackets and sit while shells and rockets exploded around us. Worst of all was the noise, the screeching whine of rockets that flew so fast and burned so hot that they could melt their way through two layers of sandbags and kill everyone inside by sheer concussion.

The violence without and the silence within were terrifying. I do not know what the other men did to contain their fear, but I was moved for the first time in my life to real prayer. Since I had not been raised in a religious family the only prayer that came to mind was one I had learned in high school Latin—*Agnus Dei, qui tollis peccata mundi, miserere nobis, et dona nobis pacem*—and by grace it was perfect: "O, Lamb of God who takest away the sins of the world, have mercy upon us and grant us Thy peace."

Then the world turned yellow, and we were deafened by the loudest crack yet. I must have blacked out momentarily, but then I remember looking into the faces of my comrades—something we all had avoided doing before—and sharing the realization that we were all still alive. Then someone broke the silence with some good old Army cursing: *"S–t! Those mother-effers almost almost blew our effing s–t away."* The next morning, two members of our squad set about digging like ghouls in search of that rocket's nosecone and found their souvenir at the bottom of a hole about eighteen inches deep, just six inches from the edge of our culvert right outside the wall from my cot.

When the shelling stopped, we feared a ground attack, and evidently the enemy did probe our perimeter. But the Cambods and our gun crews fired madly into the blackness until around midnight, when the Air Force arrived in the form of a F4C jet, which dropped napalm around our perimeter. We received a trickle of new ammunition the next day but feared another determined attack come nightfall. It sounds melodramatic now, but many of us wrote "just in case" letters to our loved ones. I was on duty that night, waiting nervously in the artillery fire-control bunker. As usual, we had a transistor radio tuned to the armed forces station: soul music for the blacks, country and western for rural whites, and top 40 hits for the rest of us. About five o'clock in the afternoon an announcer broke into the music with a news flash from Hanoi. Ho Chi Minh, the leader of North Vietnam, had just died, and to mourn his passing the Communists declared a forty-eight-hour ceasefire effective at once! So there would be no attack that night after all, and ever since then I have had a warm spot in my heart for Uncle Ho. At least he knew when to die.

By the time the war resumed, we were not only resupplied but reinforced by units of the First Air Cavalry Division. Colonels and even a brigadier general descended on our little base, and a fleet of helicopters arrived with battalions of riflemen. By day they would search for the NVA regiment. By night the B-52s would bomb to smithereens suspected enemy locations. During a couple of nights we could not sleep for the thunder of bombs. Then one morning a rumor spread around camp: helicopters had neglected to extract some cavalrymen from the jungle the night before. Had they been wasted by the B-52s? That would have been the worst SNAFU imaginable. But the choppers who searched for them found them alive and eagerly waving their arms. Perhaps the bombs had fallen a quarter mile away, or perhaps the soldiers found cover at the bottom of bomb craters. But the conclusion I drew from the episode was that something was very wrong with this war if B-52 bombers could not make a dent against personnel spread out over thousands of square miles of jungle and mountains. From that day forth I ceased to think of our own artillery as offensive weapons and instead viewed them as defensive weapons protecting our behinds until our one year of duty was over.

Until our one year was over. Nothing so illustrates the poor judgment of the Johnson administration and dereliction of duty by the Pentagon brass as their policy of limiting the Vietnam tour of duty to one year (six months for officers). No army in history had ever been sent into battle with the promise that it could go home in 365 days whether or not the war had been won. That is no way to motivate soldiers to fight fiercely and win. That is the way to motivate soldiers to take no risks, invest no emotional capital in their country's cause, and indeed resent the fact that they had to be there a single day. The "short-timer" syndrome was doubly defeating. First, it meant that as soon as soldiers became battle-hardened veterans they were sent home and replaced by another batch of rookies. Second, it meant that the closer any soldier got to his DEROS (date of expected return from overseas), the more risk-averse he became. I saw men get so agoraphobic near the end of their time that they feared walking from the bunker to the mess tent lest the enemy choose that moment to lob in a mortar round. With good reason, too. Six members of our sister battery whose DEROS had arrived were en route to Long Binh when their truck struck a mine. All six were killed.

My own year was up in February 1970. I made it to Long Binh safely only to come down with a temperature of 104 degrees and miss my freedom bird. The doctors slapped me in the malaria ward and proceeded to draw blood from me six times a day for eight days until my arm looked like that of a heroin junkie. I took ice-cold showers whenever the fever was up, re-read jungle-smeared copies of J. R. R. Tolkien's *Lord of the Rings* whenever the fever was down, and all the while wondered why there was no discharge from this war. On the ninth day, a new doctor looked at my chart and said, "Son, I don't know what you've got, but I'm going to shoot you up with tetracyclene and see what happens." The antibiotic worked at once. The fever broke, and sixteen hours later I was on my way home.

Only it turned out that home was as lonely as 'Nam. Among fellow graduate students at the University of Chicago, among friends, even among family my status as a Vietnam veteran was clearly a source of embarrassment, as if my mere presence were a judgment upon hawks and doves alike. It was as if Vietnam veterans were both morally superior *and* inferior to everyone else. Not until 1982, when the Vietnam Veterans Memorial was inaugurated, did the nation hold a parade and pretend at least to honor our service. It so happened I was in Washington, D.C., at the time, doing research for my next book. So I donned my old Army jacket and marched with the New Hampshire contingent. All the way down Constitution Avenue I wanted nothing so much as to bawl out the grief I had repressed for twelve years. But since I was "on display" with the other vets I choked back the tears and waved to the sparse crowds as if to say "Thank you."

In what ways has America itself been Vietnamized? The subject could fill a large book, but let me propose some of the more important ways in which the nation was profoundly altered by the Vietnam War. I attach no value judgments to them. I leave it to readers to ponder whether these effects have been good, bad, ugly, or just ironic. First out of the box was the professionalization of the armed forces following abolition of the draft. National service, the privilege of bearing arms for one's country, has been a civic principle of democracies since ancient Greece and, in modern times, since the French and American revolutions. Free citizens of a republic (which means "public thing") obligated themselves to share the responsibility of defending their heritage of liberty for future generations. But President Johnson's decision to send a conscripted army into a limited, undeclared, unpopular guerilla war in which the security of American democracy was not even at stake proved to be a capital blunder. So President Nixon, in hopes of defusing anti-war protests, ended the draft and not coincidentally extended the vote to eighteen-year-olds. Today, young Americans of either sex have no obligation whatsoever to serve their country in a military or civilian capacity. Instead, the United States, like monarchies of old Europe, has a professional career military hired by the taxpayers to do our fighting for us. Some experts fear that an unhealthy divergence of civil and military cultures is occurring and/or that the military may acquire too much autonomy.

Secondly, our failure in Vietnam helped to sustain a Congressional counterattack on the military prerogatives of the president. All through our history, Capitol Hill and the executive branch have battled for control over foreign policy. But the long national emergency that began with Pearl Harbor and continued throughout the Cold War made the wartime institution of an "imperial presidency" a permanent reality. Since Korea in 1950 the Congress was no longer asked to declare wars anymore. They became "police actions," "conflicts," and later "humanitarian interventions" in which Congress just approved budgets which presidents used to send armed forces anywhere, anytime, at his discretion. A backlash was bound to come, and it came in the early 1970s, with an unpopular war dragging on, Nixon in the White House, and the Democrats with majorities in Congress. Future historians may well interpret the Watergate scandal, which led to Nixon's resignation, as part of this counterattack against what Senator J. William Fulbright called "the arrogance of power." For the attack on Nixon himself was matched by the War Powers Act limiting the right of a president to send U.S. forces overseas, Senator Frank Church's hearings and the resulting intelligence reforms that reined in the CIA and required a president to consult with Congressional committees before approving covert operations, the Jackson–Vanik Amendment and other legislative acts signaling the White House that it could no longer take major foreign initiatives without Congressional input, and the congressional refusal to vote for any more funds for military assistance to South Vietnam. When the final North Vietnamese offensive was launched in 1975 President Gerald Ford was unable to provide the Saigon regime with any more weapons, much less the air support Nixon had promised after the 1973 Paris Peace Accords.

Since 1975 the struggle over foreign policy has continued because Congress, the executive branch, the media, the public at large, and even (or especially) the Pentagon were gripped by the so-called Vietnam Syndrome, that is, the fear that foreign involvements could metastasize into new Vietnams. Hence, secretaries of defense and chairmen of the Joint Chiefs of Staff endorsed the (Caspar) Weinberger Doctrine, the (Colin) Powell Doctrine, and other lists of stringent conditions that ought to be met before American forces are committed to battle. To be sure, President George H. W. Bush won Congressional support for the 1991 Gulf War, but just barely, while Bill Clinton met stubborn resistance from members of Congress over his military interventions in Somalia and the former Yugoslavia.

A fourth way in which the Vietnam War changed American society derived from the fact that in Vietnam the nation fielded its first fully integrated army in history. We know that Vietnam was traumatic for many blacks who had to serve, especially because of the criticism they received from their own civil rights leaders such as Martin Luther King, Jr., not to mention radicals like the Black Panthers. We know, too, that race relations within the Army grew strained. But the fact of the matter was that, even though blacks were somewhat over-represented in combat duty, more than 75 percent of the U.S. Army in Vietnam was Caucasian. And whatever racial tensions existed in the Army during the Vietnam War, the fact also was that it was the first occasion when tens of thousands of Americans of all races were placed in close contact with each other, told to work with each other, fight for each other, and rely on each other. That is why the Vietnam War will someday be considered a big step forward for integration. What is more, Vietnam launched the careers of thousands of successful black officers and non-commissioned officers. Thousands more black veterans went to college under the GI Bill or else made careers for which their military service helped to prepare them.

What of the soldiers and airmen who never came home? The Prisoner of War and Missing in Action (POW/MIA) issue is a fifth way in which the United States was Vietnamized. Not only do our diplomatic relations with Vietnam hinge on whether Hanoi has accounted for all of our dead but U.S. politics are still shaken by it. Ross Perot destroyed Bush's presidency primarily because he suspected that Bush, as vice president, had ignored or impeded the campaign on behalf of MIAs. That in turn raises a broader question: does it matter anymore what the answer is to the question, "What did you do in the sixties?" Statistically, non-veterans are a far larger voting bloc than veterans and their families even today. Twenty years from now the American electorate may have almost no connection with, or memory of, the 1960s or even of those who may serve in subsequent wars. Even in the Vietnam era just 40 percent of draft-age men served in the military, only a quarter of those served in Vietnam, and only one-eighth of those (or about 1 percent of all draft-age men) saw serious combat there. Not long ago it was thought that it would matter a great deal whether a given candidate had served in the military. But President George H. W. Bush began to move beyond the sixties when he selected Dan Quayle as his running mate. Quayle had avoided Vietnam by joining a National Guard unit that did not get called up. Finally, the victory of the draft-dodger Clinton over the war hero Bush in 1992 laid the matter to rest once and for all.

In what other ways has America been Vietnamized? Just look around you. American universities began their great transformation (or some would say, deformation) when "tenured radicals" from the 1960s conducted their "long march through the institutions" which had begun with the anti–Vietnam War protests. Foundations likewise accelerated their lurch to the left. Rock music, once joyous or plaintive, turned angry, negative, and at times downright ugly. Popular culture generally, once supportive of traditional values and national myths, flipped 180 degrees during and after the Vietnam War. Just contrast the patriotic films made by the director Frank Capra during the World War II and early Cold War eras with the films of Francis Ford Coppola such as *Apocalypse Now* and Oliver Stone such as *Platoon* and *Born on the Fourth of July*. Likewise, the adversarial, investigative journalism later made famous by Bob Woodward and Carl Bernstein during the Watergate scandal had first been provoked by LBJ's infamous credibility gap as mainstream reporters began to suspect the White House of not telling the truth about Vietnam (a suspicion confirmed by the leak of the Pentagon Papers in 1971). Point to any major institution in American society and you are likely to find that it was fundamentally altered by that war from which there is no discharge.

A final important and touching Vietnamization was the one made by the Vietnamese themselves, those tens of thousands of courageous refugees (including the "boat people") who fled the Communists during and after the fall of Saigon. Like returning veterans those Vietnamese were ignored by the American people because they were reminders of a nightmare everyone wanted to forget. But the Vietnamese quietly went to work for themselves, their families, and their adopted country by restoring one blighted neighborhood after another.

I myself witnessed them doing it in Oakland, California, and I've since taught their children in class, where they are among the brightest, most diligent students.

American military forces occasionally committed war crimes in Vietnam, but the war itself was not criminal. If anything, its motives were shockingly altruistic, a product of hubris but also of misguided ideals. Never before had a great power spent so many lives and so much treasure so far away, with so little at stake for itself. Ironically, the war that "wasted" Vietnam wasted so much of what it used to mean to be American that the nation will probably still pay penance into the twenty-first century, by which time two or three new generations will have grown up who do not remember Vietnam. But one is left to wonder what traumatic conflicts younger Americans will experience and from which they will find there is no discharge.

★ 10 ★

CAN THE UNITED STATES DO GRAND STRATEGY?[1]

In spring 2003, following the last lecture in my survey course on American diplomatic history since 1776, a brilliant student approached me in the hall to ask a final, confidential question. She said that my course had helped her appreciate how swiftly the United States had become the mightiest nation in history with unprecedented military, economic, and cultural power. But how long would it last? How long did I think America could remain on top?

At first I was tongue-tied, because I was loath to inject a future American leader with either complacency or despair. Then an answer occurred to me. It all depends on whether our country is as unique as we like to believe. If the United States instead follows the pattern of previous nations and empires, then demographic and technological trends, rising foreign threats, strategic folly, hubris, and/or domestic decadence must hurl it into decline, perhaps within fifty years. If, however, our institutions, values, and national character really do amount to a new order for the ages—a potent mix enabling the United States to reinvent itself and force other nations to adapt to the challenges it posed to others—then America may stay on its asymptotic trajectory. I stopped there, but as I walked to my office I recalled Arnold J. Toynbee's historical law to the effect that empires die by suicide, not murder.

As recently as the 1990s the buzzwords in our foreign policy discourse included New World Order, End of History, Unipolar

Moment, Benevolent Hegemony, Indispensable Nation, Assertive Multilateralism, and Washington Consensus. How fast are the mighty fallen, through strategic and financial malpractice, into a reprise of the terrible 1970s, when the buzzwords were imperial overstretch, exhaustion, and decline. Does another Morning in America, as President Ronald Reagan promised, still await us so long as her citizens keep faith with each other, or has the nation reached a climacteric like that of the British Empire during the first twenty years of the twentieth century? In other words, is "American exceptionalism" a source of energy, ingenuity, resilience, and civic virtue which propels our society ever upward? Or is a complacent *belief* in "exceptionalism" the source of profligacy, adventurism, amnesia, and civic vice that portends decline and fall? The defense intellectual Angelo Codevilla, who held that what passes for strategy in the United States is mostly wishful or sloppy thinking, made the same point in operational terms: "Because doing the right thing is important to Americans as to no other people, American politics is like politics nowhere else.... Basing statecraft on the American people's penchant for trying to do the right thing, as did [Abraham] Lincoln and Theodore Roosevelt, brings forth awesome energy.... But using the American people's righteousness as a propellant for private dreams, as did [Woodrow] Wilson, or as cover for tergiversation, as did George W. Bush, is ruinous."[2]

Why begin on such a skeptical, gloomy note? I think it is because my training was that of an old-school European historian, which gave me an outside vantage point from which to view our New World shibboleths more objectively than do most American historians. I suspect my training in European history also inclines me to think about foreign policy in terms of realism, balance of power, contingency, tragedy, irony, folly, unintended consequences, and systemic interactions—all of which are foreign if not repugnant to Americans. Finally, I am a Vietnam veteran skeptical of nation-

and state-building, the winning of hearts and minds, and making the world over in America's image. As the Foreign Policy Research Institute's Paul Dickler recently pointed out, I asked explicitly in the 1997 book *Promised Land, Crusader State*, "can Americans be better Iraqis than Iraqis themselves, or presume to tell Chinese how to be better Chinese? If we try, we can only be poorer Americans."[3] That book was well received except at the *Weekly Standard* and other venues where neoconservatives were already calling for the forcible removal of Saddam Hussein and a "muscular" foreign policy in the name of "national greatness." Following 9/11 they got their way while I dropped out of sight to study early American history. But the invasion of Iraq in 2003 gave us diplomatic historians an excellent case study to impress on students how hard it can be to discern motives in history. We were variously told—with equal conviction—that Operation Iraqi Freedom was "all about" oil, Israel, the war on terror, weapons of mass destruction, the Pentagon's new way of war, neoconservative ideology, the Bush family feud with Saddam, the Bush advisor Karl Rove's re-election calendar, or democratizing the whole Middle East. That suggests one reason why the Iraq campaign was doomed from the outset: too many constituencies had irons in the fire.

Which directly bears on our subject today, to wit: can America do grand strategy? I assume that does not mean, can *Americans* do grand strategy, because an easy answer would be of course they can and usually do so, if poorly. Rather I assume the title means, can the relevant agencies of the U.S. federal government plan, coordinate, and execute grand strategy with sufficient competence to secure the nation and defend its vital interests. That is a complex question that has inspired a recent spate of diagnoses of what ails U.S. strategic planning and what prescriptions are indicated.[4] I do not intend to choose among those expert assessments, much less add to them, since I claim no authority on the subject apart from what diplomatic history can teach. Instead, I imagine my task as that of a rapporteur and provocateur regarding issues that must be addressed if the nation's elites are ever to reach a consensus on what U.S. grand strategy ought to look like in this post–Cold War era.

Two recent quotations may serve to introduce those issues, the first of which is from George W. Bush's 2005 inaugural address, which a shrewd veteran of the Richard Nixon administration pithily described as a "crazy speech":

> We are led, by events and common sense, to one conclusion: The survival of liberty in our land increasingly depends on the success of liberty in other lands. The best hope for peace in our world is the expansion of freedom in all the world. America's vital interests and our deepest beliefs are now one. From the day of our Founding, we have proclaimed that every man and woman on this earth has rights, and dignity, and matchless value, because they bear the image of the Maker of Heaven and earth. Across the generations we have proclaimed the imperative of self-government, because no one is fit to be a master, and no one deserves to be a slave. Advancing these ideals is the mission that created our Nation. It is the honorable achievement of our fathers. Now it is the urgent requirement of our nation's security, and the calling of our time. So it is the policy of the United States to seek and support the growth of democratic movements and institutions in every nation and culture, with the ultimate goal of ending tyranny in our world.[5]

If that was indeed crazy, a second quotation suggests why:

> Strategic planning for American foreign policy is dead, dying, or moribund. This, at least, has been the assessment of several

> commentators and policy-makers in recent years. Michèle Flournoy and Shawn Brimley observed in 2006, "For a country that continues to enjoy an unrivaled global position, it is both remarkable and disturbing that the United States has no truly effective strategy planning process for national security." At an academic conference in 2007, a former director of the State Department's policy planning staff complained that "six years after 9/11, we still don't have a grand strategy".... [And] Council on Foreign Relations president Richard Haass argues that the United States has "squandered" its post-cold war opportunity, concluding, "Historians will not judge the United States well for how it has used these twenty years."

That was the lament of Daniel Drezner, editor of a Brookings Institution study on the forgotten art of grand strategy in 2009.[6]

Such breathtaking vitality in terms of strategic ambition combined with the certifiable death of strategic planning would suggest a disconnect between the muscles and brain of the sole superpower: a disconnect which, Drezner writes, was just as evident in the prideful "ad hoc-ery" of the Bill Clinton years as in the prideful crusade of the second Bush years. Has that disconnect always, or usually, existed, or not? Most contemporary critics agree with Aaron Friedberg's judgment that the United States "has lost the capacity to conduct serious, sustained national strategic planning," which implies that it once had that capacity. Of course, Friedberg and most others held that the United States had that capacity during the early Cold War, as proven by George C. Marshall's 1947 promotion of Policy Planning in the State Department and President Dwight D. Eisenhower's 1953 promotion of strategic planning in the Pentagon. The grand strategy designed and executed over the long haul was George F. Kennan's Containment, hence the corollary that ever since 1991 the United States has been awaiting some new Kennan to tell us what new grand strategy ought to focus American energies. Thus, there is a tendency in our strategic discourse, as illustrated by the Brookings volume, to assume that Containment represented the norm and post–Cold War drift the aberration.[7]

A broader *tour d'horizon* of American history, however, might suggest otherwise, as illustrated by another glaring juxtaposition of quotes, the first of which is from Alexis de Tocqueville's celebrated 1835 study *Democracy in America:* "There are two men who have imparted to American foreign policy a tendency that is still being followed today; the first is Washington and the second Jefferson...." Their principles of neutrality, no permanent alliances, and no granting or soliciting special privileges from foreign nations, "so plain and just as to be easily understood by the people, have greatly simplified the foreign policy of the United States. As the Union takes no part in the affairs of Europe, it has, properly speaking, no foreign interests to discuss, since it has, as yet, no powerful neighbors on the American continent.... The foreign policy of the United States is eminently expectant; it consists more in abstaining than in acting."

Tocqueville continues:

> It is therefore very difficult to ascertain, at present, what degree of sagacity the American democracy will display in the conduct of the foreign policy of the country; upon this point its adversaries as well as its friends must suspend their judgment. As for myself, I do not hesitate to say that it is especially in the conduct of their foreign relations that democracies appear to me decidedly inferior to other governments.... Foreign politics demand scarcely any of those qualities which are peculiar in a democracy; they require, on the contrary, the perfect use of almost all those in which it is deficient. Democracy is favorable to the increase of the internal resources of a state; it diffuses wealth and comfort... [but] a democracy can only with great

> difficulty regulate the details of an important undertaking, persevere in a fixed design, and work out its execution in spite of serious obstacles. It cannot combine its measures with secrecy or await the consequences with patience.[8]

So democracies cannot do grand strategy, or else cannot do it well or for long: such was the judgment rendered by the Frenchman 170 years ago. What then, does one make of the even more famous conclusion to his chapter on the "three races" populating the continent?

> There are at the present time two great nations in the world, which started from different points, but seem to tend towards the same end. I allude to the Russians and the Americans.... The conquests of the American are gained by the plowshare; those of the Russian by the sword. The Anglo-American relies upon personal interest to accomplish his ends and gives free scope to the unguided strength and common sense of the people; the Russian centers all the authority of society in a single arm. The principal instrument of the former is freedom; of the latter, servitude. Their starting-point is different and their courses are not the same; yet each of them seems marked out by the will of Heaven to sway the destinies of half the globe.[9]

Bottom line: in that era of Jacksonian Democracy and Manifest Destiny Tocqueville observed a nation that was uninterested in practicing grand strategy as Europeans understood it and yet was destined to achieve grand strategic success in terms of growth, power, and security that no other empire save gigantic Russia could match. Talk about a disconnect! Can it be that the United States flourished over its first century despite, or because of, its government's lack of any self-conscious grand strategy? Or can the elements, however passive, of nineteenth-century American foreign and military policy be rightly deemed grand strategy? Or can a civil faith—faith that divine Providence, historical progress, or one's own righteousness mystically guarantees the national destiny—function as a sort of force multiplier or self-fulfilling prophecy?

According to Tocqueville's analysis the U.S. government needed to do little to realize the nation's destiny except to avoid gratuitous interventions overseas that would risk making North America a target of Europe's Great Powers. The unilateral neutralism of Thomas Jefferson's "no entangling alliances," the ideological prudence of John Quincy Adams's "not going abroad in search of monsters to destroy," the republican separatism of James Monroe's Doctrine, and the expansionist Manifest Destiny heralded by Andrew Jackson appear to be mutually reinforcing principles that amounted to a brilliant strategy which could exploit the United States' diplomatic, economic, and military advantages to maximum effect. They just do not look like grand strategy of the sort the Prussian General Staff or British Admiralty understood during the nineteenth century or would have expressed in so many words.

Hence, two big issues that scholars and strategists need to address are whether grand strategy needs to be articulated for it to be said to exist at all, and if not whether grand strategy can be said to move a nation even when its fluctuating roster of less than competent leaders are unsure why they do anything. Auguste Comte said that demography is destiny and Robert Strausz-Hupé that you cannot argue with geography, but what if there can be logic to statecraft even though its practitioners are just acting on instinct? Why not? That is what experts at poker or bridge call "card sense." By contrast, the great French diplomat Charles Maurice de Talleyrand defined the art of statecraft as the ability to foresee the inevitable and expedite its occurrence. The great German diplomat Otto von Bismarck defined politics as the art of the possible and said statecraft amounted to hearing "the steps of God sounding through events" and "grasping the hem of His garment." The American statesman Henry Kissinger praised as wise leaders those who can look destiny in the eye without flinching, but without attempting to play God. So it would seem that successful grand strategy is a mix of acquiescence and aspiration, observation and imagination, prudence and audacity, prideful mastery of men and humble service of Providence, not to mention meticulous intellectual analysis and (here's where the instinct comes in) a deft sense of timing which to the victimized or the envious seems to be contemptible luck.

To those who doubt the U.S. government can do grand strategy well (something on which "beltway bandits" and critical bloggers seem to agree),[10] the online STRATFOR Geopolitical Diary has a definitive answer. In anticipation of the Fourth of July it posted an essay celebrating what it professed to be Americans' overarching, automatic, and now 230-year-old grand strategy. It began (rightly) by tracing strategic thought back to eighteenth-century Britain inasmuch as the thirteen colonies could aspire to their mother country's geopolitical advantages as an insular, maritime, commercial power benefiting from the rivalries and balance of power prevailing among its continental Europe rivals. Another idea it failed to mention, however, was the impressive, exemplary, hard-won unity among England, Wales, Scotland, and Ireland. That was what freed the Crown, Parliament, Bank of England, Board of Trade, and Royal Navy to mobilize national resources for the pursuit of power and wealth abroad. Following 1776 the Founders of the United States had the United Kingdom (and the United Provinces of the Netherlands) very much on their minds.

STRATFOR went on to postulate the existence of "five core rules" or "geopolitical imperatives" that have allegedly "determined the behavior" of the United States. The first was to secure strategic depth by pushing inland from the Atlantic coast, crossing the Appalachians, and (in the 1783 treaty following the War of Independence) obtaining title to all the land east of the Mississippi. The second was to expand that strategic depth across the continent. That was accomplished through the Louisiana Purchase, the War of 1812, treaties demilitarizing the U.S.–Canadian boundary, annexation of half of the Oregon Territory, and especially the Mexican War of 1846–48, which yielded all of Texas, California, and the lands in between.

The third step was "to gain control of the ocean approaches," an aspiration accomplished in the Caribbean and the Pacific by the dawn of the twentieth century. "Once a nation controls its approaches, the next logical step—the fourth imperative—is to reach farther and control the oceans themselves": That goal was achieved in World War II and its aftermath when the United States secured its grip on both oceans and made alliances with the littoral nations of Europe and Asia. All that remained was the fifth imperative, which was to prevent any other power from dominating the Eurasian landmass. That is what mandated the Containment strategy and deterrence of the Soviet bloc and Communist China. STRATFOR concludes: "These five strategic imperatives are not found anywhere in the Constitution of laws of the United States. But every one of the country's 44 presidents, regardless of intention, has conformed to them, compelled by the inexorable logic of geography.... And the same geopolitical imperatives that drove these actions will shape American efforts into the future—just as they have since 1776."[11]

How credible is that? I would certainly dispute the assertion that every single president conformed to this programmatic template. On the contrary, presidents who have given evidence of strategic vision are a decided minority. But the very notion of American traditions of foreign policy as described in my book *Promised Land, Crusader State* implies continuities even, or especially, when the president and secretary of state are ignorant, distracted, or running on autopilot because no crisis beckons. I argued that (1) Liberty, Unity, and Independence at home; (2) Unilateralism as urged in Washington's Farewell and Jefferson's Inaugural; (3) the American System of States declared in the Monroe Doctrine; and (4) continental Expansion comprised a mutually reinforcing set of principles which enabled the American Union's spectacular growth in spite of the catastrophic civil war which nearly tore the nation apart.[12]

A measure of how successful the United States has been might be glimpsed in the failed trajectories of Germany and Japan. The historian Paul Kennedy, in his classic *The Rise and Fall of the Great Powers*, described those countries as in effect "middle powers" hoping to join the world powers—the British, Russian, and American empires—that seemed likely to dominate the twentieth century to come. He thus discarded the usual periodization of international history with its watersheds in the years 1871, 1890, and 1914, and instead began his chapters on the rise of Meiji Japan and Imperial Germany in the year 1885.[13] In two world wars over the following sixty years the German and Japanese armies and navies conducted military operations at the highest level and won serial stunning triumphs. But they both erred in believing that successful campaigns on the operational or strategic level might alter *grand* strategic realities...and both suffered cataclysmic defeats in the end. Indeed, a good definition of sound grand strategy might simply postulate an equation of ends and means so sturdy that a nation or alliance triumphs in spite of serious *setbacks* in specific campaigns, an obvious example being Allied grand strategy during World War II.[14]

During the nineteenth century, of course, the United States was so blessed it was able to realize the first three of STRATFOR's geopolitical steps without much resistance and indeed on a pittance. Moreover, Americans could defend what they had and grasp what they wished without much aforethought. To be sure, the authors of our grand foreign policy traditions understood what they were doing and why. As early as 1787 Alexander Hamilton wrote in *Federalist* No. 8: "If we are wise enough to preserve the Union we may for ages enjoy an advantage similar to that of an insulated situation. Europe is at a great distance from us. Her colonies in our vicinity will likely to continue too much disproportioned in strength to be able to give us any dangerous annoyance. Extensive military establishments cannot, in this position, be necessary to our security.... This is an idea not superficial or futile, but solid and weighty." Throughout the ante-bellum era a number of statesmen such as John Quincy Adams and James K. Polk, and a handful of military professionals such as General Winfield Scott and naval Lieutenant Matthew Maury, meditated on grand strategy. But they accomplished their goals with a mostly miniature army and modest navy (what political scientists would call "free security") such that American pioneers and merchants took expansion for granted. Henry James did not wonder at that insouciance because, he wrote in 1879, "That generation which grew up with the century witnessed during a period of fifty years the immense, uninterrupted material development of the young Republic...there seems to be little room for surprise that it should have implanted a kind of superstitious faith in the grandeur of the country, its duration, its immunity from the usual troubles of earthly empires.... From this conception of the American future the sense of its having problems to solve was blissfully absent; there were no difficulties in the programme, no looming complication, no rocks ahead."[15]

By the 1870s and 1880s, however, responsible American officials noticed that their heretofore friendly environment was in rapid flux. The industrial revolution had spread throughout Europe and had begun in Japan. Commerce, shipping, and communications were fast becoming global, as illustrated by the bulk-cargo steamships, the trans-Atlantic telegraph cable, the Transcontinental Railroad and Suez Canal of 1869, and the shift in 1876 of the global futures market for cereals from Danzig, Germany, to the Chicago Board of Trade. Soon not only the British but many new challengers for naval and colonial power were penetrating parts of the world where American elites believed they had vital interests. In other words, it was high time they began to institutionalize a grand strategy.

Among those who did were Commodore Stephen B. Luce, founder of the Naval War College in 1884; Captain Alfred Thayer Mahan, who wrote *The Influence of Sea Power upon History*; Secretary of the Navy Benjamin Tracy, who persuaded Congress to begin constructing a modern two-ocean navy in 1890; the steel and shipbuilding magnates who forged America's first military-industrial complex; and Progressive publicists, both secular and religious, who promoted assertive foreign policies beginning in the 1890s. (It was they who first coined the term "isolationist" as a pejorative.) So even though the Spanish–American War of 1898 came as a surprise the drift into Yankee imperialism during and after the war was long prepared. No one personified the new era so much as Theodore Roosevelt.[16] Ironically, the only aspect of overseas empire which did not serve the nation well was the allegedly humanitarian, "white man's burden" gloss on colonization because it naively implied that the U.S. government possessed the means, the wisdom, and indeed the right to reign over and presumably uplift foreign cultures.

Nevertheless, that nation- or state-building component explains why I identified Progressive Imperialism as the first in a new, twentieth-century series of foreign policy traditions. For ever since then American policy elites, responding in many cases to wars and revolutions abroad, have quit trying to prevent the outside world from perturbing American life and instead have endeavored to use American power to reshape the outside world. Thus Wilsonianism, the fifth U.S. foreign policy tradition, universalized the faux humanitarianism of Progressive Imperialism and purported to do for the world what America had manifestly been unable to do for

Cuba or the Philippines. But quixotic Wilsonianism failed during and after both world wars, which is why the Truman administration adopted a sixth tradition, Containment, to frame its struggle against the Communist bloc. The execution of Containment, not least in the Vietnam War, proved to be costly, morally compromising, and ultimately futile. But since the strategy was grounded in realism and was periodically updated in creative ways (for instance during the first terms of Harry Truman, Dwight Eisenhower, Richard Nixon, and Ronald Reagan) Containment managed to prevail in the end.[17]

The eighth and final new tradition in my matrix is something I call Global Meliorism: the belief that Americans, whatever their self-interest, have a mission, a calling, to spread peace, prosperity, and human rights around the world. From Herbert Hoover's humanitarian projects to the Harry Truman administration's Marshall Plan to the Jimmy Carter administration's emphasis on human rights American leaders have repeatedly justified their foreign policies with appeals to Global Meliorism. Hoover said the way to fight Communism in Russia was with food, not with guns. John F. Kennedy's "best and brightest" advisors said the way to defeat Communism in the Third World was to offer South Vietnam and other nations a better social and political revolution than our adversaries. George W. Bush said the way to defeat terrorism in the Muslim world was to drain the swamps of despair and disaffection by democratizing the whole Middle East.[18]

That list of eight major foreign policy traditions would seem to suggest Americans have indeed had rich and varied experience with grand strategy. During the nineteenth century they pursued, if only intuitively, principles which ensured their nation's growth into a continental giant. Beginning in 1898 Americans reacted to revolutions (e.g., the Mexican, Chinese, and Russian) and wars (especially the Great War) which threw up new threats and opportunities that seemed to compel Washington, D.C., to react. It did react, on an enormous scale, throughout most of the twentieth century. But the way I read the historical record, the American strategies based mostly on realist premises have been mostly successful. The American strategies based mostly on idealistic or ideological premises have been at least partly abortive.

Robert Kagan, the neoconservative pundit, does not agree. Indeed, he is embarked on a decade-long mission to write narrative histories presuming to debunk those of us in the realist school who advocate prudence and restraint in foreign policy. His first volume, *Dangerous Nation*, simply insists (for its evidence proves nothing) that unilateralism and non-intervention did not characterize U.S. foreign policy, but rather that Americans (or at least their elites) have asserted their nation's mission to liberate the whole human race, and not just by example but by force, if necessary. Kagan has even called George Washington a neocon.[19] As history this is rubbish, pure propaganda written to justify President Bush's War on Terror and "freedom agenda" in the mid-2000s. It only seemed for a few years back in the 1990s that the neocons might be on to something. Thus did Francis Fukuyama herald the universal triumph of liberal democracy and free markets and called the end of the Cold War the end of history itself. Thus did Michael Mandelbaum celebrate the "ideas that conquered [past tense] the world."[20] But history has a way of happening, and by the 2000s it should have been obvious that the trillions of dollars the Bush administration was squandering on the War on Terror would accomplish next to nothing and redound to the benefit only of revisionist powers such as China, Russia, and Iran.

Where do more credible analysts of American grand strategy stand on the issues raised so far? They are seemingly all over the place, although all make some good points.

Andrew Bacevich takes exception to my schematic of U.S. foreign policy traditions for the opposite reason of Kagan's. Rejecting both my emphasis on geopolitics and Kagan's emphasis on ideology he advances an economic interpretation of what he calls "the new American militarism" reminiscent in many respects of William Appleman Williams's "Open Door" school of history. Its adherents were not strictly Marxist, but did advance a mono-causal economic theory for what Williams called the tragedy of American diplomacy. The real driving force behind U.S. foreign relations during all eras of history was the capitalist appetite for new markets, resources, and customers abroad. Therein lay the roots of tragedy because in order to meet the growing expectations of their growing population American elites were ineluctably drawn to imperialism that belied their liberationist rhetoric. Bacevich blames America's strategic folly on an iron triangle of business, political, and military elites who alone benefit from the nation's peripatetic crusades. Indeed, the statistics he cites on American debt and overextension suggest a Ponzi scheme at the end of its tether.[21]

Christopher Layne, a paleoconservative political scientist of libertarian leanings, is just as critical of American imperial overstretch. But his research on its origins leads him to spy an essential continuity in American grand strategy after and *before* 9/11, after and *before* the Cold War, even after and *before* World War II. He identifies the abiding U.S. grand strategy as one of "extra-regional hegemony" and traces its roots to the postwar planning of the Franklin D. Roosevelt administration, which began in 1940 a year and a half prior to Pearl Harbor. FDR's brain trust was tasked with drafting the blueprints for the American Century, that is, American economic and political dominance over Europe, the Middle East, and East Asia. The later emergence of an intransigent Soviet Union merely added another incentive to the mix.

Most political science theorists would not have predicted such behavior. But FDR knew that American power would be so overwhelming at victory in the war that for the good of the world as well as Americans the nation must bid for hegemony. The foreign policy and business elites (especially the financial sectors) needed no persuasion. For they, too, believed for the most part that peace and prosperity would not be wholly secure until democracy and open markets prevailed everywhere. So they actively promoted hegemony through global engagement under the guise of an *anti-hegemonic* theory, be it deterrence, modernization, democratic peace, or liberal regime theory. The world that FDR made has never faded away, not during the Cold War and not after the Cold War. Instead, American pretensions have only grown, involving the United States in "forever wars" that systematically drained that nation's military, economic, and financial strength.

Layne then surveys the grand strategies available to the United States, concluding that the most sustainable is offshore balancing. Accordingly, he would terminate U.S. security treaties with NATO, Japan, and South Korea; stop pestering China and Russia about their internal affairs; stand offshore of the Persian Gulf; and launch crash programs to escape dependence on foreign oil.[22] Other prestigious scholars of international relations such as the realist political scientists Barry Posen (MIT), Stephen Van Evera (MIT), and Stephen Walt (Harvard) also plead for a grand strategy based on restraint, while Colin Dueck (George Mason) has recently criticized American strategic culture for its susceptibility to utopian commitments sold to the public with lofty rhetoric and the promise of minimal costs. "It was an illusion," he writes, "to think that a stable, secure, and democratic Iraq could arise without a significant long-term U.S. investment of both blood and treasure." But the Bush administration seemed really to believe Secretary of Defense Donald Rumsfeld when he claimed the 9/11 attacks were a golden opportunity "to refashion the world." So Bush pursued "extremely ambitious and idealistic foreign policy goals without initially providing the full or proportionate means to achieve those goals. In this sense George

W. Bush was very much a Wilsonian."[23] Dueck concludes that the choice between a strategy of hegemony and a strategy of liberal internationalism is "almost beside the point. Neither strategy will work if Americans are unwilling to incur the full costs and risks that are implied in either case."[24]

In any event, as the wizened veterans Richard Betts and Leslie Gelb have observed, no government, whether authoritarian or democratic, can really "do" grand strategy. For that would require accurate forecasting of future crises, foreknowledge of the outcomes of alternative choices, accurate calculation of the variables and stakes in specific conflicts, accurate prediction of adversaries' reactions, and the avoidance of bureaucratic incompetence. As Betts and Gelb observed during the Vietnam War era, the bargaining processes which occur between the White House and the bureaucracies and the executive branch and Congress invariably privilege "Option B," i.e., incremental half-measures that never meet the requirements of coherent strategy.[25]

Finally, as Drezner wrote after the electorate repudiated the George W. Bush administration in the 2006 midterm elections, the government had been hurled back to square one, awaiting a new George Kennan who, like Samuel Beckett's Godot, never shows up. But if the gloom-sayers are right we may be even worse off than that because the "greatest generation" that was "present at the creation" of Cold War grand strategy was not even as successful as we think. For instance, John Lewis Gaddis has made a strong historical case that NSC 68 was really a deeply flawed blueprint.[26] Thomas Wright has indicted the Truman administration and argued that the only lessons to be learned are from its mistakes.[27] Finally and most obviously, what reason is there to assume that strategic principles from the 1940s have any relevance in the twenty-first century? The defense analyst Andrew Krepinevich has written chillingly of the "seven deadly scenarios" threatening the world today, none of which even existed during the latter half of the twentieth century.[28] Not that self-nominated candidates for Kennan's mantle do not abound. Jeffrey Legro, Michael Mandelbaum, Anatol Lieven and John Hulsman, John Ikenberry and Anne-Marie Slaughter, Benjamin Page and Marshall Bouton, Amitai Etzioni, and Drezner himself have all thrown hats into the ring at one juncture or another.[29] But all of them fall flat because none has anything particularly original to propose. Instead, they just reflexively damn the Bush administration's hubris while reaffirming human rights, democracy, and an open economy as the proper American goals. The result is some rhetorical hybrid reminiscent of Dr. Dolittle's Pushmi-Pullyu, the beast with two heads and no rump. We are told to be visionary yet pragmatic (Legro), ethical yet realistic (Lieven and Hulsman), realistic yet Wilsonian (Fukuyama), moral yet muscular (Eztioni), focused yet flexible (Drezner himself).[30]

Having witnessed so many deflating cycles in politics and foreign defense officials, let us inwardly digest this list of common strategic blunders authored by a UCLA professor of business:[31]

1. Failure to recognize or take seriously the fact that resources are scarce
2. Mistaking strategic goals for strategy
3. Failure to recognize or state the strategic problem
4. Choosing unattainable or poor strategic goals
5. Failure to define the challenge competitively
6. Making false presumptions about one's competence
7. Loss of focus due to too many stakeholders and bureaucratic processes
8. Inaccurate determination of one's competitive advantages
9. Failure to realize that few people have the cognitive skills needed for strategy
10. Failure to understand the adversary.

To that I would add only this:

11. *Failure to understand ourselves.*

In his "Silent Majority speech" President Richard Nixon assured listeners that North Vietnam could not defeat America; "only Americans can do that." I suspect that were we to run our minds over the whole sweep of history we could readily trace our nation's disasters and detours in good part to our own leaders' foibles. They are legion. We are human. But chief among them is a tendency to be so dazzled by our destiny and sure of our purity that we cannot see ourselves as others see us. That is why we must hearken to the great eighteenth-century British statesman Edmund Burke, who warned, "Among precautions against ambition it may not be amiss to take one precaution against our own. I must fairly say, I dread our own power and own ambition; I dread our being too much dreaded.... [W]e may say that we shall not abuse this astonishing and hitherto unheard of power. But every other nation will think we shall abuse it. It is impossible but that, sooner or later, this state of things must produce a combination against us which may end in our ruin."[32]

Grand strategy, whatever other ambitions it serves, cannot aim to abolish itself. Rather, the most the statesman can do, in the wise words of the Harvard political scientist Samuel Huntington, is to imagine his ship of state on an infinite sea, with no port behind and no destination ahead, his sole responsibility being to weather the storms certain to come, and keep the ship on an even keel so long as he has the bridge.

★ 11 ★

THE CONSTITUTIONAL HISTORY OF U.S. FOREIGN POLICY, PART I

The First American Century as Promised Land[1]

Four months after his inauguration President George Washington and Secretary of War Henry Knox tried to perform a Constitutional duty by seeking the advice and consent of the Senate with regard to a treaty with the Creek Indian nation. Accordingly, on Saturday, August 22, 1789, they visited the Senate chambers at Federal Hall, 26 Wall Street, in New York City. Knox handed a list of seven questions to Washington, who passed them on to the president of the Senate, John Adams, whose effort to read them was drowned out by street noise. Raising his voice, Adams repeated the first query and asked for a simple yes or no answer. A nervous silence followed until Pennsylvania's William Maclay insisted on having all the documents concerning the treaty read aloud and made a motion to refer the whole matter to an ad hoc committee. Washington "started up in a violent fret," barked, "This defeats every purpose of my coming here," then muttered on his way out the door that he would be damned if he ever went there again.[2]

Thus began the contentious courtship between the executive and legislative branches of government over the conduct of American foreign relations: a sort of perennial *pas de deux* in which the parties are not sure whether to dance or to wrestle over the delegated and implied powers granted them under the Constitution. The dean of legal scholars in the field, Columbia University Professor Louis Henkin, called it "the tension in the twilight zone" that resulted from a design for government that was "a mosaic of everyone's second choices" and established "a strange system, the strangest in the world." For all that, it has been made to work most of the time under radically different and rapidly changing circumstances precisely because of the vagaries, ambiguities, and yawning silences of our amazingly terse Constitution.[3]

Just for starters, the Washington anecdote illustrates a fundamental conundrum of our representative, constitutional, and more or less democratic republic. Trusting foreign relations—issues of war and peace—solely to executive fiat was anathema to Americans then as now. But trusting such grave matters solely to the fractious, feckless committee known as Congress seemed even worse. That is why the constitutional history of U.S. foreign relations has challenged every generation of Americans to shun extremes and draw instead on their deep reserves of pragmatism, pretense, and compromise.

Washington, the indispensable man whose availability to serve as the first president undoubtedly reassured skeptics among Anti-Federalists and Federalists alike, established the precedents and principles that shaped U.S. foreign policy for a century. He eschewed royal pomp, yet bestowed on his office a high republican dignity. He worked with Congress to create the executive departments of State, War, and Treasury. He established the doctrines of executive privilege and prerogative in foreign affairs with the full support of Secretary of State Thomas Jefferson, who declared in 1790: "The transaction of business with foreign nations is executive altogether."

Likewise, Washington took the initiative when the wars of the French Revolution erupted. Not only did he judge neutrality the only wise posture for the fragile new nation but he claimed for the executive the power to declare peace, as it were, even though Congress had the power to declare war. So Washington decreed in April 1794 that the United States "should in sincerity and good faith adopt and pursue a conduct friendly and impartial toward the belligerant [sic] Powers."[4]

Pursuant to that Washington dispatched John Jay, then Chief Justice of the Supreme Court, overseas. He was the first in a long line of presidential alter egos in foreign affairs that would include James Monroe (for Jefferson), Nicholas Trist (for James K. Polk), Thurlow Weed (for Abraham Lincoln), Edward M. House (for Woodrow Wilson), Harry Hopkins (for Franklin Roosevelt), Henry Kissinger (for Richard Nixon), and Richard Holbrooke (for Bill Clinton and Barack Obama). The commercial treaty with Britain that Jay brought home sparked bitter controversy in 1795, but its ultimate ratification meant Senate acceptance of a pattern whereby the executive hammered out deals with foreign governments before submitting their terms to his own. Washington also received foreign envoys and, in the case of the egregious Citizen Edmond-Charles Genêt for example, demanded their recall. Washington served as commander-in-chief in person and in uniform during the Whiskey Rebellion on the Pennsylvania frontier. But in all things he honored the Constitution; deferred to Congress over appointments, treaties, and appropriations to meet crises such as those caused by the Barbary Pirates; and used the presidency as a "bully pulpit" when he warned against factional strife over foreign affairs. In nearly every case Washington's acts became precedents that shaped the process whereby U.S. foreign policy practice evolved ever since.

Finally, Washington issued a Farewell Address in September 1796 that established "the true policy" of the United States, indeed a grand strategy which nearly every American statesman and citizen held sacred for one hundred years.[5] It is worth dwelling upon, not only because it pronounced all four of what I call the "Promised Land" traditions that informed U.S. foreign policy in the nineteenth century but because it remains especially salient today.

Washington began with an invocation: "Heaven may continue to you the choicest tokens of its beneficence; that your union and brotherly affection may be perpetual; that the free constitution, which is the work of your hands, may be sacredly maintained; that its administration in every department may be stamped with wisdom and virtue; that the happiness of the people of these States, under the auspices of liberty, may be complete, by so careful a preservation and so prudent a use of this blessing, as will acquire to them the glory of recommending it to the applause, the affection, and adoption of every nation, which is yet a stranger to it." He then said, "Here, perhaps, I ought to stop," but in fact he had only begun because Washington meant to instruct his countrymen on the sorts of behavior they must nurture in order to earn that blessing. He spoke first of unity, "the main pillar in the edifice of your real independence, the support of your tranquillity at home, your peace abroad; of your safety; of your prosperity; of that very Liberty, which you so highly prize." He warned lest internal divisions born of personal ambition, faction, party, economic or regional interest dissolve the bonds of the Union that American independence, liberty, and opportunity all presupposed. Since the Constitution had forged a more perfect Union, "Respect for its authority, compliance with its laws, acquiescence in its measures, are duties enjoined by the fundamental maxims of true Liberty." Indeed, Washington used the word liberty *fifteen times* in his brief address.

A liberty-loving people endowed with a good Constitution must still be vigilant because "The spirit of encroachment tends to consolidate the powers of all departments in one, and thus to create, whatever the form of government, a real despotism.... The necessity of reciprocal checks in the exercise of political power, by dividing and distributing it into different depositories, and constituting each the Guardian of the Public Weal against invasions by the others, has been evinced by experiments ancient and modern." But to Washington the most "indispensable supports of political health" were spiritual, because "reason and experience both forbid us to expect, that national morality can prevail in the exclusion of religious principle." Moving to particulars, Washington preached *prudence regarding money*: "As a very important source of strength and security, cherish public credit. One method of preserving it is to use it as sparingly as possible; avoiding occasions of expense by cultivating peace, but remembering also that timely disbursements to prepare for danger frequently prevent much greater disbursements to repel it; avoiding likewise the accumulation of debts, not only by shunning occasions of expense, but by vigorous exertions in time of peace to discharge the debts which unavoidable wars may have occasioned."

Washington then preached *prudence regarding power*. The United States should "Observe good faith and justice towards all Nations; cultivate peace and harmony with all. Religion and Morality enjoin this conduct; and can it be, that good policy does not equally enjoin it? It will be worthy of a free, enlightened, and at no distant period, a great Nation, to give to mankind the magnanimous and too novel example of a people always guided by an exalted justice and benevolence.... In the execution of such a plan, nothing is more essential, than that permanent, inveterate antipathies against particular Nations, and passionate attachment for others, should be excluded; and that, in place of them, just and amicable feelings towards all should be cultivated. The Nation, which indulges towards another an habitual hatred, or an habitual fondness, is in some degree a slave." Alluding to the rancor in the 1790s over the Citizen Genêt Affair and Jay Treaty with Britain, Washington warned: "Against the insidious wiles of foreign influence...the jealousy of a free people ought to be constantly awake; since history and experience prove, that foreign influence is one of the baneful foes of Republican Government." Indeed, "The Great Rule of conduct for us, in regard to foreign nations, is, in extending our commercial relations, to have with them as little political connexion [sic] as possible.... Europe has a set of primary interests, which to us have none, or a very remote relation.... Our detached and distant situation invites and enables us to pursue a different course. If we remain one people, under an efficient government, the period is not far off, when we may defy material injury from external annoyance...when belligerent nations, under the impossibility of making acquisitions upon us, will not lightly hazard the giving us provocation; when we may choose peace or war, as our interest, guided by justice, shall counsel. Why forgo the advantages of so peculiar a situation? Why quit our own to stand upon foreign ground? Why, by interweaving our destiny with that of any part of Europe, entangle our peace and prosperity in the toils of European ambition, rivalship, interest, humor, or caprice? It is our true policy to steer clear of permanent alliances with any portion of the foreign world."

Then, hopeful realist to the last, Washington closed: "In offering to you, my countrymen, these counsels of an old and affectionate friend, I dare not hope they will make the strong and lasting impression I could wish; that they will control the usual current of the passions, or prevent our nation from running the course which has hitherto marked the destiny of nations. But, if I may flatter myself that they may be productive of some partial benefit, some occasional good; that they may now and then recur to moderate the fury of party spirit, to warn against the mischiefs of foreign intrigue, to guard against the impostures of pretended patriotism; this hope will be full recompense for the solicitude for your welfare, by which they have been dictated."[6]

Those who have read my book *Promised Land, Crusader State: The American Encounter with the World since 1776* may recall the four great traditions that shaped U.S. foreign relations during the nineteenth century: Liberty, Unity, and Independence at Home (usually misconstrued as "American Exceptionalism"); Unilateralism (usually misconstrued as "Isolationism"); an American System of States; and Continental Expansion.[7] At first glance my choices would seem, if you will, unexceptional. But the historical evidence imposed on me interpretations of those traditions that differ from conventional wisdom. For instance, I was persuaded that the Founders did believe, or wanted to believe, that the United States would be exceptional in the sense of New Order for the Ages endowed with civil and religious liberty and a grand destiny under Providence. But contrary to myth the Founders did *not* conclude that U.S. foreign policy need be especially idealistic, pacifist, ideological, or militant. On the contrary, the Founders and their successors were realists who understood that flawed human nature required that power be checked and balanced. They likewise understood that naive, reckless, or arrogant behavior toward other countries, even or especially for the best of motives, could put at risk what really bestowed on the nation its Liberty, Unity, and Independence. In other words, the United States was to be rendered exceptional by what it *was* at home, not by what it *did or did not do* abroad. Hence the purpose of foreign and defense policy was to prevent Old World empires from corrupting the American experiment so it might prove that self-governing peoples can survive and prosper.

The second foreign policy tradition was a natural corollary. Call it Neutralism or Unilateralism, but *don't* call it Isolationism, a disparaging term of domestic propaganda not even coined until the 1890s. In fact Americans were always deeply engaged in the Atlantic and Pacific worlds, while Washington urged friendship and commerce with all nations. His Great Rule simply warned against gratuitous meddling in European affairs lest Americans harm their own interests, surrender their freedom of action, invite attacks from foreign powers, and forfeit the geographic advantages a beneficent God had bestowed on them.

Unilateralism in turn required that Europe abstain from meddling in the Americas. Hence the third tradition was invocation of an American System of republics off-limits to Old World monarchies. This aspiration was not given full expression, of course, until the Monroe Doctrine of 1823, and it remained something of a bluff for seventy years. But the notion of a separate sphere is already there in Washington's Farewell Address.

The fourth tradition, Expansionism, was a natural corollary of all the above. It was labeled Manifest Destiny by the Jacksonian publicist John O'Sullivan in 1839, but was bred in Americans' bones ever since Jamestown and Plymouth Rock. It inspired Benjamin Franklin to insist that the British cede to the new nation all the lands east of the Mississippi River (save Florida). It inspired Washington to plunge into private land speculations on the Virginia frontier. It inspired the Jefferson administration's spectacular Louisiana Purchase. It was an ulterior motive behind the Monroe Doctrine because—if North America was to be off-limits to new foreign colonial claims—then unoccupied western lands must be annexed by the United States itself. Finally, territorial expansion would allow each generation of Americans to bequeath liberty and opportunity to their children and grandchildren.

Washington's Farewell Address thus conflated moral and material messages in the manner of Moses's farewell to the Israelites in Deuteronomy. He promised Americans their nation would surely become what Jefferson called an Empire of Liberty, the freest, richest, mightiest nation in history, but only if Americans obeyed his commandments to remain united, virtuous, frugal, prudent, and vigilant, insulating their Promised Land and spreading its blessings throughout North America. To put it another way, Washington sketched out a grand strategy to transform the loose chain of Atlantic settlements into a continental empire, but only if its principles were faithfully followed. Indeed they were, for the most part, which is why the *Oxford History of the United States* volume on foreign relations is titled "From Colony to Superpower."[8]

But before examining that strategy in operation we should make a brief excursus regarding a question relevant both to historical and contemporary diplomatic debates. How did late-eighteenth-century Anglo-American statesmen understand the word "empire"? What did they mean to connote when they used it themselves? Americans always boasted that their nation was born in a revolt *against* empire, and have wanted to believe—usually with good reason—that the United States opposes colonial empires such as the British or French or ideological empires like the Nazi or Soviet. Yet after the Cold War and especially since 9/11 the notion has been advanced that an American empire would be a positive good. An unnamed member of the George W. Bush administration bragged after the invasion of Iraq, "We're an empire now, and when we act, we create our own reality."[9] Neoconservative pundits such William Kristol and Robert Kagan have predictably called for an American "benevolent hegemony," but so, too, have distinguished historians such as Andrew Roberts and Niall Ferguson. They suggest it is high time Americans accept the fact that their nation bears imperial responsibilities similar to those of Victorian Britain. Authors both for and against empire have published scores of books and articles on the theme.[10] Should we feel more comfortable with that notion after learning that many of our Founders referred to America as an embryonic empire?

The answer is no, because what the Founders had in mind was not even remotely akin to the global alliances, military bases, and interventions the United States has pursued nearly nonstop since

1941. Rather, the word "empire" meant one of three things to the Founders. The obvious first usage was autocratic rule by a capricious emperor who crushed the liberties of his subjects. Americans abominated that sort of empire. A second usage connoted a vast region larger than the typical European kingdom and singled out for some characteristic. It might be political, as in the cases of the Chinese, Ottoman, or Holy Roman empires or the Athenian, Roman, and Venetian republics in their expansive heydays. But the defining characteristic might just as well be spiritual or economic. That is the sense in which Jefferson wrote of an Empire of Liberty, and it is what Secretary of State William Henry Seward meant when he spoke of an oceanic empire to be won by spreading "the twin gospels of Christ and commerce." But a third meaning of empire in Early Modern English connoted a specific identity in law and philosophy: to wit, utter, untrammeled sovereignty. When Henry VIII broke with the papacy—a milestone in the history of liberty in the minds of the American Founders—he bade Parliament pass a statute declaring that "this realm of England is an Empire," meaning a realm subject to no temporal or spiritual authority on the face of the earth. The Founders and Framers of the Constitution assuredly held that when the Continental Congress in turn broke with the English Crown it was declaring the new nation an empire in the sense of being "utterly sovereign." Indeed, Washington gave eloquent voice to that sense in his final orders to the Continental Army on April 18, 1783: "For, happy, *thrice* happy, shall they be pronounced hereafter, who have contributed anything, who have performed the meanest office; in erecting this *stupendous fabric of freedom and empire on the broad basis of independency*; who have assisted in protecting the rights of human nature, and establishing an asylum for the poor and oppressed of all nations and religions."[11]

In short, the American empire Washington and Jefferson imagined was not the sort advocated by those today who imagine that

"George Washington was a neocon" and that America in 1776 already a "neocon nation" dangerous to tyrants all over the world.[12] The brutal Jacobins and Bolsheviks of the French and Russian revolutions would define their regimes thusly. But American revolutionaries (even Tom Paine, if you read *Common Sense* carefully) contemplated no republican crusades overseas. The Founders were not even confident their own citizenry could summon the wisdom and virtue needed to preserve their republic. (Aaron Burr gave the Constitution fifty years before it succumbed to monarchy.) In any event, Americans could hardly have been proto-neoconservatives eager to export their system because they had just ratified a Constitution that inhibited foreign adventures through its division of powers and contained no instructions at all regarding the use of those powers except, of course, to "preserve, protect, and defend the Constitution of the United States."

Hold on there! If America's survival, destiny, and providential mission relied so heavily on wisdom and prudence in foreign relations, and the willingness of her new Chosen People to obey the law handed down by their new Moses in his Farewell Address, why then did the Framers *not* include instructions and warnings to that effect? Were they naive, absent-minded, or oblivious to the complexities of foreign relations? Of course not. The very impotence of the Articles of Confederation to command foreign respect for American sovereignty was what persuaded the Federalists to convene a Constitutional Convention in the first place. Moreover, the first thirty articles of the *Federalist Papers* urged ratification on foreign policy grounds. Yet when one looks at the Constitution itself, all one finds are those few, familiar clauses. First, Article I, Section 8 grants Congress power to (1) regulate foreign commerce; (2) define and punish piracy on the high seas; (3) declare war; and (4) raise and support armies for no more than two years at time; provide for a navy; and call up state militias in need. Article II, Section 2 is sparer still, simply granting the president power to (1) serve as Commander-in-Chief; (2) appoint ambassadors with advice and consent of the Senate; and (3) make treaties with the advice and consent of two-thirds of the senators present.

That is all. No one is delegated authority to make or execute foreign policy. No mention is made of a power to recognize or derecognize foreign regimes, terminate treaties as opposed to make them, make peace as opposed to war, declare neutrality in the wars of others, annex or cede territory, bestow or deny foreign aid, impose sanctions, regulate immigration and the status of aliens, proclaim Great Rules like Washington's or Doctrines like Monroe's, or for that matter prescribe or proscribe any specific behavior at all.

What were the Framers thinking? I believe they were thinking just what we would expect them to think if we study the political and intellectual history of their time and place, the political and intellectual history they themselves studied, and of course their own highly articulate arguments. The only people who may be surprised by their thinking are those who imagine America's Founders to have been disembodied demigods obeying the dictates of universal natural laws and designing an instrument to impose such laws on all humanity—in other words, people who think America's Founders were indeed akin to Jacobins. They were not. As the very first sentence of Forrest McDonald's great book on the subject states: "The Framers of the Constitution were, for the most part, intensely practical men who were skeptical, even contemptuous, of abstract schemes of political theory."[13] The Framers were not Neo-Platonists, Thomists, Kantians, Rousseauians, or proto-Straussians. They were Anglo-Americans steeped in the Common Law, Protestant theology, the Scottish and English Enlightenments, and not least the failures of other republics both ancient and modern. They meant to fashion a government able to defend the United States whatever that may require, hence they left the government's foreign policy powers vague and elastic. But they also meant to fashion a government whose powers would not threaten their own liberty. So they separated the powers to raise and command armies, to declare and wage war.[14]

The lessons of history, not least the War of Independence itself, persuaded Federalists of the need for a single robust executive to conduct foreign relations and command the military. Sound philosophy supported that judgment. John Locke considered executive prerogative to include "the power of war and peace, leagues and alliances, and all the transactions with all persons and communities without the Commonwealth." The alternative, he warned, must be "disorder and ruin." Baron Charles-Louis de Montesquieu praised the unwritten British constitution that deemed domestic policy primarily the business of the legislature and foreign policy of the executive. Sir William Blackstone's voluminous commentaries on the Common Law found ample precedent for the Crown's exclusive authority over war and diplomacy so long as it was exercised for the public good in a Constitutional manner. But Americans also identified strongly with Britain's counter-tradition, the "Country Party" or Whig philosophy which damned executive caprice and upheld Parliamentary supremacy and cabinet government. Even Alexander Hamilton, who insisted that foreign affairs be "executive altogether" in the interest of unity, secrecy, decisiveness, dispatch, and intelligence, nonetheless conceded in *Federalist* No. 75 that the "history of human conduct does not warrant that exalted opinion of human virtue which would make it wise to commit interests of so delicate and momentous a kind, as those which concern its intercourse with the rest of the world, to the sole disposal of... a president of the United States." Abraham Lincoln would echo that wisdom when he noted the Framers "resolved to so frame the Constitution that *no one man* should hold power of bringing this oppression upon us."[15] James Madison was sufficiently worried about executive malfeasance that he wanted all residual or implied

Constitutional powers to rest with Congress or the States. In sum, the office of American president was a novelty, and the intentions or expectations of the Framers regarding its evolution cannot be fully guessed. All we can be sure of is that nobody wanted to court executive tyranny, be it that of a monarch like George III or demagogue like Oliver Cromwell.

Otherwise, the Constitution bequeathed to the nation a malleable mix of powers either assigned or imputed to the president, or to the president *cum* Senate, or to Congress, with endless opportunities for disputes which the judicial branch has adamantly refused to umpire. Driven by an "uncertain blend of patriotism with judicial humility" (in Louis Henkin's words) the courts ever since Chief Justice John Marshall have ritually bowed to increases in executive war powers. But it would be mistaken to conclude that all is strife between Congress and the president in foreign affairs. Aside from the common devotion to the national interest both branches presumably feel, and the common interest they share if the president and Congressional majority are of the same party, there operates a brilliant Constitutional serendipity. The very separation of powers almost always obliges the branches to cooperate just to get anything meaningful done. So even though American history blushes with examples of political discord thwarting effective foreign policy, it boasts even more examples of collaboration or at least toleration between branches.

Nevertheless, patterns can be discerned over time, including a cyclical one traced by eras of relative Congressional or executive energy and predominance in foreign relations. For instance, President Washington tried to attenuate somewhat the Senate's influence over the making of treaties, but the Senate retaliated by attaching to treaties various amendments such that on forty-three occasions since 1789 the president himself has rejected the final result. Likewise, from 1815 to 1869 the uppity Senate rejected thirty-one of

220 treaties and amended 80 percent of the rest. The most famous antagonist in a treaty fight, Senator Henry Cabot Lodge, later defined a diplomatic text sent to the Senate as "not properly a treaty but merely a project."[16]

Still, the most imposing long-range trend is unquestionably the accretion of executive powers as serial presidents have seized opportunities, exploited crises, or expanded bureaucratic purview in response to new technological, political, and economic complexities. The results of that long-term trend would probably shock the Framers because their initial purpose in naming the president commander-in-chief was just to ensure civil supremacy over the military. Yet by the end of World War II the power of the president had grown so great, in Harry Truman's sarcastic remark, as to make Genghis Khan green with envy.[17] Nevertheless, the road to that result was long and winding, and sometimes doubled back on itself.

So let us walk, or rather sprint, down that road if only to notice the peaks and valleys Americans encountered during their first century under the Constitution, a century during which their foreign relations were based on coherent, mutually reinforcing principles that permitted the nation to grow with phenomenal speed into a potential world power, but one whose greatest source of strength was her liberty under law at home.

In retrospect, that original U.S. grand strategy succeeded because the legislative and executive branches passed four tests, with mostly flying colors, in foreign policy, that enabled the nation to expand to the Pacific Ocean with the Constitution intact.

None of them happened on George Washington's watch because he sent no U.S. forces into combat abroad. John Adams did when the French Republic, drunk with victories in Europe and angry about Jay's Treaty with Britain, began to attack U.S. merchant ships in 1798. The U.S. Navy, abetted by numerous privateers licensed with letters of marque, paid the French commerce raiders back with interest in a so-called Quasi-War. The 1800 Treaty of Mortefontaine ended the combat (as well as the Franco-American alliance still on the books since 1778), but it is instructive to note that the U.S. government's first conflict under the Constitution was both an undeclared war and a limited war. Yet it posed no Constitutional test because it was a cooperative effort on the part of the president and the Congress. To be sure, the Jeffersonian party vilified Adams for waging war against a sister republic and using it as a pretext to restrict civil rights. But Congress authorized the hostilities through a dozen legislative acts, while the Alien and Sedition Acts were precisely that: Acts of Congress. Finally, the Supreme Court established its hands-off precedent by ruling it all Constitutional. It reasoned that if Congress had the power to declare general war, then *a fortiori* it could authorize limited war.

Jefferson, political posturing aside, agreed with the Federalist precedents. His inaugural address echoed Washington's call for unity by instructing the American people that "we are all Federalists; we are all Republicans." His first foreign initiative echoed Adams when on May 15, 1801, his cabinet decided to dispatch a naval squadron to punish the Barbary Pirates. He did not think he needed Congressional assent for a mission of self-defense, but nonetheless requested and got multiple statutes to support the campaign.

What posed the first serious Constitutional test in U.S. foreign relations was the danger posed by Napoleon's ambition to carve out an empire on the Mississippi River and the likelihood that the only way the United States could prevent it was by war or by purchase. Jefferson wondered whether the Constitution permitted acquisition of new territory, especially without the consent of its inhabitants. But he had to act quickly and sort out legalities later. So he sent James Monroe and Robert Livingston to Paris with orders to bid up to $10 million for New Orleans. When the French instead offered to sell all of Louisiana for $15 million, the Americans leapt at the bargain. What they brought home was not strictly a treaty. It could even be deemed a receipt for stolen goods since the French dictator Napoleon Bonaparte had pried Louisiana from Spain. But despite or because of the irregularities Jefferson sent it to the Senate, where, after serious debate, he won a two-thirds majority. It was a high-wire act and no mistake, but a splendid example of how a president could both take initiative now and defer to Congress later when it served the national interest.

Jefferson's Embargo of 1808 did not. By way of protesting the British and French economic blockades that interfered with neutral rights at sea, Jefferson ordered his party's majorities in Congress to pass a law prohibiting Americans from engaging in any foreign trade. That wrecked the economy and so embarrassed the Democratic-Republicans that by 1812 their western and southern factions, the so-called War Hawks led by John Calhoun and Henry Clay, beat the drums for a declaration of war against Britain. That posed a second critical test because it exposed the country to attacks (indeed, the burning of Washington City itself), risked losing New Orleans and the trans-Mississippi frontier, and threatened the unity of the eastern states because the unpopular war tempted Federalists in New England to secede from the Union. Finally, the federal government itself was woefully ill-prepared to wage or even finance the war. But the conflict ended well insofar as Andrew Jackson's victory at New Orleans saved the Louisiana Purchase and the Democrats learned how right the Federalists had been to insist on a professional military and a national bank.

Enter John Quincy Adams, who deserves a whole lecture to himself.[18] Pious, prudent, and ethical, President Monroe's Secretary of State believed the United States was destined to absorb all North America since no power could stand in the way following the War of 1812. But Americans would become their own worst enemy if they succumbed to passion and either fractured the Union or else charged off on ideological crusades. Thus, when some Congressmen urged Monroe to assist the Latin American juntas fighting for independence from Spanish colonialism, Adams chose a Fourth of July oration in 1821 to deliver a thunderous rebuke:

> [America] goes not abroad in search of monsters to destroy. She is the well-wisher to the freedom and independence of all. She is the champion and vindicator only of her own.... She well knows that by once enlisting under other banners than her own, were they even the banners of foreign independence, she would involve herself, beyond the power of extrication, in all the wars of interest and intrigue, of...avarice, envy, and ambition, which assume the colors and usurp the standard of freedom. The fundamental maxims of her policy would insensibly change from liberty to force. The frontlet upon her brows would no longer beam with the ineffable splendor of freedom and independence; but in its stead would soon be substituted an imperial diadem, flashing in false and tarnished lustre the murky radiance of dominion and power. She might become the dictatress of the world: she would be no longer the ruler of her own spirit.

Thus did John Quincy Adams give fulsome expression to the *genuine* American creed consisting of Liberty, Unity, and Independence at home and no ideological crusades abroad. He was also a shrewd and flexible champion of Unilateralism, the American System, and Continental Expansion. In 1816, the Tennessee militia chieftain Andrew Jackson pursued hostile Native Americans into Spanish Florida and executed two British gun-runners he captured there. Adams drafted a stinging indictment of Spain (and Britain) for sowing anarchy in Florida and threatened to seize the province if the Spaniards refused to sell it. He then negotiated the Transcontinental Treaty of 1819, in which the Spaniards agreed to cede Florida as well as their claims to the Oregon Territory in the Northwest.

Finally, Adams guided the federal government through its third critical test in foreign affairs when he crafted the Monroe Doctrine. Following the Napoleonic Wars the restored King of Spain spoke of reconquering Mexico and South America. Adams was not upset by that crazy whim, but was greatly upset when the British Foreign Secretary made a gratuitous offer of joint Anglo-American opposition to prevent a Spanish reconquest. The Royal Navy hardly needed American help to patrol the Atlantic, so why were the British tempting Americans with such a démarche *unless* their ulterior motive was to curb U.S. expansion in the Western Hemisphere? Adams waged a lonely battle in the cabinet and in public opinion but at last persuaded Monroe to issue a unilateral declaration in his 1823 Annual Message to Congress. That event was a big leap forward for the executive branch, because Monroe simply declared his Doctrine to Congress rather than submitting it for approval. But since the president did not ask Congress to vote any funds or risk any conflict no one objected. (Congress has always been pleased to cheer brave words that require no action.) The contents of the Monroe Doctrine were fourfold: (1) no new European colonization in the Americas; (2) no transfer of existing colonies to other empires; (3) no reimposition of colonial rule where it had been thrown off; and (4) no *American* crusades in monarchical Europe. The last point was simply reciprocity. If Americans warned Europeans not to meddle in the affairs of the New World then Americans must promise not to meddle in the affairs of the Old World. The Monroe Doctrine in practice was really a bluff throughout most of the nineteenth century because the federal government lacked the military power to enforce Monroe's principles. But Adams's bluff was never called (save briefly by France during the Civil War) and by 1846 the Russians (in Alaska) and British (in what became Canada) assented to treaties that recognized U.S. claims to the Pacific Northwest. In 1841 President John Tyler even draped the Monroe Doctrine's mantle over the Sandwich Islands (Hawaii) when the Royal Navy briefly threatened their independence.

Clearly, U.S. expansionism had a long history by the time a Jacksonian Democrat editor sanctimoniously christened it Manifest Destiny in 1839. The reason he did so was to make America's westward march seem to be God's will, thereby obscuring the fact that the hoped-for annexation of Texas, New Mexico, and California faced serious political and perhaps Constitutional barriers. First, the territories in question were provinces of the Republic of Mexico (even though Anglo-Texans declared independence in 1836 and the Californians were virtually autonomous). Second, President Jackson could not annex the Republic of Texas by treaty because two-thirds of the senators—divided by now over the issue of slavery—would never vote in favor of admitting the slave-holding Texans. So if Manifest Destiny was not to be thwarted some Manifest Design was in order. First, President Jackson recognized the Republic of Texas on his last day in office in 1837. Then President Tyler slipped annexation through Congress in 1845 by means of a joint resolution that required only simple majorities.

Such expansion of slavery in the United States by such dubious means prompted John Quincy Adams to call the Texan annexation "the apoplexy of the Constitution." But the president elected in 1844, Jackson protégé James K. Polk, played even faster and looser with Constitutional niceties. Hoping to purchase or conquer the rest of Texas, New Mexico, and California, Polk maneuvered the enemy into firing the first shot. In 1846 he ordered a reconnaissance in force under General Zachary Taylor to occupy the Rio Grande, thereby inviting a Mexican attack and creating a *casus belli*. Democrats in Congress, quoting the president to the effect that "American blood has been spilled on American soil," closed off debate after a single day and proceeded to declare war against Mexico. Nor did the Whigs, who remembered how the Federalist Party had self-destructed by opposing the War of 1812, dare to object.

This was expansionism of a different sort insofar as the president used his war powers prior to a declaration of war to spark a conflict which presented Congress with a fait accompli. Frustrated Whigs suspected the war was a Democrat conspiracy to expand the number of slave states, but their legislative protests, including the Proviso proposed by Congressman David Wilmot of Pennsylvania and the so-called Spot Resolutions sponsored by a one-term Congressman from Illinois named Abraham Lincoln, hung fire. When in 1848 the diplomat Nicholas Trist brought home the Treaty of Guadalupe Hidalgo, in which Mexico ceded to the United States what became the entire Southwest, Whigs felt pressured to vote in favor lest Democrats accuse them of prolonging a war they professed to despise. The precedent was scary, as Lincoln told his law partner William Herndon: "Allow the president to invade a neighboring nation whenever he shall deem it necessary to repel an invasion, and you will allow him to do so whenever he may choose to say he deems it necessary for such purpose.... If to-day he should choose to say he thinks it necessary to invade Canada to prevent the British from invading us, how could you stop him? You may say to him, 'I see no probability of the British invading us'; but he will say to you, 'Be silent. I see it, if you don't.'"[9]

The 1846 Oregon Treaty with Britain and 1848 Treaty of Guadalupe Hidalgo with Mexico realized America's coast-to-coast destiny. But the way that was done eroded cooperation in foreign affairs between the branches of government. After the falsely named Compromise of 1850 the sectional breach grew so wide that the Northern and Southern states even began to pursue their own foreign policies. Democrats trolled for chances to annex slave-holding territories in the Caribbean and Central America. Whigs looked to expand Yankee trade, for instance by opening Japan in 1853. There followed the dissolution of the Whig Party and rise of the Republican Party, the fracture of the Democratic Party, the election of Lincoln in 1860, Southern secession and Civil War, thus bringing to terrible fruition a schism in the American Civil Religion such that two American sects waged what both imagined to be a holy war. But however one apportions the blame, the Confederates' fracture of the Union was the unforgivable sin against the Holy Spirit because the United States could never fulfill God's plan if they ceased to be united at all. Indeed, secession risked *all* the strategic traditions on which American greatness depended. For if two or more rival nations emerged on their soil, Americans would themselves undermine the peculiar advantages identified in Washington's Farewell Address. Liberty at home would devolve into "half-slave, half-free." Unilateralism would become impossible as both nations competed for foreign allies. The Monroe Doctrine could no longer exist even as bluff. American Continental Expansion would also go into reverse. Indeed, secession might even have bred more secession if Texas, New Mexico, Utah, California, and Oregon decided to go their own ways.

Foreign policy was also critical to the outcome of the Civil War because the Confederate strategy, consciously modeled on that of Washington and the Continental Army, counted on foreign assistance, whereas President Lincoln and Secretary of State William Henry Seward worked frantically to keep Britain and France neutral. Congress was often an unhelpful ally in war and diplomacy alike, because the Radical Republicans who inherited a majority when the Southern Democrats walked out were impatient and ideological. For instance, most did not understand the diplomatic delicacy required by the declaration of a Union blockade which had no standing under international law. Thus, most members bristled when Lincoln and Seward avoided a war with Britain over the *Trent* Affair by releasing two Confederate agents the *U.S.S. San Jacinto* had captured from a British mail packet. Most telling, perhaps, was an amusing contretemps that occurred in 1864 when members of Congress made inflammatory remarks about French Emperor Napoleon III's occupation of Mexico. When the French minister dropped by the State Department to express indignation, Seward politely assured him that Congress did not speak for the United States. The remark was leaked, whereupon the House *unanimously* resolved "that Congress has a Constitutional right to an authoritative voice in declaring and prescribing the foreign policy of the United States... not less in diplomatic negotiations than in the use of national forces when authorized by law; and the propriety of any declaration of foreign policy by Congress is sufficiently proved by the vote which pronounces it."[20]

Facile historians often commit the fallacy of prolepsis, which in effect is to read history backward. Thus, one reads in many textbooks that the Civil War somehow prepared America for its later career as a world power and a champion of freedom abroad as well as at home. The war supposedly achieved that by obliging the Lincoln administration to mobilize the nation's manpower and economy and enabling the Radical Republicans to launch the first "nation-building project," known as Reconstruction. But the truth was otherwise. For Lincoln, the great stake in the war was not the fate of self-government *everywhere*, but rather the fate of self-government *anywhere*. That is what he meant when he warned Congress that "we shall nobly save, or meanly lose, the last, best hope of earth."[21] Nor was post-bellum America prepared to bid for world power—not for over a generation—because the federal government shrank back nearly to nothing, Congress vigorously reasserted itself in foreign policy, and both branches slashed federal spending in order to pay down the national debt. The army would have disbanded entirely if not for the need to patrol Indian country. Even expansion went on hold after 1867, when a penurious, skeptical Senate barely ratified — thanks to some bribes by the Russian ambassador—Secretary of State Seward's purchase of Russian America (Alaska) for $7.2 million. Most telling, both presidents and senators during the Gilded Era reaffirmed their faith in the traditional foreign policy creeds established by Washington and John Quincy Adams.

Once again, however, to recognize that traditional principles of foreign policy were honored on down to the end of the nineteenth century is by no means to suggest that the United States turned "isolationist." Indeed, the last decades of the 19th century were the era when American exports flooded world markets and American scholars, tourists, missionaries, and merchants traveled abroad as never before. Those were the decades when the United States helped draft conventions to regulate international shipping, postal service, telegraphy, time zones, and commercial law. The White House and State Department simply kept a low profile during those peaceful decades, while the public was reassured when President Grover Cleveland promised in his 1885 inaugural address scrupulously to avoid "any departure from that foreign policy commended by the history, the traditions, and the prosperity of our Republic. It is the policy of independence, favored by our position and defended by our known love of justice and by our power. It is the policy of peace suitable to our interests. It is the policy of neutrality, rejecting any share in foreign broils and ambitions upon other continents and repelling their intrusion here. It is the policy of Monroe and of Washington and Jefferson: peace, commerce, and honest friendship with all nations; entangling alliance with none."

Yet that same year a book called *Congressional Government* appeared in print which damned the "inordinate" powers of Congress and concomitant restraints on the presidency, especially in foreign policy. The author, a supercilious professor of political science, advocated amending the Constitution in order to make the president a British-style prime minister in whom legislative and executive authority would be united. His ideas were little noticed outside the ivory tower. But American society and world politics were in rapid flux, and within just fifteen years the challenges mounted by industrialism and imperialism called into being the activist presidency longed for by a Princeton professor named Woodrow Wilson.

★ 12 ★

THE CONSTITUTIONAL HISTORY OF U.S. FOREIGN POLICY, PART II

The Second American Century As Crusader State[1]

On September 16, 1898, Senator Albert J. Beveridge (R-Ind.) delivered a ringing keynote address to his state's political convention. He spoke just a month after the truce in the Spanish–American War left U.S. armed forces in occupation of Manila in the Philippine Islands, Guam in the Marianas, and Puerto Rico in the West Indies, plus the Hawaiian Islands (annexed during the war through a joint resolution of Congress) and Cuba, whose independence had been the ostensible aim of the American war effort. The question before President William McKinley, the Senate, and voters in the midterm elections was whether the United States should, would, or could retain those conquests.

Beveridge couched his appeal in the evangelical rhetoric that resonated with mainstream Americans. He asked why God had made the United States

> a greater England with a nobler destiny...? Have we no mission to perform, no duty to discharge to our fellow man? Has

> the Almighty Father . . . marked us as the people of his peculiar favor, merely to rot in our own selfishness, as men and nations must, who take cowardice for their companion and self for their Deity. . .? The Opposition tells us that we ought not to govern a people without their consent. I answer, the rule of liberty that all just government derives its authority from the consent of the governed, applies only to those who are capable of self-government. We govern the Indians without their consent, we govern our territories without their consent, we govern our children without their consent. How do they know that our government would be without their consent? Would not the people of the Philippines prefer the just, humane, civilizing government of this Republic to the savage, bloody rule of pillage and extortion from which we have rescued them?

Thus did Beveridge instruct Americans that far from feeling guilty about imperialism, they ought feel guilty only if they spurn it! Beveridge's boldest appeal was to precedent: "And, now, obeying the same voice that Jefferson heard and obeyed, that Jackson heard and obeyed, that Monroe heard and obeyed, that Seward heard and obeyed, that Grant heard and obeyed, that Harrison heard and obeyed, our president to-day plants the flag over the islands of the seas, outposts of commerce, citadels of national security, and the march of the flag goes on!"[2] That same year the British author Rudyard Kipling sent his poem "The White Man's Burden" to Theodore Roosevelt with the same object in mind: to shame Americans into embracing imperialism.

What a contrast to Grover Cleveland's 1885 inaugural address, which had foresworn foreign entanglements in obedience to Washington's Great Rule and the Monroe Doctrine! How to explain so sudden and thorough a shift? First, by observing that the shift was not all that sudden. It occurred over two decades during which the global strategic and domestic economic environments were utterly transformed and the rapidly industrializing United States began to adjust. Congress authorized construction of a modern steel navy, and big businessmen competed aggressively for raw materials and markets overseas. The Cuban revolt against Spain proved to be the occasion for the American exertion of world power, but the potential for it was obvious. The U.S. population had reached 71 million, greater than any European country save Russia. U.S. agriculture was so bountiful that its exports undersold European producers in their own countries. U.S. coal production matched Britain's, and its steel output doubled that of second-place Germany. U.S. technology and enterprise were making American corporations world leaders in such revolutionary industries as chemicals, pharmaceuticals, electricity, petroleum, and soon internal combustion. But their very success caused business and government leaders to fret about the dangers of overproduction, hence their belief in the need to capture foreign markets. Likewise, the closing of the western frontier proclaimed by the historian Frederick Jackson Turner in 1893 implied that the United States must now pioneer frontiers overseas if its freedom and opportunity were to pass to new generations. Likewise, new waves of immigrants, including Catholics and Jews from southern and eastern Europe, made American society vastly more cosmopolitan, but also anxious about the assimilation of "hyphenated Americans" suspected of dual loyalties.

Most of all, those were the decades when the so-called New Imperialism captivated large and small powers alike as Britain, France, Germany, Italy, Russia, Spain, Portugal, the Netherlands, Belgium, and Japan carved out colonial empires in Africa, Asia, and Oceania and built blue water navies. The world was shrinking and Americans noticed. In 1890 Secretary of the Navy Benjamin Tracy persuaded Congress to fund a modern, two-ocean fleet, and Captain Alfred Thayer Mahan published *The Influence of Sea Power on History.* Mahan would popularize a new term meant to disparage opponents of expansion when he boasted, "I am imperialist simply because I am not isolationist."[3] In 1894 even the stodgy Cleveland administration breathed fire when the British appeared to challenge the Monroe Doctrine in a dispute with Venezuela. Secretary of State Richard Olney proclaimed: "Today the United States is practically sovereign on this continent and its fiat is law upon the subjects to which it confines its interposition."[4] That same year the treaty ending the first Sino-Japanese War granted Tokyo dominance over Korea, Manchuria, and the Ryukyu Islands. The European powers hastened to scramble for concessions of their own in the decrepit Qing Empire, which in turn inspired the McKinley administration's "Open Door policy" in hopes of keeping the China market open to American trade and investment.

The executive branch, though mostly passive during the late nineteenth century, had nevertheless been growing in size and agency as the government began to address the problems of urban, industrial society. The Supreme Court even contributed to the trend through its recondite 1890 decision *In re Neagle.* The case turned on whether a federal marshal, assigned as bodyguard to a Supreme Court Justice, was subject to prosecution by the State of California for shooting an innocent suspect. The court ruled 6–2 with one abstention to grant *habeas corpus* to the agent David Neagle on the grounds that the Constitution endows the executive branch with the power to do whatever was needed to enforce "the rights, duties and obligations growing out of the Constitution itself, our international relations, and all the protection implied by the nature of government under the Constitution." Theodore Roosevelt would later invoke this "stewardship theory" to claim extra-Constitutional powers, especially under the "pressures of international relations."[5]

Such powerful trends might readily explain the new assertiveness in foreign affairs. Only efforts to promote American trade in the Far East were not new: they dated from the 1840s and 1850s. Nor was American acquisition of non-contiguous territory such as Alaska in 1867 and Samoa in 1887. Rather the truly shocking novelty during and after 1898—the one which explains Beveridge's ecstatic rhetoric—was the moral pretension that Americans *had a mission* to uplift alien cultures. In other words, what most historians have labeled new and bad about American policy in 1898 was in fact old and benign, and what most historians think was traditional and good about the war of 1898 was in fact new and dangerous.[6] For the first time in their history Americans succumbed to the temptation to claim that they possessed the power, wisdom, charity, patience, the right, and indeed the duty to rule over colonial peoples.

The United States, by the twenty-first century, would have such long (and checkered) experiences with nation-building crusades that contemporary advocates of "regime change" easily gull the public into believing their nation's foreign relations have *always* been about "humanitarian interventions" and the "democracy promotion." But it just is not so. The federal government began to play the Crusader State during a discrete era—the Progressive Era—during which it greatly expanded its regulation of domestic life as well. Overseas imperialism was simply the external expression of the same spirit driving internal reform. That explains why leading Progressives were nearly all imperialists and nearly all imperialists were Progressives. Herbert Croly, founder of the influential journal the *New Republic*, even thought the Spanish American War launched the Progressive Era because of its "tremendous impulse to the work of reform."[7]

What is more, the Progressive Era, like previous reform movements in American history, had a strong religious component, and that of the late nineteenth century—the muscular Christianity of the Social Gospel movement and the missionary societies—made it an article of faith that America possessed a divine mission to uplift the downtrodden abroad as well as at home. The Reverend Josiah Strong's best-selling books combined Social Gospel with Social Darwinism. He ascribed to the American people "the largest liberty, the purest Christianity, the highest civilization," and a destiny to dispossess, assimilate, and mold all weaker races "until, in a very true and important sense, it has Anglo-Saxonized mankind."[8] Such messianic pretensions on behalf of one's nation would have struck nineteenth-century preachers and politicians as idolatry. But as the historian Arthur Schlesinger, Jr., observed, when American Protestantism turned liberal in the late nineteenth century, "shucking off such cardinal doctrines as original sin, one more impediment was removed to belief in national virtue and perfectibility."[9]

The Spanish–American War is of compelling interest for all sorts of reasons. It should not be forgotten that its origins lay not in some imperialist plot but in Cuba's struggle for independence and Spain's brutal counter-insurgency just ninety miles off the Florida coast. Neither Cleveland nor his successor McKinley wanted to wade into the bloody morass, but the latter came under increasing pressure from a jingoist war party, the Hearst and Pulitzer newspaper chain that publicized Spanish atrocities (the "CNN effect" of that day), and the outcry over the mysterious explosion of the *U.S.S. Maine* in the harbor at Havana. So the reluctant president, not unlike James Madison in 1812, asked Congress to decide whether to authorize U.S. intervention, which it did by votes of 311 to 6 in the House and 42 to 35 in the Senate. McKinley insisted American motives were humanitarian. Congress passed the Platt Amendment denying territorial designs on Cuba itself. But a good deal of historical evidence has since come to light suggesting the real motive of the McKinley administration was to supplant Spanish suzerainty with its own in order to *prevent* the emergence of a genuine *Cuba Libre.*[10]

In the wake of that "splendid little war" (to quote Secretary of State John Hay) the U.S. military remained in occupation of

Cuba and the other insular conquests, causing an Anti-Imperialist League to protest the annexationist Treaty of Paris which ended the conflict. Such opposition infuriated Theodore Roosevelt, who groused that some "evidently consider the prerogatives of the Senate as far more important than the welfare of the country."[11] In the end, however, TR got his way. The Senate advised and consented to the treaty by a 57 to 27 vote, barely exceeding the required two-thirds majority.

A final aberration of 1898 was the imposition by the U.S. government of colonial rule over foreigners to whom Americans had no intention of granting statehood. Yet advocates of empire such as Senator Knute Nelson (R-Minn.) insisted their cause was not only just, but holy: "Providence has given the United States the duty of extending Christian civilization. We come as ministering angels, not despots."[12]

That is a measure of how far the nation had drifted from the wisdom of James Madison in *Federalist* No. 51: "If men were angels, no government would be necessary. If angels were to govern men, neither external nor internal controls on government would be necessary."[13] After 1898 Americans came to be told that Providence called them to govern others without their consent, and the Supreme Court promptly concurred. In a series of six "Insular Decisions" beginning in 1901 the justices ruled that Filipinos, Guamanians, Hawaiians, and Puerto Ricans had no rights the U.S. government was bound to respect and therefore the Constitution did *not* necessarily follow the flag.[14]

The Spanish–American War merits in-depth discussion because it illustrates when, how, and why Americans began to invent new diplomatic traditions ostensibly to meet the challenges of a new century. Progressives in government, academia, journalism, and Protestant churches now deemed the principles dating back to Washington's Farewell Address to be inadequate to a new era characterized by a global economy, colonial and naval competition, political and technological revolution, and soon enough, world war. To Progressives it now seemed that Americans must exert their power overseas in order to secure themselves at home. Whereas their original Promised Land traditions had aimed to deny the world the chance to perturb America's future, their new Crusader State traditions aimed to afford America the chance to perturb the world's future. In the fullness of time the federal government would conceive of four twentieth-century traditions, the first of which was Progressive Imperialism, a nationalist, power-political, but paternalistic response for which the war to free Cuba was the occasion. The second would be Wilsonianism, an internationalist legal and institutional response for which the two world wars would provide the occasion. The third would be Containment, a military and diplomatic response to ideological threats for which the Cold War was the occasion. The fourth was Global Meliorism, for which all the twentieth-century conflicts provided occasion. Global Meliorism was based on the notion that American foreign policy must not only treat the symptoms of tyranny, revolution, and war but address their causes through humanitarian aid, economic development, social engineering, democracy promotion, and nation-building. What the republic clearly lost when it became America the Crusader State was the humility and the prudence which had characterized America the Promised Land. The Constitutional consequences of that sea change could not have been more profound.

Progressive Imperialists believed the United States could no longer ignore "foreign broils" but must "speak softly and carry a big stick," in Teddy Roosevelt's famous words. Industrialism and imperialism were submerging the old European balance of power into a world balance of power which now required the United States to guard its maritime approaches while expanding its military and commercial reach throughout the seven seas. But the United States, the Progressives believed, would be a "good imperialist" which bestowed, in paternalistic fashion, moral and material progress on backward colonial peoples. President Roosevelt's 1904 Corollary to the Monroe Doctrine explicitly claimed a duty to intervene in what we now call "failed states" and said that in the Western Hemisphere it was up to the United States, "however reluctantly, in flagrant cases of such wrongdoing and impotence, to the exercise of an international police power."[15]

Roosevelt's motives included the old ones of warding off European interventions in the hemisphere and protecting American lives and property, plus the tasks of civilizing peoples deemed incapable of self-government. But the Roosevelt Corollary raised the question of whether the president had the Constitutional prerogative to decide when or whether to exercise such "police power." The State Department solicitor-general J. Reuben Clark answered yes in 1912. He drew a distinction between an intervention which involved taking over a country's sovereign affairs (which would require the approval of Congress) and an intervention designed to protect lives and property (which fell under the authority of the commander-in-chief). Senator Augustus Bacon (D-Ga.) mounted a forlorn protest in the form of a bill to deny appropriations to any military deployment made without Congressional assent. But the War Department's counsel carried the day by arguing that the president could send armed forces anywhere if he deemed it necessary to protect American citizens.

In his autobiography published the following year Roosevelt explained his theory of government: "I declined to adopt the view that what was imperatively necessary for the nation could not be done by the president unless he could find some specific authorization for it. My belief was that it was not only his right but his duty to do anything that the needs of the nation demanded unless such action was forbidden by the Constitution or by the laws.... I did not usurp power, but I did greatly broaden the use of executive power.... I acted...whenever and in whatever manner was necessary, unless prevented by direct constitutional or legislative prohibition.... The course I followed [was] of regarding the Executive as subject only to the people, and, under the Constitution, bound to serve the people affirmatively in cases where the Constitution does not explicitly forbid him to render the service." That bold assertion prompted the anti-Progressive Speaker of the House Joseph Gurney Cannon (R-Ill.) to observe that Roosevelt had "no more use for the Constitution than a tomcat has for a marriage license."[16] License or not, he got his way nearly all of the time.

Historians customarily draw a sharp distinction between Roosevelt's Progressive Imperialism and Woodrow Wilson's Liberal Internationalism (as, for instance, in John Milton Cooper's title *The Warrior and the Priest*).[17] TR is depicted as a realist devoted to power politics in the national interest, whereas Wilson is depicted as the idealist who despised power politics and what he called selfish interest. The contrast is overdrawn. Both were Progressive reformers. Both believed in executive energy and cheered the Spanish–American War in the belief that it would empower the president. Both engaged in gunboat diplomacy. TR pronounced the Corollary to the Monroe Doctrine and arrogated to the United States an international police power (which he then used to stage a phony revolution in Panama to enable the digging of the canal). Wilson ordered Marines to Nicaragua and Haiti, bombarded Veracruz, and invaded Sonora on the pretense of "teaching the Mexicans to elect good men." TR sent the Navy's Great White Fleet around the world. Wilson pledged to build a navy "second to none." TR merrily confessed, "I took the Canal Zone, started the canal and let Congress debate me" (prompting his Secretary of War to quip: "Mr. President, you have been accused of seduction and have conclusively proved you were guilty of rape").[18] Wilson believed the ends justify means so deeply that in 1917 he persuaded Congress to wage a discretionary total war in pursuit of "a universal dominion of right by such a concert of free peoples as shall bring peace and safety to all nations and make the world itself at last free."[19]

So far as the Constitution is concerned, the real distinction between the two Progressive presidents was this. Roosevelt's prudence and sense of proportion bred successes which an otherwise jealous Congress had to acknowledge. Wilson's folly and self-righteous zeal bred disasters which obliged Senators to resist. Roosevelt, not Wilson, was the first American to win a Nobel Peace Prize (for mediating the Russo-Japanese War). Roosevelt, not Wilson, repented of the annexation of the Philippines ("our Achilles' heel," he called it as early as 1907). Roosevelt, not Wilson, grew so skeptical of nation-building that he likened annexing the Dominican Republic to a boa constrictor swallowing a porcupine "wrong-end to."[20] In other words, Wilsonianism was less a reaction *against* Progressive Imperialism than a moralistic caricature of it. Wilson deemed foreign policies which merely served the national interest to be degrading. It was he who lectured the cadets at the Naval Academy that "The idea of America is to serve humanity."[21] Wilson firmly believed that the measure of his nation's virtue was not what America *was* but rather what America *did*. So where TR waged finite struggles in pursuit of tangible goals such as the balance of power and the Panama Canal, Wilson waged infinite struggles in pursuit of abstractions such as a "war to end war" and "to make the world safe for democracy." Wilson, like Herman Melville's Captain Ahab, pursued a white whale and destroyed himself in the process.[22]

Wilson enunciated his specific war aims in his Fourteen Points address of January 1918. They included open diplomacy, freedom of the seas, free trade, disarmament, self-determination (for Europeans, not colonies), and a League of Nations to ensure perpetual peace. French Premier Georges Clemenceau sniffed that Wilson's agenda would be splendid if only men were not men, and indeed the agenda failed for all-too-human reasons. Wilson grew so intoxicated with his messianic role and apparent popularity, and so exaggerated America's leverage and his own war powers, that by Armistice Day he evidently expected to dictate terms to the Germans, the Allies, and the U.S. Senate. He broke precedent by personally negotiating the Treaty of Versailles and insisting the League Covenant be part of it. He appointed no senators to the American delegation and asked none for advice even though Republicans had won a majority in the November 1918 elections. Upon hearing of opposition on Capitol Hill, he retorted: "The Senate must take its medicine."[23]

Myth has it that Wilson was a prophet martyred by mossback isolationists. In truth, Senator Henry Cabot Lodge (R-Mass.), chairman of the Foreign Relations Committee, was a distinguished scion of Boston bluebloods and PhD historian conversant in six languages. He was far more cosmopolitan than Wilson. Nor did Lodge represent "isolationists" because he tried to build a coalition to ratify the treaty *in defiance of* the dozen or so Irreconcilables led by Senator William Borah (R-Ida.). Finally, Lodge addressed real Constitutional issues by drafting fourteen reservations to ensure that U.S. membership in the League of Nations would not contravene the powers of Congress to declare war and regulate commerce and immigration. Wilson refused all compromise, leaned on Democrats to oppose all reservations, and killed the last chance for ratification. Wilson then killed himself when he embarked on an exhausting whistle-stop tour to stump for the League of Nations and suffered a massive stroke.

Twenty-five years after U.S. rejection of the Treaty of Versailles President Franklin D. Roosevelt's publicity juggernaut popularized the myth of the saintly Wilson martyred by mossback isolationists in order to pre-empt opposition that might arise to his United Nations. That partisan branding of Republicans as opponents of internationalism proved so effective that it soon tainted the history of the whole interwar era. School children learned that Wilson's tragic defeat had restored Congressional primacy in foreign relations, hurled the nation back into isolationism, and caused provincial Republicans from the Great Plains to pass the 1930s Neutrality Acts, which prevented FDR from confronting the growing fascist threat.

The truth was almost the opposite. The administrations of Warren G. Harding, Calvin Coolidge, and Herbert Hoover were bastions of Progressive Republican internationalism. They even promoted such Wilsonian goals as disarmament, collective security, and the Open Door. The difference was that instead of relying on ideological appeals the Republicans practiced deft diplomacy, deployed private capital, and made informal ententes with foreign governments and businesses to resolve international conflicts. Secretary of State Charles Evans Hughes sponsored the 1921–22 Washington Naval Conference that pacified the Pacific and the 1924 Dawes Plan, which stabilized the European economies and enabled France and Germany to embrace collective security. Of course, none of those settlements would survive the Great Depression beginning in 1929, but even then the Republican President Herbert Hoover hoped to save international cooperation. It was Roosevelt who ran on an isolationist platform in 1932, and it was the large New Deal Democrat majorities in Congress that passed the Neutrality Acts from 1935 to 1938. When at last FDR moved to rearm the United States in light of the fascist threat he got decisive support from "Fortress America" Republicans.[24]

In terms of Constitutional issues in foreign affairs, however, by far the greatest surge in presidential authority occurred on Roosevelt's watch. The Pearl Harbor attack triggered, not a five-year, but a *fifty-year emergency* during which the United States fought totalitarian rivals for the soul of the world. That permanent crisis ineluctably expanded the president's war powers and peace powers to the near emasculation of those exercised by Congress. During the 1940s and 1950s presidents increasingly conducted business with foreign governments through executive agreements rather than formal treaties, which would require the Senate's consent.

It all began with a quiet inflection point in 1936 when *United States v. Curtiss-Wright* reached the Supreme Court. Bolivia and Paraguay were waging their bitter Chaco War, and Congress gave the president the option of imposing an arms embargo, which Roosevelt did. But Curtiss-Wright Export defied the ban and was sued by the Justice Department. The aviation firm's defense was that Congress had improperly surrendered its power over foreign trade to the president's "unfettered discretion." The court, as usual, found for the executive, but Justice George Sutherland rendered a breathtaking *obiter dicta* suggesting that presidential authority in foreign affairs was *virtually limitless*. Sutherland argued that in 1776 the union of the thirteen states became sovereign and thus assumed all the "right and power of the other members of the international family." Therefore, "the powers to declare and wage war, to conclude peace, to make treaties, to maintain diplomatic relations with other sovereignties, [even] if they had never been mentioned in the Constitution, would have vested in the federal government as a necessary concomitant of nationality." But where in the federal government? Sutherland, citing (out of context) an opinion of the first Chief Justice John Marshall, decided the president is vested with "plenary and exclusive power . . . as the sole organ of the federal government in the field of international relations—a power which does not require as a basis for its exercise an act of Congress. . . ."[25]

Sutherland's history was as flawed as it was gratuitous. In 1776 the several states declared *themselves*, not the Continental Congress, to be sovereign vis-à-vis Britain. The Articles of Confederation likewise declared that each state retained its sovereignty, freedom, and independence, and defined the United States as a "firm league of friendship." It was precisely to replace that (not so firm) league with a genuine government that Federalists convened in Philadelphia in 1787. The Constitution, by reserving some powers to Congress, belied the notion of the executive as "sole organ." No wonder that legal scholars to this day concur that *Curtiss-Wright* was a "radical, path-breaking act" that invited White House and State Department lawyers to arrogate powers to the president, while excusing the courts from interfering.[26]

That meant presidents might make deals of all sorts with foreign governments without the Senate's advice and consent. To be sure, if such agreements required appropriation then of course Congress must approve, but only by a simple majority in both houses. Not coincidentally, 1937 was the year the "curves crossed" on the chart such that ever since the number of executive agreements has far exceeded the number of treaties. Between 1900 and 1933 presidents concluded 388 executive agreements versus 411 treaties. Between 1933 and 1979 they made 8,405 executive agreements versus 550 treaties.[27]

Such was hardly the original intent of the Constitution's Framers. In *Federalist* No. 64 John Jay cautioned against *any* delegation of the power to make treaties, naming it just as important as war, peace, and commerce. Madison considered the making of treaties a legislative function insofar as they become part of the highest law of the land. Even Hamilton conceded in *Federalist* No. 75 that the treaty power belonged "properly neither to the legislative nor the executive" but was a shared responsibility. Presidential scruples reflected those judgments. When Monroe received the 1817 Rush–Bagot Accord—an exchange of notes with Britain demilitarizing the Great Lakes—he sent it to the Senate with a query as to whether it *needed* to be sent to the Senate![28] By the late nineteenth century executive agreements became gradually more common and less controversial because most were just postal conventions, fishery accords, and the like. But starting with Theodore Roosevelt presidents began to do serious business through executive agreements that bypassed the Congress. The Root–Takahira and Lansing–Ishii Accords of 1908 and 1917, for instance, defused war scares between the United States and Japan through painful compromises which probably could not have won two-thirds support in the Senate. Under FDR executive agreements became the norm. Did that amount to a dangerous usurpation of power by the executive? The answer was not as much as it might appear because senators usually approved of the executive agreements presidents made, or else did not know or care about their substance, or else were happy to skip tiresome hearings. What did and does exercise Congress and the public are cases where presidents appeared—if only in retrospect—to have exploited executive privilege to make war.

The latest example has been George W. Bush's notorious decision to invade Iraq in 2003. But the origins of *every* American war—from the War of Independence to the War of 1812, Mexican War, Civil War, Spanish–American War, First World War, and Second World War—became controversial once historians began to comb the archives in search of their murky and complex causes. In the 1941 case historians have found strong circumstantial evidence that FDR hoped his executive acts, such as the undeclared war against German U-boats in the Atlantic and economic sanctions against Japan, might provoke an attack that would force the hand of Congress.[29] The controversy is still relevant today because the Pearl Harbor Syndrome—fear of a sneak attack—is still the strongest justification for presidents to contemplate pre-emptive strikes against terrorists and states that harbor them. But the other Pearl Harbor Syndrome—fear of presidential chicanery—has been the strongest justification for restriction of presidential prerogatives. As early as August

1940, when Roosevelt made an executive agreement to trade U.S. destroyers for British bases, the Republican presidential candidate Wendell Willkie called it "the most dictatorial and arbitrary act of any president in the history of the United States."[30]

After Pearl Harbor Dr. New Deal morphed overnight into Dr. Win-the-War, and in that guise FDR committed far more "dictatorial and arbitrary" acts with the full support of Willkie, the Congress, and the American public. One such act was his immediate creation of a military tribunal to condemn suspected German saboteurs with the ex post facto compliance of the Supreme Court (it was said the justices "did not want to be perceived as just standing by while six men were executed").[31] Another was the internment of Japanese American citizens in concentration camps. The *nisei* did get their day in court, but in December 1944 the Supreme Court, in *Korematsu v. United States,* found in the government's favor. Justice Hugo Black wrote for the 6–3 majority that they were "unable to conclude that it was beyond the war power of Congress and the Executive to exclude those of Japanese ancestry from the West Coast area at the time they did."[32] That was later damned as a Constitutional breach as chilling as the 1857 Dred Scott decision on slavery, yet the issues it raised were revisited during the Red Scare of the early Cold War and again after the Al Qaeda terrorist attacks of September 11, 2001.

Foreign and military policy during World War II were not only confined to the executive branch but were usually confined to the president himself. Roosevelt made all the big decisions, especially during his summit meetings with Winston Churchill, and then with Churchill and Josef Stalin at the Teheran and Yalta conferences. Indeed, the most far-reaching executive agreements in history were the Yalta Accords and the follow-on Potsdam Accords negotiated by FDR's successor Harry Truman. What is more, those executive agreements ended up substituting for the treaties of peace which the Big Three allies never would draft. The Senate did get to vote on whether the United States ought to join the United Nations, but otherwise its power to advise and consent to a great postwar settlement simply expired. No subsequent war has ever ended with a formal treaty submitted to the Senate for its approval. All subsequent wars have ended in accords, truces, or U.N. resolutions.

Of course, the mere fact that the United States joined and expected to lead the United Nations represented a sea change in the legal context of foreign relations. It seemed that Americans, having learned their lesson, now fully embraced a Wilsonian world order. FDR had certainly unfurled the banner of Wilsonianism, beginning with the Atlantic Charter of 1941, but he did so because it served as a moral and ideological weapon in the war against fascism. He was not really a true believer. Rather, FDR had witnessed Wilson's blunders close up when he served as Assistant Secretary of the Navy during and after World War I and meant not to repeat them in 1945. He had also admired the bluff nationalism of his cousin Theodore. So FDR's real blueprint for the postwar era was for a Great Power condominium. He imagined the United Nations would be led by a Security Council dominated by "Four Policemen"—the United States, Soviet Union, Great Britain, and Nationalist China—whose leaders would not abolish force from world politics so much as exert a monopoly of force. Unfortunately that, too, proved naive because the only interest shared by the Communist Soviet Union, monarchical British Empire, and democratic United States was defeat of the Axis, and once that was achieved the alliance promptly dissolved.[33] By the end of 1946 it was also clear that the Soviets and Americans could not agree on U.N. control of atomic energy, which doomed them to a nuclear arms race. By early 1947 the rapid decline of British power threw the burden of defending whole theaters of the Eurasian land mass on the United States. It was then that Senator Arthur Vandenberg (R-Mich.) advised Truman and Secretary of

State Dean Acheson they must "scare the hell out of the American people" if they wanted Congress to fund their foreign commitments. The Truman Doctrine not only did that but universalized the Cold War commitments such that the president theoretically pledged to defend any country anywhere whose freedom was threatened. Congress responded with $400 million for Greece and Turkey and then billions more in Marshall Plan grants for European recovery. In 1949 Congress even repealed the Great Rule ("no entangling alliances") established by George Washington and Thomas Jefferson when it ratified the Treaty of Washington founding NATO, America's first permanent peacetime alliance since the year 1800, by a vote of 82 to 13.

The most ominous watershed followed almost at once. Communist North Korea invaded South Korea in June 1950. Truman ordered General Douglas MacArthur to hurl American forces into combat without consulting Congress at all. He mobilized the nation for protracted combat, revived conscription, called up reserves, and later authorized offensive action across the 38th parallel into North Korea. When the Communist Chinese intervened (something MacArthur failed to anticipate), Truman made the command decisions *not* to carry the war to the enemy, *not* to use all the weapons in America's arsenal, and *not* even to try to win—all on his own authority. To be sure, he still had to defer to Congress to obtain appropriations to pay for the war, but he and his legal advisors did not seek approval from Congress for their unilateral military support of United Nations resolutions.

Truman's feisty defense of South Korea had since received nearly universal acclaim in the United States. But legal scholar Louis Fisher has bluntly concluded that "the Truman Administration violated the plain language and the clear legislative history of the U.N. Charter and U.N. Participation Act. Nothing supports the notion that Congress, by endorsing the United Nations as an international peacekeeping body, had amended the Constitution by reading itself out of the war-making power. Congress did not—and could not—do so." What is more, Truman implicitly granted that fact by resorting to wordplay. When asked in a news conference on June 29, 1950, whether the United States was at war again, he replied, "We are not at war." Would it be more accurate, asked the reporter, to call this Korean conflict a sort of "police action under the United Nations?" To which Truman replied, "That is exactly what it amounts to."[34]

When is a war not a war? When a president does not dare or desire to ask Congress to declare it. Senator Robert Taft (R-Ohio) cried that Truman had "simply usurped authority" in violation of the Constitution. Secretary of State Acheson rebutted that the president had the authority to commit armed forces abroad and that it "may not be interfered with by the Congress." At the time, the historian Arthur M. Schlesinger, Jr., scorned Taft for a primitive. He ate his words later, during the Vietnam War, and became one of the harshest critics of what he damned as "the imperial presidency."[35]

The Truman administration also won almost unanimous praise for adopting the grand strategy of Containment, which—notwithstanding the enormous cost and occasional blunders made in its name over the course of nine presidencies—proved ultimately to be a success. But the Cold War, the limited hot wars it sparked, and the nuclear arms race all tested the flexibility of American government in unprecedented ways. The machinery of the international obligations assumed by the United States did not mesh well with the machinery of its domestic procedures, and if forced together they would have stripped their gears. Consider the Truman Doctrine. The journalist Walter Lippmann feared it might someday get American boys sent into battle in obscure Asian countries, and the Korean War soon proved him right. But was it technically true that a presidential doctrine or the U.N. Charter or treaties like NATO obligate Americans to fight in defense of other nations? If not, then American commitments would lack credibility with friends and foes alike. If so, then such commitments in fact violate the Constitution. As the Senate Foreign Relations Committee officially stated (in a report on the retrocession of the Panama Canal in 1978): "A treaty may not declare war."[36]

That is a sensitive issue all branches of government prefer to ignore. In literal fact, all the collective security pacts of that era specified that their obligations would be carried out "by the Parties in accordance with their respective constitutional processes" (Article 43 of U.N. Charter). The 1945 U.N. Participation Act authorized the president to furnish troops only with the approval of both houses of Congress. The NATO treaty requires each party to take "such action as it deems necessary, including the use of armed force, to restore and maintain the security of the North Atlantic area." Moreover, Acheson himself assured the Senate on April 12, 1949: "This does not mean that the United States would automatically be at war if we or one of the Parties to the Treaty were attacked. Under our Constitution, only the Congress can declare war." That is why the legal scholar Michael Glennon concludes: "The evolution of Anglo-American constitutionalism is in no small part a history of the decline of the war-making power as a 'prerogative' power, a history of its transfer to legislative authorities.... So the negotiators wrote into the treaties the fullest measure of commitment that their domestic legal and political systems would allow—which was zero.... To pretend otherwise is to undermine the very constitutional processes that the treaties were intended to preserve."[37]

Presidents pretend otherwise, and Congress almost always welcomes the pretense. All parties realize that the world had become much smaller and more lethal since 1787 and that U.S. foreign policy must aim to prevent, not just respond to, hostile acts from abroad. So ever since the Korean War the United States has maintained a strong military posture and global network of alliances which almost all Americans now take for granted. But Constitutionally speaking the era since 1950 has been anomalous. The Framers could not conceive of a cold war or hot peace which puts the nation on a permanent war footing and enables the president to project force at a moment's notice. Or, if some of them did, they recoiled. Thus did James Madison write:

> Of all the enemies to public liberty war is, perhaps, the most to be dreaded, because it comprises and develops the germ of every other. War is the parent of armies; from these proceed debts and taxes; and armies, and debts, and taxes are the known instruments for bringing the many under the domination of the few. In war, too, the discretionary power of the Executive is extended; its influence in dealing out offices, honors, and emoluments is multiplied; and all the means of seducing the minds, are added to those of subduing the force, of the people. The same malignant aspect in republicanism may be traced in the inequality of fortunes, and the opportunities of fraud, growing out of a state of war, and in the degeneracy of manners and of morals engendered by both. No nation could preserve its freedom in the midst of continual warfare.[38]

Nor (as former Secretary of the Navy John Lehman observed) could the Framers have conceived of the Congress being obliged to authorize huge defense expenditures beyond the two-year Constitutional limit or to create a huge defense bureaucracy that has become a virtual fourth branch of government.[39]

President Eisenhower's 1961 Farewell Address warned of the dangers to democratic governance posed by a permanent military-industrial complex and scientific-technological elite. He confessed he had no solutions, but understood that the Cold War placed an even greater premium on bipartisanship in foreign affairs. Politics must stop at the water's edge. So Ike ended the divisive Korean war, repudiated the Communist witch-hunt led by Senator Joseph McCarthy (R-Wisc.), and reached out to Democrats, especially Majority Leader Lyndon Johnson (D-Tex.), for bipartisan support on national defense. But neither did Eisenhower relinquish the new presidential prerogatives. His administration in fact designed a new military strategy called the New Look, which made Containment dependent on blunt nuclear deterrence (Massive Retaliation); forged alliances systems that encircled the Soviet bloc; and in 1957 declared the Eisenhower Doctrine, which specifically applied the Truman Doctrine to the whole Middle East. Ike also added to the executive branch's toolkit the use of the Central Intelligence Agency for covert operations beginning in Iran, Guatemala, and the Congo. Not least, he angrily opposed an amendment by Senator John Bricker (R-Ohio) that sought to prohibit the substitution of executive agreements for treaties.[40]

President John F. Kennedy pushed bipartisanship and brinkmanship to the limit in 1962 when he ignored international law and risked nuclear war by subjecting Fidel Castro's revolutionary regime in Cuba to a naval quarantine. He then resolved the crisis through an executive agreement with Nikita Khrushchev the very terms of which were not even made public. Nor did Kennedy consult Capitol Hill when he sharply increased the U.S. Special Forces (Green Berets) in South Vietnam and extended security guarantees to authoritarian regimes such as Francisco Franco's Spain.[41] He even persuaded Congress to relinquish another serious Constitutional duty through the 1962 Trade Expansion Act, which gave the president "fast-track authority" to negotiate tariff reductions under the General Agreement on Tariffs and Trade.

When President Johnson likewise sought bipartisan sanction for regional military deployments it seemed so routine that Chairman of the Senate Foreign Relations Committee J. William Fulbright

(D-Ark.) willingly sponsored the 1964 Tonkin Gulf Resolution. It granted the president authority to take whatever military measures he deemed necessary to prevent Communist aggression in Southeast Asia. Two years later, when the Vietnam "conflict" (again, not a war) escalated with no end in sight, Congressmen decided they had been tricked, and Fulbright himself damned the Johnson administration for having succumbed to "the arrogance of power." But the real issue at stake in the Vietnam debacle was not whether Secretary of Defense Robert McNamara lied about the alleged Tonkin Gulf attacks on a U.S. Navy destroyer or that Johnson exploited the resolution. The real issue was how easily a president's otherwise legitimate powers could be abused to create a situation that all but compels Congress to support in the U.S. armed forces in undeclared wars. That dilemma has frustrated *some* members of Congress in every conflict since Vietnam. But it has probably been a source of relief to *most* members because deferring to the president frees them to share the glory when things go well yet blame the White House when they do not.[42]

In any event, the original intent of the Tonkin Gulf Resolution was moot. A federal district judge ruled in 1968 that the Vietnam war effort was Constitutional on the simple grounds that a majority in Congress had the power to cut off funds for it whenever it chose. In fact, the Democrat majority after 1969 gradually withdrew support for what it now called Richard Nixon's War beginning with the repeal of the Tonkin Gulf Resolution in 1971. Following the 1973 Paris Peace Accords the Democrats voted to prohibit any future military actions in Southeast Asia. Nixon vetoed that bill and was barely sustained when an override failed.

What Congress did pass over Nixon's veto was the notorious War Powers Resolution (WPR) in 1973, perhaps the most ambitious legislative attempt to bridle a president since the post–Civil War struggle with President Andrew Johnson over Reconstruction. The

WPR is worth reading—once—then forgetting, because its convoluted, contradictory, and probably unconstitutional mix of instructions, restrictions, and ticking clocks has never been honored by any administration or upheld by any court. Presidents Gerald Ford, Jimmy Carter, Ronald Reagan, George H. W. Bush, Bill Clinton, and George W. Bush all dispatched U.S. forces into combat situations without paying the WPR more than lip service. In 1990, following Saddam Hussein's invasion of Kuwait, President Bush stationed 100,000 personnel in Saudi Arabia, having sought no authorization and having informed just one member of Congress: Senator Sam Nunn (D-Ga.). When he then prepared Operation Desert Storm to liberate Kuwait, fifty-four Congressmen, led by the chairman of House Armed Services Committee, the Berkeley radical Ron Dellums (D-Calif.), filed for an injunction to stop the war. U.S. District Judge Harold H. Greene ran for cover. Noting that 54 fell far short of a majority he judged the case "not ripe for judicial determination."[43]

Even if upheld the War Powers Resolution could not possibly fulfill its intentions. First, no one wants the president to be prohibited from acting in emergencies. Second, the sixty- or ninety-day periods after which the president must get Congressional authorization do not begin until the president, at his leisure, reports the deployment. Third, once U.S. troops are in a combat zone it is hardly likely that the Congress would publically ensure the defeat of their mission. In the first Gulf War, the real clock was set by the U.N. Security Council, whose Resolution 678 required Iraqi forces to withdraw from Kuwait by January 15, 1991. That put *Congress* under a deadline. Three days of frantic debate ensued until, on January 12, the sullen chambers voted to authorize force by 250 to 183 in the House and 52 to 47 in the Senate. House Speaker Tom Foley called it "the practical equivalent of a declaration of war." By then it was crystal clear that the War Powers Resolution was "a bad idea whose time has come and gone."[44]

Far from rolling back presidential war powers in the wake of the Vietnam War, Congress failed to prevent another serious arrogation on the part of the least likely president, Jimmy Carter. He suddenly announced that the United States would grant full recognition to the People's Republic of China on January 1, 1979. To be sure, that act was blessed by the Constitution. But as part of the package Carter had to terminate the 1955 Mutual Defense Treaty with the Nationalist Chinese regime on Taiwan—a treaty which had been approved by two-thirds of the Senate. Did the president alone have the right to un-ratify? Senators led by Barry Goldwater (R-Ariz.) filed a Constitutional challenge, but the Circuit Court of Appeals ruled against them, while the Supreme Court refused the case on the familiar grounds that it "involves the authority of the president in the conduct of our national foreign relations."[45] (This time, however, Congress got a last laugh of sorts. Just as senators learned in the early years of the republic to attach amendments to treaties *made* by a president, so now they passed a law that amended a treaty *unmade* by a president. Thus did the April 1979 Taiwan Relations Act mandate the continued sale of weapons to the Taipei regime and give the Mutual Defense Treaty new de facto life.)

The rapidity with which the executive branch reasserted its "sole organ" status was perhaps most evident when Carter used his 1980 State of the Union address to add his own name to the growing list of presidential doctrines. He had begun his term as a post-Watergate, post-Vietnam Democrat who in 1977 implicitly repudiated Truman's heritage as well as Nixon's in his "inordinate fear of Communism" speech at Notre Dame University. But following the Soviet invasion of Afghanistan he declared the Carter Doctrine, warning that the United States would take whatever measures were necessary to defend the Persian Gulf from aggression and thus ensure the free flow of oil. Since Great Britain had retreated from all its bases "east of Suez" in 1971 the United States needed to fill the Middle East vacuum just as it had with the eastern Mediterranean at the time of the Truman Doctrine in 1947. Only Carter, unlike Truman, did not invite Congress to vote.[46]

Ronald Reagan's administration acted as if the WPR simply did not exist. It dispatched 1,200 Marines to Beirut, launched an invasion of Grenada, sent advisors to El Salvador, and funneled aid to the Afghan Mujaheddin and Nicaraguan Contras, whom Reagan called Freedom Fighters resisting Communist regimes. In a column for *TIME* magazine Charles Krauthammer dubbed this policy the Reagan Doctrine.[47] Democrats in Congress hated such *noblesse oblige* on the part of a conservative president. So they passed three amendments named for Congressman Edward Boland (D-Mass.), which prohibited aid to the Contras. The increasingly tortuous terms of those amendments—designed to close every possible loophole—gave officials in the National Security Council the bright idea of funneling funds gleaned from foreign arms sales to the Nicaraguan resistance movement. When the scandal broke Reagan took responsibility, but thanks to sensational televised hearings featuring Colonel Oliver North Congress emerged from this Iran-Contra Affair nearly as embarrassed as the White House.

Meanwhile, an interesting novelty emerged in the "twilight zone" regarding the federal government's war powers. The executive branch, having rendered the WPR anodyne, but having recognized the need for accountability and prudence in the wake of the Vietnam War, began to check and balance itself. Secretary of Defense Caspar Weinberger delivered a stunning speech to the National Press Club in November 1984 that laid out what immediately came to be known as the Weinberger Doctrine. Never again, he said, should an American president send forces into combat unless six severe conditions were met and only after all alternatives had been exhausted. The short-range cause of that initiative was Reagan's disastrous deployment of U.S. Marines in Lebanon, where 241 were killed by a terrorist bomb. The longer-range causes included the determination by the Joint Chiefs of Staff as well as the Congress and public that there must be "no more Vietnams." Not surprisingly, the strongest internal opposition came from Secretary of State George Shultz, because effective diplomacy often requires a threat of force behind it. But for a number of years thereafter, the idea of the executive branch placing checks on itself gained some traction. Thus did General Colin Powell, in the run-up to the First Gulf War in 1991, add his own list of prerequisites prior to sending Americans into overseas combat.[48]

After the 9/11 attacks, needless to say, not only Congress but cautious voices in the executive branch were silenced. George W. Bush requested a resolution granting him authority "to deter and preempt any future acts of terrorism or aggression against the United States." The House Committee on International Relations changed "preempt" to "prevent" (which in any case could be construed to include preemption), after which it passed the Authorization to Use Military Force by votes of 420 to 1 and 98 to 0.[49] The resolution gave the president authority "to use all necessary and appropriate force against those nations, organizations, or persons he determines planned, authorized, or aided the terrorist attacks that occurred on September 11, 2001, or harbored such organizations or persons. . . ."[50] The George W. Bush administration would invoke that authority to overthrow the Taliban regime in Afghanistan, then invade Iraq in 2003 on the basis of flawed intelligence regarding Saddam Hussein's programs for weapons of mass destruction. Both operations provoked local counter-insurgencies which dragged on year after year and which cost *trillions* of dollars.

By now it should be clear why one chapter in a book on this subject is entitled "Why the President Almost Always Win in Foreign Affairs" and why a recent article is entitled "Why Hawks Win." First, the executive almost always takes the initiative; second, Congress almost always acquiesces; third, the courts always demur on the grounds that war and diplomacy are in the domain of the "political branches."[51] For better or worse the U.S. government has changed a great deal since the great Federalist lawyer James Wilson assured the Pennsylvania Ratifying Convention: "This system will not hurry us into war; it is calculated to guard against it. It will not be within the power of a single man, or a single body of men, to involve us in such distress."[52]

But before we praise or blame the assertive chief executives or passive legislatures and jurists who have wrought or acquiesced in such Constitutional devolution it is necessary to place events in their historical contexts. Every change has been a response to a challenge born of new circumstances at particular times. We may judge them to have been wise or foolish by their results, and worthy or unworthy of being precedents by the persistence of the challenges that inspired them. But we would be wise to listen to Louis Henkin, who delivered the prestigious Cooley Lectures at the University of Michigan Law School on the Constitution's bicentennial. Henkin worried about presidential abuse of the war powers, yet held to the dictum "if it ain't broke, don't fix it" because a healthy "tension in the twilight zone" had enabled the federal government to adapt to America's role as a world power in an era of revolutionary change. He prescribed no major amendments to the Constitution and concluded that even if the British critic Thomas Macaulay was right that our Constitution is "all sail and no anchor," perhaps what it most needs is a rudder.[53]

Perhaps, but that begs the question of who or what can serve as rudder of the American ship of state. Congress is unable or unwilling to do so, serving primarily as a squeaky brake that engages too late to prevent executive blunders.[54] Courts are unable and unwilling to do so. So that leaves the ultimate arbiters in our Constitutional system: the American people themselves. Presidents may abuse their war powers and/or commit malpractice in foreign affairs, but so long as they do not arrogate to themselves the power to suspend elections "for the duration" the voters are empowered to oust the people or party in charge every two or four years. Granted, public opinion is a crude instrument subject to all sorts of manipulation, short-sightedness, folly, and overreaction: *vox populi* is scarcely *vox dei*. But in our democratic system it is sovereign, which is why Americans have little choice but to trust Theodore Roosevelt's principle embedded in the Progressive "Bull Moose" Party platform of 1912: "We hold with Thomas Jefferson and Abraham Lincoln that the people are the masters of their Constitution, to fulfill its purposes and to safeguard it from those who, by perversion of its intent, would convert it into an instrument of injustice."[55]

Finally, before rendering judgment on 220 years of Constitutional adaptation we must perform another more pressing task, which is to define what we now mean by "war" in an era of nuclear weapons, cold war, limited war, counter-insurgency, and terrorism by non-state actors. For instance, if the War on Terror is indeed a war as traditionally understood, then pre-emptive strikes, restrictions on civil liberties, and deadly, permanent nation-building programs in darkest Asia fall under presidential authority. But one may retort, if the War on Terror is indeed a war as traditionally understood, then it ought to be *declared by Congress and re-declared every two years*. But to that one may retort, if the War on Terror is a indeed a war as traditionally understood, then *against whom would Congress declare it?* Underground terrorist movements, religious zealots, and non-state actors of various grounds? World politics have moved so far from the era of blatant fascist or monarchical aggression that our Constitutional language seems no longer adequate. Yet its very sparseness and ambiguity allow us to hope that the United States government can continue to adjust, if not always quickly or smoothly, to whatever new challenges loom in the future.

Justice Louis Brandeis put the point elegantly in a dissenting opinion of 1926. "The doctrine of the separation of powers," he wrote, "was adopted by the Convention of 1787, not to promote efficiency but to preclude the exercise of arbitrary power. The purpose was, not to avoid friction, but, by means of the inevitable friction incident to the distribution of governmental powers among three departments, to save the people from autocracy."[56] So stipulated! As long as We the People revere our Constitution it cannot do permanent harm to the national interest, because—when all is said and done—the Constitution *is* our national interest.

ACKNOWLEDGMENTS

Given that the lectures printed in this book were written over the course of thirty-odd years I cannot possibly recall all the family members, friends, colleagues, literary agents, and editorial staff members who were contributors to my career accomplishments. I shall, however, acknowledge the most important of them. My long-suffering "wonder wife" Jonna Van Zanten McDougall has been indispensable throughout our thirty-six years of marriage, and I cannot thank her enough for patiently putting me up with the thousands of hours I have devoted to extracurricular research and writing. My co-director of the International Relations Program at the University of Pennsylvania, Dr. Frank Plantan, was also indispensable because his bureaucratic expertise and imaginative program-building freed from the day-to-day hassle of administering an undergraduate major which has attracted several thousand students over the decades. Frank has now retired, but not without gifting me with an equally bright and energetic successor as co-director, Dr. Tomoharu Nishino. I owe a great deal to the late Harvey Sicherman, who served as president of the Foreign Policy Research Institute (FPRI) in Philadelphia from around 1990 until his untimely death in 2011, and also to his successor Alan Luxenberg, who sponsored many of my lectures and steered most of the programs in which I participated. I also wish to thank my colleagues in the history departments of the University of California, Berkeley, where I taught from 1975 to 1988, and those at the University of Pennsylvania, where I have been teaching ever since. Finally, I would be woefully remiss if I did not mention the great friend and mentor of my old age, Emeritus Professor James

Kurth of Swarthmore College. His wise counsel, brilliant insights into history, politics, and religion, and sheer inspiration have sustained me throughout my seventh and eighth decades.

This is also the place to acknowledge and thank the publishers and editors who granted me rights to reprint many of the lectures herein. The essay comprising Chapter 1 was presented as the FPRI Ginsburg-Satell Lecture #1, delivered at the Museum of the American Revolution in Philadelphia in May 2018 and published in *Orbis: A Journal of World Affairs* 62, no. 4 (2018). The essay comprising Chapter 2 was presented as the FPRI Ginsburg-Satell Lecture #2, delivered at the Museum of the American Revolution in July 2019 and published online by the FPRI Center for the Study of America and the West. The essay comprising Chapter 3 was presented as the FPRI Ginsburg-Satell Lecture #3, delivered at the Museum of the American Revolution in Philadelphia in June 2020 and published in *Orbis: A Journal of World Affairs* 62, no. 4 (2018). The essay comprising Chapter 4 was presented as the FPRI Ginsburg-Satell Lecture #4, delivered at the Museum of the American Revolution in June 2021. The essay comprising Chapter 5 was presented as the FPRI Ginsburg-Satell Lecture #5, delivered at the Museum of the American Revolution in Philadelphia in May 2022. The essay comprising Chapter 6 was written for the FPRI Center for the Study of America and the West and published online by FPRI (July 4, 2004). The essay comprising Chapter 7 was published online by *Law and Liberty* on October 2, 2017. The essay comprising Chapter 8 was first published as an E-Note by FPRI in December 2003. The essay comprising Chapter 9 is adapted from the R. Patricia Trickey Lecture in American Studies, delivered at the Agnes Irwin School, Rosemont, Pennsylvania, in October 1994 and published in *Orbis: A Journal of World Affairs* 39, no. 4 (1995). The essay comprising Chapter 10 was presented at the Temple University Consortium on Grand Strategy in October 2009 and published in *Orbis: A Journal of World Affairs*

54, no. 2 (2010). The essays comprising Chapters 11 and 12 were presented at the National Constitution Center in Philadelphia and published by the FPRI Center for the Study of America and the West in July 2010. Last but not least, I gratefully acknowledge the people who accepted this manuscript and expertly shepherded it through the publishing process, especially Daniel McCarthy, John A. Burtka IV, and Hannah Rowan of the Intercollegiate Studies Institute and Elizabeth Bachmann of Encounter Books.

—Walter A. McDougall,
Bryn Mawr, Pennsylvania, August 2024

NOTES

CHAPTER 1

1 This essay was written as the Foreign Policy Research Institute's Ginsburg-Satell Lecture #1 at the Museum of the American Revolution, Philadelphia, Pennsylvania, on May 15, 2018, and was published by *Orbis: A Journal of World Affairs* 62, no. 4 (2018): 505–17.

Additional Sources

Adams, John. *A Defense of the Constitutions of Government of the United States of America* (1787–88) In *The Works of John Adams*, edited by Charles Francis Adams, vol. 6 of 10. Boston: Little, Brown and Company, 1850–56.

Bailyn, Bernard. *The Ideological Origins of the American Revolution.* Cambridge, Mass.: Harvard University, 1967.

Bouwsma, William J. *Venice and the Defense of Republican Liberty in the Age of the Counter-Reformation.* Berkeley: University of California, 1968.

Brucker, Gene A. *Renaissance Florence.* Berkeley: University of California, 1969.

Clarke, J. C. D. *The Language of Liberty 1660–1832: Political Discourse and Social Dynamics in the Anglo-American World.* New York: Cambridge University, 1994.

Fink, Zera S. *The Classical Republicans: An Essay on the Recovery of a Pattern of Thought in Seventeenth-Century England* (1945). Evanston, Ill.: Northwestern University, 1962.

Fischer, David Hackett. *Albion's Seed: Four British Folkways in America.* New York: Oxford University Press, 1994.

Gamble, Richard M. *In Search of the City on a Hill: The Making and Unmaking of an American Myth.* London: Continuum, 2012.

Guicciardini, Francesco. *Selected Writings, Including Considerations on the Discourses on Livy of Machiavelli.* Oxford, Eng.: Oxford University, 1965.

Halbertal, Moshe and Stephen Holmes. *The Beginning of Politics: Power in the Biblical Book of Samuel.* Princeton, N.J.: Princeton University, 2017.

Kirk, Russell. *The Roots of American Order.* La Salle, Ill.: Open Court, 1974.

Machiavelli, Niccolo. *The Prince* (1535). Translated by Angelo M. Codevilla. New Haven, Ct.: Yale University, 1997.

——— *Discourses on Livy* (1531). Translated by Harvey C. Mansfield. Chicago: University of Chicago, 1997.

Mansfield, Harvey. *Machiavelli's Virtue.* Chicago: University of Chicago, 1966.

McDougall, Walter A. *Freedom Just Around the Corner: A New American History, 1585–1620.* New York: HarperCollins, 2004.

Najemy, John M. *Italy in the Age of the Renaissance: 1300–1550.* New York: Oxford University, 2004.

———*A History of Florence, 1200–1575.* Malden, Mass.: Blackwell, 2006.

Nelson, Eric. *The Hebrew Republic: Jewish Sources and the Transformation of European Political Thought.* Cambridge, Mass.: Harvard University, 2010.

Norwich, John Julius. *A History of Venice.* New York: Knopf, 1982.

Pocock, J. G. A. *The Machiavellian Moment: Florentine Political Thought and the Atlantic Republican Tradition.* Princeton, N.J.: Princeton University, 1975.

Rahe, Paul A. *Republics Ancient and Modern: Classical Republicanism and the American Revolution.* Chapel Hill: University of North Carolina, 1992.

———*Machiavelli's Liberal Republican Legacy.* New York: Cambridge University, 2006.

———*Against Throne and Altar: Machiavelli and Political Theory under the English Republic.* New York: Cambridge University, 2008.

Robbins, Caroline. *The Eighteenth-Century Commonwealthman: Studies in the Transmission of English Liberal Thought.* Cambridge, Mass.: Harvard University, 1959.

Sacks, Jonathan, "The Politics of Freedom." *Chabad* (blog). August 9, 2012," https://www.chabad.org/parshah/article_cdo/aid/1928705/jewish/The-Politics-of-Freedom.htm.

———"The Consent of the Governed." *The Rabbi Sacks Legacy*. August 21, 2017, http://rabbisacks.org/consent-governed-shoftim-5777/.

Shalev, Eran. *American Zion: The Old Testament as a Political Text from the Revolution to the Civil War.* New Haven, Ct.: Yale University, 2014.

Strauss, Leo. *Thoughts on Machiavelli.* Chicago: University of Chicago, 1958.

Walzer, Michael. *Exodus and Revolution.* New York: Basic Books, 1985.

———*In God's Shadow: Politics in the Hebrew Bible.* New Haven, Ct.: Yale University, 2012.

Wood, Gordon S. *The Creation of the American Republic, 1776–1787.* Chapel Hill: University of North Carolina, 1969.

CHAPTER 2

1 This essay was originally the second annual Ginsburg-Satell Lecture at the Museum of the American Revolution, Philadelphia, Pennsylvania, and was published online by the Foreign Policy Research Institute's Center for the Study of America and the West on July 18, 2019.

2 The letters had come into Franklin's possession in December 1772, but he never revealed his source, which remains unknown to this day. Of the

half-dozen persons variously nominated for the source my own favorite was Franklin's old rival turned protégé, Hugh Williamson. A medical doctor trained at the College of Philadelphia, he went on to become a surgeon-general in the Continental Army and a heroic delegate to the Continental Convention. After his death in 1819 his eulogist David Hosack claimed Williamson had purloined the letters and given copies to Franklin. But the latest scholar to plumb the mystery concludes that the most likely leaker was Thomas Pownall, a former governor of Massachusetts and Member of Parliament who shared Franklin's hopes for reconciliation between Britain and the colonies, and whose brother served in the Colonial department under Lord Hillsborough. Thus, Pownall had the motive, means, and opportunity.

3 Benjamin's belated decision to sail home and sign the Declaration of Independence caused a breach between father and son that never healed. When Ben urged his son to embrace the colonial cause William not only refused, he tried to use his prerogatives and prestige as governor of New Jersey to organize a Loyalist resistance to Congress. Colonial militias deposed him in January 1776 and after the Declaration of Independence Congress condemned him to solitary confinement in a cruel prison. He was released in a prisoner exchange in 1778 and moved to New York City, then under British occupation, where he established an active network of Loyalist partisans and spies. In 1782 he went into exile in England and never saw his father again save for a brief and cold meeting in London in 1785.

4 John Adams later recalled that Franklin expressed a "personal animosity and very severe resentment" toward the King. As late as 1773 he had faith that George III would prevent the Westminster Parliament from ever revoking colonial charters or suborning the rights of the assemblies. So he took it personally when the King refused even to read the Olive Branch Petition and sided with Parliament. What is more, George came to hate Franklin in return, so much so that when a lightning strike caused an explosion at a royal ordnance depot in England and a Royal Society investigation found the fault in a metal cramp inside the structure, the King refused to believe that Franklin had not sabotaged the arsenal by providing it with a defective lightning rod!

Additional Sources

Bailyn, Bernard. *The Ordeal of Thomas Hutchinson.* Cambridge: Harvard University, 1974.

Baltzell, E. Digby. *Puritan Boston and Quaker Philadelphia.* New York: Free Press, 1979.

Beeman, Richard. *Our Lives, Our Fortunes, and Our Sacred Honor: The Forging of American Independence, 1774–1776.* New York: Basic Books, 2013.

Black, Jeremy. *Crisis of Empire: Britain and America in the Eighteenth Century.* London: Continuum, 2008.

Bowen, Catherine Drinker. *Miracle at Philadelphia: The Story of the Constitutional Convention.* Boston: Little, Brown, 1966.

——— *The Most Dangerous Man in America: Scenes from the Life of Benjamin Franklin.* Boston: Little, Brown, 1974.

Brands, H. W. *The First American: The Life and Times of Benjamin Franklin.* New York: Doubleday, 2000.

Bridenbaugh, Carl and Jessica Bridenbaugh. *Rebels and Gentlemen: Philadelphia in the Age of Franklin.* New York: Reynal & Hitchcock, 1942.

Clark, J. C. D. "British America: What If There Had Been No American Revolution?" In *Virtual History: Alternatives and Counterfactuals,* edited by Niall Ferguson, 125–74. New York: Basic Books, 1999.

Doerflinger, Thomas M. A. *In Vigorous Spirit of Enterprise: Merchants and Economic Development in Revolutionary Philadelphia.* Chapel Hill: University of North Carolina, 1986.

Epstein, Daniel Mark. *The Loyal Son: The War in Franklin's House.* New York: Ballantine, 2017.

Franklin, Benjamin. *Autobiography* (1791). Edited by Peter Conn. Philadelphia: University of Pennsylvania, 2005.

Goodwin, George. *Benjamin Franklin in London: The British Life of America's Founding Father.* New Haven: Yale University, 2013.

Griffin, Patrick. *The Townshend Moment: The Making of Empire and Revolution in the Eighteenth Century.* New Haven: Yale University, 2017.

Hay, William Anthony. "These States United." *Claremont Review of Books.* June 11, 2018: https://www.claremont.org/crb/basicpage/these-states-united/.

——— "An End to Empire?" *Justifying Revolution: Law, Virtue, and Violence in the American War of Independence.* Edited by Glenn A. Moots and Philip Hamilton. Norman: University of Oklahoma, 2018: 264–84.

Isaacson, Walter. *Benjamin Franklin: An American Life.* New York: Simon and Schuster, 2003.

Johnson, Paul. *A History of the American People.* New York: HarperCollins, 1997.

Maier, Pauline. *American Scripture: Making the Declaration of Independence.* New York: Knopf, 1997.

Marietta, Jack. *The Reformation of American Quakerism, 1748–1783.* Philadelphia: University of Pennsylvania, 1984.

McDougall, Walter A. *Freedom Just Around the Corner: A New American History 1585–1829.* New York: HarperCollins, 2004.

Morgan, Edmund S. *Benjamin Franklin.* New Haven: Yale University, 2002.

Nash, Gary B. *Quakers and Politics: Pennsylvania, 1681–1726.* Princeton, N.J.: Princeton University, 1968.

——— *The Unknown American Revolution: The Unruly Birth of Democracy and the Struggle to Create America.* New York: Viking, 2005.

Penegar, Kenneth Lawing. *The Political Trial of Benjamin Franklin: A Prelude to the American Revolution*. New York: Algora, 2011.

Rakove, Jack N. *The Beginnings of National Politics: An Interpretive History of the Continental Congress*. New York: Knopf, 1979.

Ryerson, Richard Alan. *The Revolution is Now Begun: The Radical Committees of Philadelphia, 1765–1776*. Philadelphia: University of Pennsylvania, 1978.

Sanford, Charles L., ed. *Benjamin Franklin and the American Character*. Boston: D.C. Heath, 1955.

Scharf, J. Thomas and Thompson Westcott. *History of Philadelphia 1609–1884*, 2 vols. Philadelphia: L. H. Everts, 1884.

Schiff, Stacy. *A Great Improvisation: Franklin, France, and the Birth of America*. New York: Henry Holt, 2005.

Simmons, R. C. and Peter D. G. Thomas. *Proceedings and Debates of the British Parliaments Respecting North America, 1754–1783*, 6 vols. New York: Kraus International, 1982–86.

Skemp, Sheila L. *The Making of a Patriot: Benjamin Franklin at the Cockpit*. New York: Oxford University, 2012.

Thomas, Peter D. G. *British Politics and the Stamp Act Crisis: The First Phase of the American Revolution 1763–1767*. Oxford: Clarendon Press, 1975.

——— *The Townshend Duties Crisis: The Second Phase of the American Revolution 1767–1773*. Oxford: Clarendon Press, 1987.

——— *Tea Party to Independence: The Third Phase of the American Revolution 1773–1776*. Oxford: Clarendon Press, 1991.

Wood, Gordon S. *The Radicalism of the American Revolution*. New York: Random House, 1991.

——— *The Americanization of Benjamin Franklin*. New York: Penguin Press, 2004.

Wright, Esmond. *Franklin of Philadelphia*. Cambridge: Harvard University, 1984.

CHAPTER 3

1 This essay was first delivered as the Foreign Policy Research Institute's third Ginsburg-Satell Lecture at the Museum of the American Revolution in June 2020 and was published online as an FPRI Special Report on June 17, 2020.

2 The Pennsylvania Delegation included Joseph Galloway: native of Maryland, moved at eighteen; Charles Humphreys: Haverford native; Samuel Rhoads: Philadelphia native; John Dickinson: Wilmington native; Edward Biddle: Philadelphia native; Thomas Mifflin: Philadelphia native; John Morton: Ridley native; George Ross: New Castle native.

3 The Pennsylvania Delegation included Andrew Allen: Philadelphia native; George Clymer: Philadelphia native; John Dickinson: Wilmington native; Benjamin Franklin: Boston; Robert Morris: England, then Maryland; Benjamin Rush: Philadelphia native; James Smith: Ireland, but Philadelphia

by age two; George Taylor: Ireland, moved age twenty; Thomas Willing: Philadelphia native; James Wilson: Scotland.

4 The Pennsylvania slate included Benjamin Franklin, David Rittenhouse, George Clymer, Owen Biddle, Timothy Matlack, James Cannon, and the zealous Germans Frederick Kuhl and George Schlosser.

5 The Pennsylvania delegates were George Clymer, a Philadelphia native; Thomas Fitzsimons, born in Ireland; Benjamin Franklin, born in Boston; Jared Ingersoll, born in New Haven; Thomas Mifflin, a Philadelphia native; Gouverneur Morris, born in New York; Robert Morris, born in England; and James Wilson, born in Scotland.

Additional Sources

Baltzell, E. Digby. *Philadelphia Gentlemen: The Making of a National Upper Class.* Glencoe, Ill.: Free Press, 1958.

——*Puritan Boston and Quaker Philadelphia.* New York: Free Press, 1979.

Beeman, Richard. *Plain, Honest Men: The Making of the American Constitution.* New York: Random House, 2009.

——*Our Lives, Our Fortunes, and Our Sacred Honor: The Forging of American Independence, 1774–1776.* New York: Basic Books, 2013.

Bowen, Catherine Drinker. *Miracle at Philadelphia: The Story of the Constitutional Convention May to September 1787.* Boston: Little, Brown, 1966.

Brands, H. W. *The First American: The Life and Times of Benjamin Franklin.* New York: Doubleday, 2000.

Bridenbaugh, Carl and Jessica Bridenbaugh. *Rebels and Gentlemen: Philadelphia in the Age of Franklin.* New York: Reynal & Hitchcock, 1942.

Buranelli, Vincent. *The King & the Quaker: A Study of William Penn and James II.* Philadelphia: University of Pennsylvania, 1962.

Clark, J. C. D. "British America: What If There Had Been No American Revolution?" In *Virtual History: Alternatives and Counterfactuals,* edited by Niall Ferguson, 125-74. New York: Basic Books, 1999.

Doerflinger, Thomas M. A. *Vigorous Spirit of Enterprise: Merchants and Economic Development in Revolutionary Philadelphia.* Chapel Hill: University of North Carolina, 1986.

Dunn, Richard S. and Mary Maples Dunn, eds. *The World of William Penn.* Philadelphia: University of Pennsylvania, 1986.

Eberlein, Harold D. and Cortlandt V. Hubbard. *Diary of Independence Hall.* Philadelphia: Lippincott, 1948.

Fleming, Thomas. "Unlikely Victory: Thirteen Ways the Americans Could Have Lost the Revolution." In *What If? The World's Foremost Military Historians Imagine What Might Have Been,* edited by Robert Cowley, 155–86. New York: G. P. Putnam's Sons, 1999.

Hutchins, Catherine E., ed. *Shaping a National Culture: The Philadelphia Experience, 1750–1800.* Winterthur, Del.: Winterthur Museum, 1994.

Irvin, Benjamin H. "The Streets of Philadelphia: Crowds, Congress, and the Political Culture of Revolution, 1774–1783." *The Pennsylvania Magazine of History and Biography* 129, no. 1 (Jan. 2005): 7–44.

Johnson, Paul. *A History of the American People*. New York: HarperCollins, 1997.

Maier, Pauline. *From Resistance to Revolution: Colonial Radicals and the Development of American Opposition to Britain, 1765–1776*. New York: Vintage Books, 1972.

——— *Ratification: The People Debate the Constitution, 1787–1788*. New York: Simon & Schuster, 2010.

——— *American Scripture: Making the Declaration of Independence*. New York: Knopf, 1997.

Marietta, Jack. *The Reformation of American Quakerism, 1748–1783*. Philadelphia: University of Pennsylvania, 1984.

McDougall, Walter A. *Freedom Just Around the Corner: A New American History 1585–1829*. New York: HarperCollins, 2004.

Moretta, John A. *William Penn and the Quaker Legacy*. New York: Pearson Longman, 2007.

Nash, Gary B. *Quakers and Politics: Pennsylvania, 1681–1726*. Princeton, N.J.: Princeton University, 1968.

——— *First City: Philadelphia and the Forging of Historical Memory*. Philadelphia: University of Pennsylvania, 2002.

——— *The Unknown American Revolution: The Unruly Birth of Democracy and the Struggle to Create America*. New York: Viking, 2005.

——— *The Liberty Bell*. New Haven, Ct.: Yale University, 2010.

Rakove, Jack N. *The Beginnings of National Politics: An Interpretive History of the Continental Congress*. New York: Knopf, 1979.

Rappleye, Charles. *Robert Morris: Financier of the American Revolution*. New York: Simon & Schuster, 2010.

Ryerson, Richard Alan. *The Revolution is Now Begun: The Radical Committees of Philadelphia, 1765–1776*. Philadelphia: University of Pennsylvania, 1978.

Sanford, Charles L., ed. *Benjamin Franklin and the American Character*. Boston: D.C. Heath, 1955.

Scharf, J. Thomas and Thompson Westcott. *History of Philadelphia 1609–1884*, 2 vols. Philadelphia: L. H. Everts, 1884.

Wood, Gordon S. *The Americanization of Benjamin Franklin*. New York: Penguin Press, 2004.

CHAPTER 4

1 This essay was first delivered as the Foreign Policy Research Institute's fourth Ginsburg-Satell Lecture at the Museum of the American Revolution on June 10, 2021.

Additional Sources

Adams, Donald R. *Finance and Enterprise in Early America: A Study of Stephen Girard's Bank, 1812–1831.* Philadelphia: University of Pennsylvania, 1978.

Arey, Henry W. *The Girard College and Its Founder.* Philadelphia: Sherman, 1852.

Baltzell, E. Digby. *Philadelphia Gentlemen: The Making of a National Upper Class.* Glencoe, Ill.: The Free Press, 1958.

Beck, James M. *Stephen Girard: Merchant and Mariner.* Philadelphia: Lippincott, 1897.

Bridenbaugh, Carl and Jessica. *Rebels and Gentlemen: Philadelphia in the Age of Franklin.* New York: Reynal and Hitchcock, 1942.

Chandler, Charles L., et al. *Philadelphia: Port of History, 1609–1837.* Philadelphia: Maritime Museum, 1976.

Hickey, Donald R. *The War of 1812: A Forgotten Conflict.* Urbana: University of Illinois, 2012.

Ingram, Henry A. *The Life and Character of Stephen Girard.* Philadelphia: Stanley Hart, 1885.

McDougall, Walter A. *Freedom Just Around the Corner: A New American History 1585–1829.* New York: HarperCollins, 2004.

McGraw, Thomas K. *The Founders and Finance: How Hamilton, Gallatin, and Other Immigrants Forged a New Economy.* Cambridge, Mass.: Belknap Press, 2012.

McMaster, John B. *The Life and Times of Stephen Girard: Mariner and Merchant,* 2 vols. Philadelphia: Lippincott, 1918.

Powell, J. H. *Bring Out Your Dead: The Great Plague of Yellow Fever in Philadelphia in 1793.* Philadelphia: University of Pennsylvania, 1949.

Sapio, Victor. *Pennsylvania and the War of 1812.* Frankfort: University of Kentucky, 2015.

Scharf, J. Thomas and Thompson Westcott. *History of Philadelphia 1609–1884,* 2 vols. Philadelphia: L. H. Everts, 1884.

Schwartz, Robert D. *The Stephen Girard Collection: A Selective Catalog.* Philadelphia: Girard College, 1980.

Simpson, Stephen. *Biography of Stephen Girard.* Philadelphia: Thomas Bonsal, 1832.

Stagg, J. C. A. *The War of 1812: Conflict for a Continent.* New York: Cambridge University, 2012.

Weigley, Russell, ed. *Philadelphia, a 300-Year History.* New York: W. W. Norton, 1982.

Whitaker, Arthur. *The United States and the Independence of South America, 1800–1832.* Baltimore: Johns Hopkins University, 1941.

Wilson, George. *Stephen Girard: America's First Tycoon.* Conshohocken, Penn.: Combined Books, 1995.

Williams, William H. *America's First Hospital: The Pennsylvania Hospital, 1751–1841.* Wayne, Penn.: Haverford House, 1976.

Zial, William F. *A Catalogue of the Personal Library of Stephen Girard.* Philadelphia: Girard College and American Philosophical Society, 1990.

CHAPTER 5

1 This essay was first delivered as the Foreign Policy Research Institute's fifth Ginsburg-Satell Lecture at the Museum of the American Revolution on May 24, 2022.

Additional Sources

Adams, Henry. *The History of the United States Under the Administrations of Thomas Jefferson and James Madison*, 9 vols. New York: Charles Scribner's Sons, 1889–91.

Bailey, Thomas A. *A Diplomatic History of the American People.* Eighth Edition. New York: Appleton Century Crofts, 1969.

Bew, John. *Castlereagh: A Life.* Cambridge, Eng.: Cambridge University, 2012.

Bickham, Troy. *The Weight of Vengeance: The United States, the British Empire, and the War of 1812.* New York: Oxford University, 2012.

Brands, H. W. *Andrew Jackson: His Life and Times.* New York: Random House, 2005.

Bemis, Samuel Flagg. *John Quincy Adams and the Union.* New York: Knopf, 1956.

———*John Quincy Adams and the Foundations of American Foreign Policy.* New York: Knopf, 1949.

Bickham, Troy. *The Weight of Vengeance: The United States, the British Empire, and the War of 1812.* New York: Oxford University, 2012.

Brown, Wilburt S. *The Amphibious Campaign for West Florida and Louisiana, 1814–1815.* Tuscaloosa: University of Alabama, 1969.

Christian, Marcus. *Negro Soldiers in the Battle of New Orleans.* New Orleans: 150th Anniversary Committee of Louisiana, 1965.

Cooke, John Henry. *A Narrative of Events in the Attack on New Orleans in 1814 and 1815.* London: T. & W. Boone, 1835.

Folk, Reau E. *Battle of New Orleans: Its Real Meaning.* Nashville: Tennessee Commission on Education, 1935.

Ford, Worthington C., ed. *The Writings of John Quincy Adams*, 7 vols. New York: Macmillan, 1913–17.

Hay, William Anthony. *Lord Liverpool: A Political Life.* Woodbridge, Eng.: Boydell Press, 2018.

Hickey, Donald R. *The War of 1812: A Forgotten Conflict.* Urbana: University of Illinois, 1989.

——— *Don't Give Up the Ship!: Myths of the War of 1812.* Urbana: University of Illinois, 2006.

LaFeber, Walter. *The American Age: United States Foreign Policy at Home and Abroad Since 1750.* New York: Norton, 1989.

Maass, Richard W. "'Difficult to Relinquish Territory Which Had Been Conquered': Expansion and the War of 1812." *Diplomatic History* 39, no. 1 (2015): 70–97. McDougall, Walter A. *Promised Land, Crusader State: The American Encounter with the World Since 1776.* Boston: Houghton Mifflin, 1997.

——— *Freedom Just Around the Corner: A New American History 1585–1828.* New York: HarperCollins, 2004.

Muir, Rory. *Britain and the Defeat of Napoleon, 1807–1815.* New Haven: Yale University, 1996.

Owsley, Frank Lawrence, Jr. "The Role of the South in the British Grand Strategy in the War of 1812." *Tennessee Historical Quarterly* 31, no. 1 (Spring 1972): 22–38.

Perkins, Bradford. *Castlereagh and Adams: England and the United States, 1812–1823.* Berkeley and Los Angeles: University of California, 1964.

———*Prologue to War: England and the United States, 1805–1812.* Berkeley and Los Angeles: University of California, 1961.

Randall, William Sterne. *Unshackling America: How the War of 1812 Truly Ended the American Revolution.* New York: St. Martin's, 2017.

Remini, Robert. *Andrew Jackson and the Course of American Empire.* New York: Harper & Row, 1977.

———*Henry Clay: Statesman for the Union.* New York: Norton, 1991.

——— *The Battle of New Orleans: Andrew Jackson and America's First Military Victory.* New York: Penguin Putnam, 1999.

———*John Quincy Adams.* New York: Times Books, 2002.

Schake, Kori. *Safe Passage: The Transition from British to American Hegemony.* Cambridge, Mass.: Harvard University, 2017.

Stagg, J. C. A. *Mr. Madison's War: Politics, Diplomacy, and Warfare in the Early American Republic, 1783–1830.* Princeton, N.J.: Princeton University, 1983.

——— *The War of 1812: Conflict for a Continent.* New York: Cambridge University, 2012.

Taylor, Alan. *The Civil War of 1812.* New York: Vintage Books, 2010.

Thompson, Neville. *Earl Bathurst and the British Empire 1762–1834.* Barnsley, Eng.: Pen and Sword Books, 1999.

Updyke, Frank A. *The Diplomacy of the War of 1812.* Baltimore: Johns Hopkins University, 1915.

CHAPTER 6

1 This essay was written for the Foreign Policy Research Institute's Center for the Study of America and the West and was published by FPRI on July 4, 2004.

Additional Sources

Albanese, Catherine L. *Sons of the Fathers: The Civil Religion of the American Revolution.* Philadelphia: Temple University, 1976.

Bailyn, Bernard. *The Ideological Origins of the American Revolution*. Cambridge, Mass.: Harvard University, 1967.

Bellah, Robert and Phillip E. Hammond. *Varieties of Civil Religion*. San Francisco: Harper & Row, 1980.

Block, Ruth. *Visionary Republic: Millennial Themes in American Thought, 1756–1800*. Cambridge, Eng.: Cambridge University, 1985.

Bloom, Harold. *The American Religion*. New York: Simon & Schuster, 1992.

Bonomi, Patricia U. *Under the Cope of Heaven: Religion, Society, and Politics in Colonial America*. New York: Oxford University, 2003.

Boyd, Julian P. *The Declaration of Independence: The Evolution of the Text*. Washington, D. C.: Library of Congress, 1943.

Bullock, Steven C. *Revolutionary Brotherhood: Freemasonry and the Transformation of the American Social Order, 1730–1840*. Chapel Hill: University of North Carolina, 1996.

Butler, Jon. *Awash in a Sea of Faith: Christianizing the American People*. Cambridge, Mass.: Harvard University, 1990.

Cherry, Conrad. *God's New Israel: Religious Interpretations of American Destiny*. Englewood Cliffs, N.J.: Prentice-Hall, 1971.

Crawford, Richard. "Music of the American Revolution: The Birth of Liberty," New York: New World Records, 1976.

Cullen, Jim. *The American Dream: A Short History of an Idea That Shaped a Nation*. New York: Oxford University, 2003.

Draper, Theodore. *A Struggle For Power: the American Revolution*. New York: Times Books, 1996.

Elson, Ruth Miller. *Guardians of Tradition: American Schoolbooks of the Nineteenth Century*. Lincoln: University of Nebraska, 1964.

Ellis, Joseph J. *American Sphinx: The Character of Thomas Jefferson*. New York: Knopf, 1997.

Ferguson, Robert A. "The Commonalities of Common Sense." *William and Mary Quarterly* 57 (2000): 465–504.

Fischer, David Hackett. *Albion's Seed: Four British Folkways in America*. New York: Oxford University, 1989.

Foner, Philip S., ed. *The Complete Writings of Thomas Paine*, 2 vols. New York: Citadel, 1945.

Gorn, Elliot J. *The McGuffey Readers*. New York: Bedford/St. Martin's, 1998.

Guthrie, William Norman. *The Religion of Old Glory*. New York: George H. Doran, 1918.

Heimert, Alan. *Religion and the American Mind From the Great Awakening to the Revolution*. Cambridge, Mass.: Harvard University, 1966.

Maier, Pauline. *American Scripture: Making the Declaration of Independence*. New York: Knopf, 1997.

Marvin, Carolyn. *Blood Sacrifice and the Nation: Myth, Ritual, and the American Flag*. New York: Cambridge University, 1999.

May, Henry F. *The Enlightenment in America*. New York: Oxford University, 1976.

McDougall, Walter A. *Freedom Just Around the Corner: A New American History 1585–1828*. New York: HarperCollins, 2004.

Middlekauff, Robert S. *The Glorious Cause: The American Revolution 1763–1789*. New York: Oxford University, 1982.

Morgan, Edmund S. *The Birth of the Republic 1763–1789*, 3rd ed. Chicago: University of Chicago, 1992.

Noonan, John T., Jr. *The Lustre of Our Country: The American Experience of Religious Freedom*. Berkeley: University of California, 1998.

Olasky, Marvin. *Fighting For Liberty and Virtue: Political and Cultural Wars in Eighteenth-Century America*. Washington, D.C.: Regnery, 1995.

O'Leary, Cecilia E. *To Die For: The Paradox of American Patriotism*. Princeton: Princeton University, 1999.

Pocock, J. G. A. "The Imperial Crisis." In *The Varieties of British Political Thought, 1500–1800*, 246–82. Cambridge, Eng.: Cambridge University, 1993.

Rakove, Jack N. *The Beginnings of National Politics: An Interpretive History of the Continental Congress*. New York: Knopf, 1979.

Ritchey, Russell E., ed. *American Civil Religion*. New York: Harper & Row, 1967.

Smith, Elwyn A. *The Religion of the Republic*. Philadelphia: Fortress, 1971.

Tuveson, Ernest Lee. *Redeemer Nation: The Idea of America's Millennial Role*. Chicago: University of Chicago, 1968.

Van Alstyne, Richard W. *Genesis of American Nationalism*. Waltham, Mass.: Blaisdell, 1970.

Whitehall Company. *The Presidents, Their Inaugural Addresses*. Chicago: Whitehall, 1968.

Wood, Gordon S. *The Creation of the American Republic 1776–1789*. Chapel Hill: University of North Carolina, 1969.

CHAPTER 7

1 This essay was first published by the *Law and Liberty* online forum on October 2, 2017.

2 Thomas Boghardt, *The Zimmermann Telegram: Intelligence, Diplomacy, and America's Entry into World War I* (Naval Institute Press, 2012), pp. 181–90.

3 Niall Ferguson, editor, *Virtual History: Alternatives and Counterfactuals* (Basic Books, 1999), pp. 1–90 (quote, p. 89).

4 "The Bible and Progress, Address by The Honorable Woodrow Wilson on the Tercentenary Celebration of the Translation of the Bible into the English Language" (Denver, May 7, 1911), http://frontiers.loc.gov/service/gdc/scd0001/2012/20120129002bi/20120129002bi.pdf.

5 Barry Hankins, *Woodrow Wilson: Ruling Elder, Spiritual President* (Oxford University, 2016). See also Malcolm D. Magee, *What the World Should Be: Woodrow Wilson and the Crafting of a Faith-Based Foreign Policy* (Baylor University, 2008).

6 See Michael Kazin, *War Against War: The American Fight for Peace, 1914–1918* (Simon & Schuster, 2017); Thomas Fleming, *The Illusion of Victory: America in World War I* (Perseus Books, 2003); and Richard M. Gamble, *The War for Righteousness: Progressive Christianity, the Great War, and the Rise of the Messianic Nation* (ISI Books, 2003) on the powerful pacifist movements during the era of U.S. neutrality.

7 Boghardt's *The Zimmermann Telegram* establishes this beyond doubt. Many editorialists scoffed at the absurdity of the German proposal, and public uproar over it quickly subsided; it was not mentioned as a *casus belli* even after the U.S. declaration of war.

8 John Milton Cooper, Jr., *Woodrow Wilson: A Biography (*Knopf, 2009), p. 4. See also Justus D. Doenecke, *Nothing Less Than War: A New History of America's Entry into World War I* (University Press of Kentucky, 2012), pp. 217–49.

9 See Walter A. McDougall, *The Tragedy of U.S. Foreign Policy: How American Civil Religion Betrayed the National Interest* (Yale University Press, 2016), pp. 141–53.

10 Michael S. Neiberg, in *The Path to War: How the First World War Created Modern America* (Oxford University, 2016), argues instead that American opinion at large had grown increasingly alarmed about the national security threat that a victorious Germany would mount. I disagree, but even if he is correct, that would seem to imply that the president ought to have argued for belligerence on realist grounds as Theodore Roosevelt always recommended.

11 Otis L. Graham, Jr., "1917: What If the United States Had Stayed Neutral," in Morton Borden, Jr. and Otis L. Graham, Jr., *Speculations on American History* (D. C. Heath and Company, 1977), pp. 103–17. Graham mentions as plausible the sorts of prohibitions against American trade, investment, and travel that Congress later enacted in the 1930s Neutrality Acts.

12 Gamble, *War for Righteousness*, pp. 149–208 (quotes, pp. 154–59, 202–03).

13 *The Nation* cited in Robert E. Osgood, *Ideals and Self-Interest in America's Foreign Relations: The Great Transformation of the Twentieth Century* (University of Chicago, 1953), pp. 321–32. *The New Republic* cited in John A. Thompson, *Reformers and War: American Progressive Publicists and the First World War* (Cambridge University Press, 1987), pp. 234–36.

14 First, the U.S. war effort, by ensuring Germany's defeat, perversely eliminated the only external force capable of suppressing the Bolshevik regime in Russia. As a condition of the Armistice, the Germans had to renounce the annexationist Treaty of Brest-Litovsk they had made with the Bolsheviks and evacuate western Russia. Second, the U.S. military interventions

in the Russian Arctic, which Wilson ordered over the summer of 1918, were too small and remote to affect the course of the civil war that broke out between the "Reds" and the "Whites," but nevertheless fed Bolshevik propaganda. Third, Wilson (wisely) refused the Anglo-French proposals at the Paris Peace Conference to intervene massively in support of the White Russian armies. Fourth, the 5,000 troops Wilson sent to Vladivostok to secure the Trans-Siberian Railway (and defend Russian sovereignty from the grasping Japanese) served only to hold the region "in escrow" until the victorious Bolsheviks arrived to claim it.

15 Kazin, *War Against War: The American Fight for Peace*, p. 25.

16 Richard Gamble, "Wilsonian Slaughter," *The American Conservative*, February 23, 2009.

17 Lloyd E. Ambrosius, in *Wilsonianism: Woodrow Wilson and His Legacy in American Foreign Relations* (Palgrave Macmillan, 2002), described the flood of books and articles celebrating Wilsonianism after the American "victory" in the Cold War.

18 C. D. McIntyre, editor, *God, History, and Historians: Modern Christian Views of History* (Oxford University, 1977), p. 375.

CHAPTER 8

1 This essay was first published as an E-NOTE of the Foreign Policy Research Institute in December 2003.

CHAPTER 9

1 This essay was adapted from the R. Patricia Trickey Lecture in American Studies at the Agnes Irwin School, Rosemont, Pennsylvania, delivered in October 1994, and was published in *Orbis: A Journal of World Affairs* 39, no. 4 (1995): 479–89.

CHAPTER 10

1 This essay was originally presented as a lecture in the Temple University Consortium on Grand Strategy, October 8, 2009, and was published in *Orbis: A Journal of World Affairs* 54, no. 2 (2010): 165–84.

2 Angelo M. Codevilla, *Advice to War Presidents: A Remedial Course in Statecraft* (New York: Basic Books, 2009), p. 273.

3 Walter A. McDougall, *Promised Land, Crusader State: The American Encounter with the World Since 1776* (Boston: Houghton Mifflin, 1997), p. 220.

4 See inter alia Aaron L. Friedberg, "Strengthening Strategic Planning," *Washington Quarterly* 31, no. 1 (2007): 47–60; Rupert Smith, *The Utility of Force: The Art of War in the Modern World* (New York: Knopf, 2007); Andrew F. Krepenivich and Barry D. Watts, *Regaining Strategic Competence: Strategy for the Long Haul* (Washington, D.C.: Center for Strategic and Budgetary Assessments, 2009); and Codevilla, *Advice to War Presidents*. For a standard classic defining the field in general see John M. Collins, *Grand Strategy: Principles and Practices* (Annapolis, Md.: Naval Institute Press, 1983).

5 George W. Bush, "Second Inaugural Address" (Jan. 20, 2007) accessed Sep. 29, 2009 at http://www.bartleby.com/124/pres67.html.

6 Daniel W. Drezner, ed., *Avoiding Trivia: The Role of Strategic Planning in American Foreign Policy* (Washington, D.C.: Brookings Institution Press, 2009), pp. 3–4.

7 Aaron L. Friedberg, "Strengthening U.S. Strategic Planning," in ibid., pp. 84–97.

8 Alexis de Tocqueville, *Democracy in America* (New York: Vintage, 1945), pp. 240–45; for other editions just see volume 1, chapter 13.

9 Ibid., pp. 450–52 (volume 1, chapter 18).

10 For instance, see Jeff Huber, "Another Krock of Krepinevich," http://zenhuber.blogspot.com/2009/09/another-krock-of-krepinevich.html.

11 STRATFOR Geopolitical Diary, "America's Indivisible Imperatives" (July 2, 2009), accessed July 22, 2009 at http://www.stratfor.com/geopolitical_diary.

12 The hardball war and diplomacy of the Polk administration that belied the benign, idealistic "Manifest Destiny" school of U.S. expansion, is summarized by McDougall, *Promised Land, Crusader State*, pp. 76–98, and described in depth by Thomas R. Hietala, *Manifest Design: American Exceptionalism and Empire* (Ithaca, N.Y.: Cornell University, 2003), and David M. Pletcher, *The Diplomacy of Annexation: Texas, Oregon, and the Mexican War* (Columbia: University of Missouri, 1973).

13 Paul Kennedy, *The Rise and Fall of the Great Powers* (New York: Random House, 1987), pp. 194–346.

14 Krepenivich and Watts, *Regaining Strategic Competence*, which cites in turn Richard Overy, *Why the Allies Won* (New York: Norton, 1995), and Andrew Rogers, *Masters and Commanders: How Roosevelt, Churchill, Marshall and Alan Brooke Won the War in the West* (London: Allen Lane, 2005).

15 Henry James, *Hawthorne* (New York: Harper & Bros., 1879), pp. 142–43.

16 See the Annapolis, Md.: Naval Institute Press publications by Robert Seager, *Alfred Thayer Mahan: The Man and His Letters* (1977), Robert G. Albion, *Makers of Naval Policy, 1798–1947* (1980), and James C. Bradford, ed., *Admirals of the New Steel Navy* (1990); also Richard D. Challener, *Admirals, Generals, and American Foreign Policy 1898–1914* (Princeton, N.J.: Princeton University, 1973), Richard H. Collin, *Theodore Roosevelt, Culture, Diplomacy, and Expansion: A New View of American Imperialism* (Baton Rouge: Louisiana State University, 1985), and Walter A. McDougall, *Let the Sea Make a Noise: A History of the North Pacific From Magellan to MacArthur* (New York: Basic Books, 1993).

17 On Eisenhower's Solarium exercise and the drafting of the New Look blueprint NSC 162/2 of fall 1953, see Robert R. Bowie and Richard H. Immerman, *Waging Peace: How Eisenhower Shaped an Enduring Cold War Strategy* (New York: Oxford University, 1998).

18 Even now British Prime Minister Tony Blair has spurned what he calls "crabbed realism" in favor of assertive idealism because "our cause is just, right, and the only way the future of the world can work." Blair, "Doctrine

of the International Community: Ten Years Later," *Yale Journal of International Affairs* 4, no. 2 (2009): 5–14.

19 Robert Kagan, *Dangerous Nation* (New York: Knopf, 2006). On the Founders see Kagan, "Neocon Nation: Neoconservatism, c. 177," *World Affairs* 1, no. 2 (Spring 2008).

20 See Francis Fukuyama, *The End of History and the Last Man* (New York: Free Press, 1992), and Michael Mandelbaum, *The Ideas That Conquered the World: Peace, Democracy, and Free Markets in the Twenty-first Century* (New York: Public Affairs, 2002).

21 Bacevich's scholarly evolution seems to have been inspired by his fierce loyalty to the U.S. military, which in turn bred righteous anger over the damage done by the excessive demands made on the Army and Marines in particular since 9/11. Compare his *American Empire: The Realities and Consequences of U.S. Diplomacy* (Cambridge, Mass.: Harvard University, 2002), to *The New American Militarism: How American Are Seduced into War* (New York: Oxford University, 2005), and *The Limits of Power: The End of American Exceptionalism* (New York: Metropolitan, 2008). His theory about the elites manipulating grand strategy is reminiscent not only of William Appleman Williams, *The Tragedy of American Diplomacy*, rev. ed. (1962), but of his contemporary, the sociologist C. Wright Mills, *The Power Elite* (New York: Oxford University, 1956).

22 Christopher Layne, *The Peace of Illusions: American Grand Strategy from 1940 to the Present* (Ithaca, N.Y.: Cornell University, 2006). Geir Lundestad's critical review ("American Grand Strategy since 1940: Politcal Science and History, *Diplomatic History* 31, no. 4 [September 2007]: 783–86) faults Layne for depicting U.S. strategy over many decades as one-dimensional and invulnerable to domestic political resistance. If so, then how can his recommended alternative of offshore-balancing be a realistic alternative? He also faults Layne for underestimating the seriousness of the Soviet confrontation and European eagerness for an American commitment. Lundestad himself has referred to the U.S.-led Western bloc as "empire by invitation."

23 Colin Dueck, *Reluctant Crusaders: Power, Culture, and Change in American Grand Strategy* (Princeton, N.J.: Princeton, 2006); quote on p. 162.

24 Ibid., p. 171.

25 Richard K. Betts, "Is Strategy an Illusion?" *International Security* 25, no. 2 (Fall 2000): 5–50; Leslie H. Gelb, *The Irony of Vietnam: The System Worked* (Washington, D.C.: Brookings Institution, 1979).

26 See the Gaddis commentary in Ernest R. May, ed., *American Cold War Strategy: Interpreting NSC 68* (Boston: St Martin's, 1993), p. 146. He asserts NSC 68 was not a strategy at all, or else a poor one, because it made all interests "vital" and thus made possible negotiations "only on the basis of Soviet capitulations." That in turn, transferred the power to define American interests to the Soviets themselves and made inevitable the militarization of an ideological conflict.

27 Thomas Wright, "Learning the Right Lessons from the 1940s," in Drezner, *Avoiding Trivia*, pp. 125–36. The lessons are 1. Be flexible because "consistency" can lead to over-extension and imprudence; 2. Don't neglect bilateral diplomacy for which institutions are no substitute; 3. Secure and retain domestic legitimacy without which no strategy can be sustained; 4. Prioritize problems and try to solve them rather than over-emphasize process and institutions; 5. Manage expectations and appeal to the President for support.

28 Andrew F. Krepinevich, *7 Deadly Scenarios: A Military Futurist Explores War in the 21*st *Century* (New York: Bantam, 2009).

29 Daniel W. Drezner, "The Grandest Strategy of Them All," *The Washington Post* (Dec. 17, 2006); Drezner is author of *All Politics is Global: Explaining International Regulatory Regimes* (Princeton, N.J.: Princeton University, 2007).

30 Jeffrey W. Legro, *Rethinking the World: Great Power Strategies and International Order* (Ithaca, N.Y.: Cornell University, 2005), defines the prerequisites for a paradigm shift in worldviews, arguing that they must be visionary but also pragmatic insofar as they recommend concrete steps to be taken. Mandelbaum, *The Case for Goliath: How America Acts as the World's Government in the 21st Century* (New York: Public Affairs, 2005), insists that the United States is the indispensable power, hence it cannot afford to starve its military of resources in favor of feeding its oil addiction and social entitlements. Lieven and Hulsman, *Ethical Realism and American Foreign Policy* (New York: Pantheon, 2006), argues a Realist case said to reflect the ethical tradition of Kennan, Hans Morgenthau, and Reinhold Niebuhr. American strategy should refocus on strengthening the home front and leading the world by example. Fukuyama, *America at the Crossroads: Democracy, Power, and the Neoconservative Legacy* (New Haven: Yale University, 2006), calls for a "realistic Wilsonianism" expressed in a "multi-multilateralism" of overlapping international institutions rather than unilateral militarism. Ikenberry and Slaughter, *Forging a World of Liberty Under Law* (Princeton, N.J.: Princeton Project on National Security, 2006), is billed as a "collective X article." The authors stress international law and institutions to channel U.S. power and a "concert of democracies" to promote human rights. Etzioni, *Security First: For a Muscular, Moral Foreign Policy* (New Haven, Ct.: Yale University, 2007), criticizes democratization and nation-building as far too expensive, uncertain, and ineffective to warrant priority. The United States ought instead to seek legitimacy for its exertion of power through multilateral enforcement institutions such as the Proliferation Security Initiative. Page and Bouton, *The Foreign Policy Disconnect: What Americans Want From Our Leaders But Don't Get* (Chicago: University of Chicago, 2006), is an outlier insofar as it agrees with Christopher Layne that U.S. business and foreign policy elites conspire to frustrate the common sense of the American people. But far from being libertarian, these authors advocate economic nationalism in the name of "fair trade."

31 The ten "common strategy sins" as presented by business professor Richard Rumelt in a CSBA seminar on Sep. 25, 2007, cited by Krepinevich and Watts, *Regaining Strategic Competence*, pp. 33–34.

32 Burke quoted by Layne, *Peace of Illusions*, p. 204. The obverse of this collective self-satisfaction is what Toynbee called "the mirage of immortality." At the height of a civilization its members "are prone to regard it, not as a night's shelter in the wilderness, but as the Promised Land, the goal of human endeavors" and thus invite their own destruction from decadence within and/or attack from without. See Samuel P. Huntington, *The Clash of Civilizations and the Remaking of World Order* (New York: Simon & Schuster, 1996), p. 301. Is America or the West an exception? Huntington cites Matthew Melko, *The Nature of Civilizations* (Boston: Porter Sargent, 1969), p. 155, who asks, "First, is Western Civilization a new species, in a class by itself, incomparably different from all other civilizations that have ever existed? Second, does its worldwide expansion threaten (or promise) to end the possibility of development of all other civilizations?" If the likely answer to either is no, then we had better guard against imagining ourselves immortal.

CHAPTER 11

1 This essay was first delivered as a lecture series at the National Constitution Center, Philadelphia, and published by the Foreign Policy Research Institute's Center for the Study of America and the West (July 30, 2010).

2 The main primary source for this delightful anecdote is Kenneth R. Bowling and Helen E. Veit, eds., *The Diary of William Maclay and Other Notes on Senate Debates* (Johns Hopkins, 1988), pp. 128–32; see also Stanley Elkins and Eric McKitrick, *The Age of Federalism* (Oxford, 1993), pp. 55–58, and Forrest McDonald, *The American Presidency: An Intellectual History* (Kansas, 1994), pp. 221–23.

3 Louis Henkin, *Constitutionalism, Democracy, and Foreign Affairs* (Columbia, 1990), pp. 17–43 (quotes, pp. 43).

4 Washington deliberately avoided using the word "neutrality" in his Proclamation of Neutrality of April 22, 1794, out of deference to Secretary of State Jefferson's francophilia. But coincident with the hot debate between Jeffersonians and Hamiltonians over whether the United States should tilt toward France or Britain was a fierce debate over whether the president or Congress had the power to declare neutrality at all. See the pseudonymous exchange between Alexander Hamilton and James Madison in *The Letters of Pacificus and Helvidius with the Letters of Americanus* (Scholars' Facsimiles, 1976).

5 Washington left office in March 1797, but issued his "farewell" the previous autumn in hopes that his prestige and advice might boost the presidential campaign of his Vice President John Adams against the Democratic-Republican candidate Jefferson. Washington had asked James Madison to compose a draft for such an address back in 1792, but four years later he relied almost exclusively on Alexander Hamilton's philosophy and essayist's

skills. See Felix Gilbert, *To the Farewell Address: Ideas of Early American Foreign Policy* (Princeton, 1961).

6 For the text online see "Washington's Farewell Address," Yale Law School, http://avalon.law.yale.edu/18th_century/washing.asp.

7 McDougall, *Promised Land, Crusader State*, and "Back to Bedrock: The Eight Traditions of American Statecraft," *Foreign Affairs* 76, no. 2 (1997): 134–46.

8 See George C. Herring, *From Colony to Superpower: U.S. Foreign Relations Since 1776* (Oxford, 2008), and Walter A. McDougall, "Can America Do Grand Strategy?" *Orbis: A Journal of World Affairs* 54, no. 2 (Spring 2010): 165–84.

9 Quoted by Ron Suskind, "Faith, Certainty and the Presidency of George W. Bush," *New York Times Magazine* (October 17, 2004). The Bush advisor is generally thought to be Karl Rove although he has denied saying it.

10 See Richard H. Immerman, *Empire for Liberty: A History of American Imperialism From Benjamin Franklin to Paul Wolfowitz* (Princeton, 2010).

11 Washington's celebratory general orders followed by just over a month the famous Newburgh Address with which he defused a mutinous conspiracy among disgruntled officers. See "Newburgh Crisis VIII—Cessation of Hostilities," *Democratic Thinker* (January 10, 2010), http://democratic-thinker.wordpress.com/2010/01/10/newburgh-crisis-viiicessation-of-hostilities.

12 This absurd claim was the basis for Robert Kagan's book *Dangerous Nation: America's Place in the World, from its Earliest Days to the Dawn of the 20th Century* (Knopf, 2006) and article "Neocon Nation: Neoconservatism c. 1776," in *World Affairs* (Spring 2008).

13 McDonald, *The American Presidency*, p. 9.

14 The contrast with Jacobinism is elaborated by Claes G. Ryn, *America the Virtuous: The Crisis of Democracy and the Quest for Empire* (Transaction, 2003). Needless to say, the classic contrast between the ideologies of the American and French revolutions is Edmund Burke, *Reflections on the Revolution in France* (1790). My own understanding of the intellectual origins of American Constitutional thought rests on classic historical accounts including J. G. A. Pocock, *The Machiavellian Moment: Florentine Political Thought and the Atlantic Republican Tradition* (Princeton, 1975); Bernard Bailyn, *The Ideological Origins of the American Revolution* (Harvard, 1992); Jack N. Rakove, *Original Meanings: Politics and Ideas in the Making of the Constitution* (Knopf, 1996); Gordon S. Wood, *The Creation of the American Republic, 1776–1787* (North Carolina, 1998); Forrest McDonald, *Novus Ordo Seclorum: The Intellectual Origins of the Constitution* (Kansas, 1985); Richard R. Beeman, *Plain, Honest Men: The Making of the American Constitution* (Random House, 2009); and my own *Freedom Just Around the Corner: A New American History 1585–1828* (HarperCollins, 2004).

15 David Gray Adler and Larry N. George, *The Constitution and the Conduct of American Foreign Policy* (Kansas, 1996), p. x.

16 W. Stull Holt, *Treaties Defeated in the Senate* (Johns Hopkins, 1933), p. 179.

17 Clinton L. Rossiter, *The American Presidency* (Harcourt, Brace, 1960), p. 30.

18 The literature on John Quincy Adams is deservedly immense, but an excellent short summary of his views on statecraft is Greg Russell, *John Quincy Adams and the Public Virtues of Diplomacy* (Missouri, 1995).

19 Arthur B. Lapsley, ed., *Writings of Abraham Lincoln* (G. P. Putnam's Sons, 1906), 2:51–52.

20 *Congressional Globe*, 38th Cong., 2d Sess. (1864).

21 Michael Burlingame is especially persuasive on this score, for instance in his recent biography *Abraham Lincoln: A Life* (Johns Hopkins, 2008).

CHAPTER 12

1 This essay was first delivered as a lecture series at the National Constitution Center, Philadelphia, and published by the Foreign Policy Research Institute's Center for the Study of America and the West (July 30, 2010).

2 I am embarrassed to confess that my book *Promised Land, Crusader State*, pp. 101–02, misdates the speech. I evidently conflated the 1898 "March of the Flag" address with Beveridge's 1900 "In Support of an American Empire" speech. Happily, the error is irrelevant to my argument, which is the sharp contrast between the spirit, if not always the substance, of Progressive Imperialism and that of all previous U.S. foreign policy traditions.

3 James C. Bradford, ed., *Admirals of the New Steel Navy* (Naval Institute, 1990), p. 42.

4 Dispatch to London, July 20, 1895: *Foreign Relations of the United States 1895* (G.P.O., 1948), pp. 545–62.

5 The passage in question is quoted by Fareed Zakaria, *From Wealth to Power: The Unusual Origins of America's World Role* (Princeton, 1998), p. 137. For the entire fascinating opinion, see *In re Neagle,* Justia (1890), http://supreme.justia.com/us/135/1/case.html.

6 McDougall, *Promised Land, Crusader State*, p. 102. The conclusion drawn by Kenneth Moss, *Undeclared War and the Future of U.S. Foreign Policy* (Johns Hopkins, 2008), pp. 218–19, lends gratifying support to my interpretation of America's transition from Promised Land to Crusader State. The Founding Fathers, he writes, would acknowledge the place of military force in national security and foreign policy generally. However, they would be appalled that military force has become the most visible instrument of foreign policy and that the president enjoys a virtual carte blanche to wield it in the absence of Congressional oversight. When did the great, gradual drift toward presidential prerogative begin? Almost all accounts trace it to the early Cold War, noting that Congress has not used its war powers since 1941: "Yet the real foundation for expanded presidential use of military force occurred at the beginning of the twentieth century. It corresponded to a global expan-

sion of U.S. interests and the rise of a conviction that the United States could use military force to improve the world as well as protect and serve its interests. The gap between Theodore Roosevelt's world policeman and George W. Bush's desire to transform and stabilize the Middle East is not very wide, especially when the bridge is a Wilsonian idealism that believes in the universal appeal of American political ideals and values."

7 Robert Dallek, *The American Style of Foreign Policy: Cultural Politics and Foreign Affairs* (Knopf, 1983), p. 30. See also Herbert Croly, *The Promise of American Life*, 1909 (Bobbs-Merrill, 1965).

8 Josiah Strong, *Our Country: Its Possible Future and Present Crisis* (1885), quoted in Julius W. Pratt, *Expansionists of 1898* (Johns Hopkins, 1936), p. 6.

9 Arthur M. Schlesinger, Jr., *The Cycles of American History* (Houghton Mifflin, 1986), p. 17.

10 See Louis A. Perez, Jr., *The War of 1898: The United States and Cuba in History and Historiography* (North Carolina, 1998).

11 W. Stull Holt, *Treaties Defeated in the Senate* (Johns Hopkins, 1933), p. 178.

12 "Knute Nelson," Law Zone, http://www.lawzone.com/half-nor/nelson.htm.

13 James Madison, *The Federalist Papers*, No. 51.

14 In time Alaska and Hawaii would be incorporated and obtain statehood in 1958 and 1959. Puerto Ricans were granted U.S. citizenship in 1917 (so they could be conscripted for the Great War) and local self-government in 1952 under a commonwealth status that survives to this day. In the Philippines the Army had to impose colonial rule through a counter-insurgency campaign that killed 4,000 American soldiers and several hundred thousand Filipinos. The islands were granted a measure of self-government in 1934 and independence in 1946. Guamanians were granted U.S. citizenship in 1950, but remain an unincorporated organized territory.

15 "Roosevelt Corollary," Wikipedia, http://en.wikipedia.org/wiki/Roosevelt_Corollary.

16 Nathan Miller, *Theodore Roosevelt: A Life* (William Morrow, 1992), p. 408. For the Cannon quote see "Joseph Gurney Cannon," Wikipedia, http://en.wikipedia.org/wiki/Joseph_Gurney_Cannon.

17 John Milton Cooper, *The Warrior and the Priest: Woodrow Wilson and Theodore Roosevelt* (Harvard, 1983).

18 H. W. Brands, *TR: The Last Romantic* (Basic Books, 1977), p. 488.

19 War Message to Congress, April 2, 1917, Ray Stannard Baker, ed., *The Public Papers of Woodrow Wilson*, vol. 1 (Harper's, 1925), pp. 6–16.

20 Lloyd Gardner, "A Progressive Foreign Policy, 1900–1921," in W. A. Williams, ed., *From Colony to Empire* (John Wiley, 1972), p. 218.

21 "The School of Cooperative Individualism," http://www.cooperativeindividualism.org/wilson-woodrow_idea-of-america.html.

22 On the tendency of Wilson and Protestant clergy to interpret America's entry into the war as an evangelical, even millenarian crusade see Richard Gamble, *War for Righteousness: Progressive Christianity, the Great War, and the Rise of the Messianic Nation* (ISI Books, 2003). The most convincing interpreter of Wilson's statecraft, in my opinion, is Lloyd Ambrosius, *Woodrow Wilson and the American Diplomatic Tradition: The Treaty Fight in Perspective* (Cambridge, 1987); *Wilsonian Statecraft: Theory and Practice of Liberal Internationalism During World War I* (Scholarly Resources, 1991); *Wilsonianism: Woodrow Wilson and His Legacy in American Foreign Relations* (Palgrave Macmillan, 2002).

23 Thomas G. Paterson, *American Foreign Policy*, p. 267.

24 See Justus Doenecke and John Wilz, *From Isolation to War: 1931–1941* (Harlan Davidson, 2003), and Doenecke, ed., *In Danger Undaunted: The Anti-Interventionist Movement of 1940–1941 as Revealed in the Papers of the America First Committee* (Hoover Institution, 1990).

25 Michael J. Glennon, *Constitutional Diplomacy* (Princeton, 1990), pp. 18–20; John Yoo, *Crisis and Command: The History of Executive Power from George Washington to George W. Bush* (Kaplan, 2009), pp. 289–93.

26 David Gray Adler and Larry N. George, *The Constitution and the Conduct of American Foreign Policy* (Kansas, 1996), p. 26. The Supreme Court reinforced its judgment in favor of the executive branch in its 1937 decision in *United States v. Belmont.* After recognizing the USSR in 1933 Roosevelt approved an executive agreement with Soviet authorities that liquidated debts to American citizens incurred by the defunct tsarist regime. Augustus Belmont sued for relief on the grounds that the agreement violated New York State property law. The court held that "in respect of our foreign relations generally, state lines disappear" and the president speaks for the nation (Yoo, *Crisis and Command*, p. 292).

27 Lawrence Margolis, *Executive Agreements and Presidential Power* (Praeger, 1986), p. 108.

28 Edward Corwin, *The President's Control of Foreign Relations* (Princeton, 1917), pp. 117–18.

29 See especially Marc Trachtenberg, *The Craft of International History: A Guide to Method* (Princeton, 2006), and his recent posts on the H-Diplo website.

30 Kenneth S. Davis, *FDR, Into the Storm, 1937–40: A History* (Random House, 1993), p. 611.

31 "Ex parte Quirin," Wikipedia, http://en.wikipedia.org/wiki/Ex_parte_Quirin.

32 Yoo, *Crisis and Command*, p. 318.

33 For the latest and best critical scholarship on FDR's postwar plans see Wilson D. Miscamble, *From Roosevelt to Truman: Potsdam, Hiroshima, and the Cold War* (Cambridge, 2007).

34 Adler and George, *The Constitution and the Conduct of American Foreign Policy*, p. 320.

35 Yoo, *Crisis and Command*, pp. 330–40. Legal scholar Edward S. Corwin in turn scorned Acheson, Schlesinger, historian Henry Steele Commager as "high-flying prerogative men" in *The New Republic*, Jan. 29, 1951, p. 15. See also Schlesinger, *The Imperial Presidency* (Houghton Mifflin, 1973).

36 Glennon, *Constitutional Diplomacy*, p. 204. On the international and domestic legal puzzles conjured by the unique American practice of declaring presidential doctrines in foreign affairs, see Heiko Meirtöns, *The Doctrines of U.S. Security Policy* (Cambridge, 2010).

37 Ibid., p. 204.

38 James Madison (Apr. 20, 1795) in *Letters and Other Writings of James Madison*, 4 vols., IV: 491 (Philadelphia: Lippincott, 1865).

39 See especially the concluding chapter in John Lehman, *Making War: The 200-Year-Old Battle Between the President and Congress over How America Goes to War* (Scribner's, 1992). The atypicality of Cold War mobilization is demonstrated by statistics that show the size of standing U.S. armed forces has ceased to be determined by whether the nation is at war or at peace. During the Civil War some 2.8 million men served in uniform on one side or the other. From the end of Reconstruction in 1876 until 1898 all the armed forces combined shrank to between 34,000 to 43,000. During the era of Progressive Imperialism, 1898–1917, standing peacetime armed forces rose to between 100,000 and 175,000. During the Great War the United States quickly mobilized 2.5 million men, but after 1918 the military shrank back to about 250,000 prior to creeping up to 450,000 by 1940. World War II put an incredible 12 million Americans in uniform, but the services shrank to just 1.4 million by 1948. The Korean War (sorry, Police Action) more than doubled that total to 3.2 million. But Eisenhower's best efforts notwithstanding, deployments did not shrink much after the Korean truce. Instead, active U.S. military personnel hovered between 2 and 3 million for the duration of the Cold War. In 2008 the Pentagon counted 1,385,122 on active duty and 1,458,500 reservists, many of whom have been deployed since 9/11.

40 In private Ike was heard to grumble, "If it's true that when you die the things that bothered you most are engraved on your skull, I am sure I'll have there the mud and dirt of France during invasion and the name of Senator Bricker." See Louis Galambos, ed., *The Papers of Dwight D. Eisenhower: The Presidency* (Johns Hopkins, 1996), document 707. During the hearings on the Bricker Amendment Senator Guy Gillett (D-Iowa) asked a State Department official to clarify the difference between a treaty and an executive agreement. He was told, "a treaty was something they had to send to the Senate to get approval by two-thirds vote. An executive agreement was something they did not have to send to the Senate." That said it all.

41 In 1963 Kennedy told the Spanish Caudillo that "a threat to either country... would be a matter of common concern to both." Franco warmly concurred. But did JFK have the power to commit America to the defense of Spain? During the Spanish Civil War in the 1930s Roosevelt and

Congress had agreed the answer was no (see Dominic Tierney, *FDR and the Spanish Civil War: Neutrality and Commitment in the Struggle That Divided America* [Duke University, 2007]), but the Kennedy administration invoked the Truman Doctrine that implied the answer was yes in every case (Schlesinger, *Imperial Presidency*, p. 202).

42 See Edwin E. Moise, *Tonkin Gulf and the Escalation of the Vietnam War* (North Carolina, 1996); J. William Fulbright, *The Arrogance of Power* (Random House, 1966). The discussion of the real issue surrounding the Vietnam is based on Henkin.

43 Adler and George, *The Constitution and the Conduct of American Foreign Policy*, p. 42.

44 Lehman, *Making War*; "come and gone" by Edward Keynes in Adler and George, *The Constitution and the Conduct of American Foreign Policy*, p. 252.

45 *Goldwater v. Carter*, 444 U.S. 996 (1979).

46 Zbigniew Brzezinski drafted key sentences in the Carter Doctrine and modeled them on the words of the Truman Doctrine Carter had hoped to supersede: Brzezinski, *Power and Principle: Memoirs of the National Security Advisor, 1977–1981* (Farrar, Straus, Giroux, 1983), p. 444.

47 "The Reagan Doctrine," *TIME* (April 1, 1985).

48 The Weinberg-Powell Doctrine included a list of conditions that must be met in advance of a deployment:

a. The United States should not commit forces to combat unless the vital national interests of the United States or its allies are involved.
b. U.S. troops should only be committed wholeheartedly and with the clear intention of winning. Otherwise, troops should not be committed.
c. U.S. combat troops should be committed only with clearly defined political and military objectives and with the capacity to accomplish those objectives.
d. The relationship between the objectives and the size and composition of the forces committed should be continually reassessed and adjusted if necessary.
e. U.S. troops should not be committed to battle without a reasonable assurance of the support of U.S. public opinion and Congress. (Some lists also mention international support.)
f. The commitment of U.S. troops should be considered only as a last resort.

49 The only nay vote was (predictably) cast by Barbara Jean Lee (D-Calif.), who represented the Berkeley/North Oakland district which had previously elected Ron Dellums.

50 "Terrorism," FindLaw, http://news.findlaw.com/wp/docs/terrorism/sjres23.es.html.

51 See the pithy political insights of Harold Hongju Koh, "Why the President Almost Always Win in Foreign Affairs" in Adler and George, *The Consti-*

tution and the Conduct of American Foreign Policy, pp. 158–80; and the pithy psychological insights of Daniel Kahneman and Jonathan Renshon, "Why Hawks Win," in *Foreign Affairs* (Jan.–Feb. 2007).

52 Jonathan Eliot, *Debates in the Several State Conventions on the Adoption of the Federal Constitution*, 4 vols. (1836), cited by Adler, "The Constitution and Presidential War-Making: The Enduring Debate," *Political Science Quarterly* 103 (Spring 1988): 1–36.

53 Letter to H. S. Randall, May 23, 1857, in G. O. Trevelyan, *The Life and Letters of Lord Macauley* (1875), pp. 409–10. The Cooley lectures were the basis for Henkin, *Constitutionalism, Democracy, and Foreign Affairs* (Columbia, 1990).

54 An excellent book by William G. Howell and Jon C. Pevehouse, *While Dangers Gather: Congressional Checks on Presidential War Powers* (Princeton, 2007) argues that whereas the Congress speaks with many voices and must usually act indirectly to restrain executive assertion, it can nonetheless wield meaningful influence through hearings, protests, budgetary procedures, and especially the media and public opinion.

55 Teaching American History, http://teachingamericanhistory.org/library/index.asp?document=607.

56 *Myers v. United States*, 272 U.S. 52, 293, in Glennon, *Constitutional Diplomacy*, p. 325.

INDEX